D1070427

PATTERNS OF CONFLICT
IN COLOMBIA

COLOMBIA

PATTERNS OF CONFLICT
IN COLOMBIA

by
James L. Payne

New Haven and London, Yale University Press, 1968

TO AARON WILDAVSKY

PREFACE

The subject of political motivation is not one that readily appeals to the empirical political scientist. There are too many possibilities for vague speculation, for untested, and often untestable, psychological theories, and for subjective, unreliable evidence. Most students of politics, anxious to measure their concepts and prove their statements, understandably view the subject with suspicion.

Although skepticism about the analysis of motives of political participants is healthy, the desire to avoid the subject is not. Explanations of political phenomena inevitably rest upon assumptions about the motives of participants. We predict that politicians will behave in a certain way under certain circumstances only because we know, or assume we know, their goals. The problem is not whether to employ the idea of motivation; we must. Since we are using the idea all the time, we may as well make our assumptions explicit. Unrecognized assumptions are dangerous; explicit assumptions often provide a starting point for theories.

My analysis of incentives and their consequences in Colombia suggests that we may have assumed wrongly that Latin American political leaders seek ideological or program rewards. From this assumption flow the discussions of "lefts" and "rights," reactionaries and revolutionaries, nationalists, modernizers, or reformers, and interpretations of political groupings as lower class, upper middle class, business-oriented, or peasant-oriented. All these categories and labels take for granted, it seems, that participants seek to realize external goals: the defense of ideologies, programs, or social groups.

This assumption, my investigations suggest, is unwarranted. The incentive of political leaders in Colombia is a quite personal one: they seek status. The most convincing evidence of this comes from a close examination of Colombian politics. A wide range of phenomena, from the patterns of legislative behavior to the factionalism within the political parties, is consistent with the assumption that leaders seek status. These many features seem inconsistent with the proposition that Colombian politicians seek program or ideological rewards. A preliminary inspection of conditions in other Latin American countries suggests that, there too, status is perhaps the most important incentive for political leaders.

American scholars have assumed that program motives are predominant in Colombia when they are not; in the United States we often assume program incentives are not important when they are. American politicians are frequently portrayed as hypocritical opportunists arranging coalitions, responding to pressure groups, straddling fences, and defending constituencies with no other objective than the continued enjoyment of the status or money political office provides. American leaders, we suppose, will do anything to get elected; with this maxim we think we explain much of American politics.

In the light of the Colombian findings it becomes necessary to reexamine this perspective. In Colombia one encounters politicians who really will do almost anything to get elected. These participants show us what we never would have imagined from only the American experience: how politicians with strong private motives actually behave. The contrast with American political practices is so striking that I am forced to conclude that American politicians do not, by and large, have strong private motives but, instead, seek satisfaction from shaping public policy. They have a program incentive. This study of Colombian politics, then, also sharpens our understanding of American politics by exploring the range of possible incentives and their different consequences.

Explanations of political phenomena, if they are to be criticized, remembered, and used in other contexts, must be clear and concise. To this end I have advanced explicit, testable hypotheses—drawn together in Appendix III—as summaries of the arguments. The hypotheses are not, of course, conclusive or final statements. They are something to shoot at, something to test. They increase the likelihood of productive, on-target volleys while reducing the number of wild shots and ricochets.

In acknowledging the assistance I have received in the preparation of this study, I would first thank the many Colombian politicians who participated in the interviews and the questionnaire. In view of the possibly delicate nature of most interview comments, I shall not identify the sources by name unless the discussion clearly requires it. In most cases interview comments quoted are merely illustrative or typical and therefore do not require attribution.

The field research was undertaken from February to September 1965. Expenses were covered by a generous Woodrow Wilson Dissertation Fellowship grant; the costs of the final preparation of the manuscript were borne by Wesleyan University faculty research funds.

For their efforts in reading and criticizing drafts of the manuscript I am indebted to David Bushnell, Anthony Maingot, Ernst B. Haas, Aaron Wildavsky, William P. McGreevey, Oliver Woshinsky, Fred Greenstein, Nelson Polsby, Stuart Fagan, and Andrew McFarland. In the struggle to communicate through so many words, editors Ruth Davis Kaufman and my father, William L. Payne, have rendered great assistance. No list of acknowledgments is complete without my wife, Suzanne, who maintained an unflagging interest in the study while I continually tested the arguments on her.

J. L. P.

Middletown, Connecticut
October 1967

CONTENTS

TABLES AND FIGURES

TABLES

FIGURES

PART ONE

INCENTIVES FOR
POLITICAL PARTICIPATION

CHAPTER 1

THE INCENTIVE APPROACH TO
POLITICAL ANALYSIS

*Now we must consider the possibility of sabotage. The most important
thing is to get our trusted men into the theater early. The event starts at
seven so we should get there by six. We must occupy the key positions:
first, we must take control of the first four rows. We want only our friends
there because if saboteurs are going to throw eggs or tomatoes, as they did
at the university, we want them far enough back so they don't stand a good
chance of hitting the target, since if they miss no real harm is done.
Secondly, our men should be stationed at the ends of the rows, so that if
any saboteurs attempt to create a disturbance we'll have them boxed in.
This was the strategy Gaitán used and it was very successful.*

*Also, tell everyone that there will be police at the door, frisking every-
one who enters. I know that many people of these neighborhoods are
accustomed to carry revolvers, so tell them not to bring any weapons or
they'll lose them. But before the police are there we will get about 50 small
wooden clubs inside, sawed from sticks. We will pass these out to our
people and they can keep them up their sleeves. Then if any saboteurs
make trouble: Bop! Bop!*

> *Excerpt of remarks made by a Liberal
> party leader at a meeting of organizers
> for the rally of Carlos Lleras Restrepo
> in the Teatro Boichica, Bogotá,
> March 30, 1965.*

To understand the turbulent politics of Colombia one must first discover what motivates Colombian politicians. Here is a system which
for a century and a half has been characterized by frequent fighting.
What has the fighting been about? What does a city councilman want
that he should throw a chair across the council chamber, breaking
up the meeting? What is a senator really seeking when he walks out
of the opening ceremonies of Congress shouting, "I can't stand imbe-
cilities"? Turning to the sweep of Colombian history, marked by

civil wars, organized assassinations, violent demonstrations, and riots, the question is always the same: what do participants seek so desperately from politics that they should take such extreme measures?

The answer to this question is the theme of this study, which attempts to explain political conflict in Colombia through an examination of political motives and the context in which these motives find expression. By "political conflict" I mean the actions that contending participants take in attempting to gain political office or influence political office-holders. The "intensity" of conflict is the costs or sacrifices the different actions entail. These costs may be relatively low in some actions—vitriolic speeches, newspaper invective, and parliamentary riots—or extremely high as in large street riots or civil wars. Using the number of political deaths alone, one can construct numerical equivalents for the level of political conflict. As more political deaths occur over a period of time, the system may be defined as low, moderate, or high in its level of conflict intensity.

On a scale of political deaths per generation, Colombia has one of the highest levels of political conflict in the world. In nearly 150 years since independence the country has been racked by ten national civil wars: 1830–31, 1839–41, 1851, 1854, 1860–61, 1876, 1885, 1899–1902, and the covert guerrilla war of 1949–53. In addition there have been countless local revolts and flare-ups, including the violence of the 1922 election campaign, the many local clashes in the period 1931–34, and in 1946–48. The national civil wars between 1830 and 1876 cost an estimated 24,600 lives.[1] The War of a Thousand Days (1899–1902) is supposed to have cost about 100,000 lives.[2] One approximation of the costs of the most recent major conflict (1949–53) and its aftereffects is 134,820 lives.[3]

Perhaps the most perplexing aspect of this system is that political conflict has never been low. One cannot say that politics has ever been "tranquil" or "harmonious" in Colombia. Even in 1965, a year of relative calm compared to other times, strong invective and heated accusations were commonplace; riots were frequent in Congress, in

1. Antonio Pérez Aguirre, *25 Años de Historia Colombiana, 1853 a 1878* (Bogotá, Editorial Sucre, 1959), p. 439.

2. Jesús María Henao and Gerardo Arrubla, *History of Colombia*, ed. and trans. J. Fred Rippy (Chapel Hill, University of North Carolina Press, 1938), pp. 518–19.

3. Germán Guzmán Campos, Orlando Fals Borda, and Eduardo Umaña Luna, *La Violencia en Colombia* (2 vols. 2d ed. Bogotá, Tercer Mundo, 1963, 1964), *1*, 292.

departmental assemblies and city councils; demonstrations, occasionally accompanied by violence, were numerous; the violent sabotage of political rallies was, as indicated above, usually expected.

In Colombia the civil wars have not represented abrupt breaks with a prior period of tranquility. Instead they were seemingly natural extensions of an always heated politics. Nor has the country entered a period of political calm following outbreaks of violence. Agitation and tension continued and the next spate of violence never seemed far away—and it usually wasn't. This pattern contrasts dramatically with the usually peaceful politics in the United States. The Civil War was, of course, a period of intense conflict. But after it ended politics returned to its usual calm rhythm. In Colombia civil wars have been like outcroppings of a continuous substratum. None of them has lessened the chances of having another.

The violent tone of Colombian politics is seen in the experience of Simon Bolívar, liberator and first president of Gran Colombia (which included Colombia, Venezuela, Ecuador, and Panama at that time). Named president in 1821 by the Congress of Cúcuta, Bolívar, finishing the War of Independence in Peru, did not assume office until 1826. Even before he arrived in Bogotá news reached him of the rebellion of José Antonio Páez in Venezuela. Bolívar patched up the Venezuelan situation temporarily and returned to Bogotá in 1827, a hero. One year later, on the night of September 25, 1828, he found himself hiding underneath El Carmen bridge after fleeing from an organized attempt on his life. He later gained the upper hand and set about punishing his political adversaries, including Vice-president Santander, who was accused of participating in the plot and eventually exiled. These events contrast remarkably with the adulation given to the American liberator, George Washington, and the relatively mild tone of American politics during his presidency.

The Colombian system, then, exhibits a marked tendency toward intense political conflict. An explanation for this tendency, I believe, lies in the basic goal of political participants.

INCENTIVE THEORY

In the approach to politics developed here, incentives constitute the cornerstone of the theory. An incentive is simply the satisfaction an individual seeks from political participation. It is the motive that explains his presence in politics and his behavior as a participant. Incentives have two dimensions. One is the object or *nature* of the satisfaction. The other is the *strength* of the motive, that is, the costs which the participant is willing to suffer to obtain the satisfaction. If we know the nature and strength of a participant's incentive and the alternatives open to him, we may predict his behavior with some accuracy.

These are common axioms of human behavior. Individuals seek satisfactions or goals. These goals have a "price tag" in terms of the sacrifices demanded. Among the alternatives open to him, the individual will select the path which best yields the desired satisfactions. We use these axioms constantly in our everyday lives to predict and explain the actions of others. In this study I adopt these assumptions but focus them into a technique for developing specific propositions about political phenomena. This adaptation requires certain qualifications to the accepted axioms mentioned above.

First, the incentive approach assumes that the goals participants seek in political activity can be treated as if they were few in number. It rejects the proposition that the goals of participants are as varied as the desires of men. For the purpose of theory-building, the investigator may treat incentives as if there were only two, three, or perhaps four. This reduction of the number of possible incentives leads to a second assumption: incentives are basic, underlying satisfactions and not momentary, incidental goals. Such objectives as winning an election, becoming committee chairman, or appointing one's son as Senate page are not profitably treated as incentives. With goals so narrowly identified the possibilities for predictive theory are correspondingly limited. By applying the concept of incentives to underlying, relatively fixed goals, such as status or money, the incentive approach will yield hypotheses about a wide range of phenomena.

A third assumption is that one may identify entire groups of participants as motivated by one incentive. Even though a certain variety of incentives may actually be found in a system, it is possible and profitable to select a dominant incentive for the system as a whole. By "system" I mean the level on which the investigator wishes to make his analysis: a nation, a region, an organization or part of an organization. Once the investigator selects a dominant incentive he may ask: what would happen in this system if everyone were seeking this satisfaction? Thus he could formulate hypotheses about the system, and predict contrasts between this system and another with a different dominant incentive.

The incentive approach assumes that political participants are continually facing action alternatives. Should they form a new party or remain in the old one? Should they run again for office or not? Should they attempt to punish a defector from their party? Should they attempt to sabotage a campaign rally? Which of the alternatives the participants select will depend on their incentives, how strong these incentives are, and which action best realizes the respective satisfaction.

To recapitulate, the elements of the incentive theory adopted in this study are:

1. Political participants have incentives.
2. An incentive is the basic, underlying satisfaction which accounts for a person's political activity.
3. Incentives have two dimensions: nature (object) and strength (costs one is willing to sustain to obtain the satisfaction).
4. Incentives for political participation can be treated as if they were few in number.
5. Participants in a system may be treated as if they all had the same incentive (the dominant incentive).
6. The dominant incentive for political participation may vary in nature and strength from system to system.
7. The action alternatives open to political participants lead to different satisfactions.
8. Political participants will select the action alternative that fulfills their incentive, provided that the costs of this action do not exceed the strength of the incentive.

OTHER USES OF THE INCENTIVE CONCEPT

The statement of the incentive approach given above parallels many existing discussions of political phenomena. Many writers have concerned themselves with the goals of political participants. Robert Lane advances a "grammar of political motives." [4] The authors of *Voting* list ten types of party workers "according to the major interests that appeared to the field staff to explain their presence in party work." [5] Such discussions of motives are generally included to complete a descriptive picture and therefore a premium is placed on constructing lengthy lists which do not lend themselves to theoretical application.

Other writers have sought to reduce motives for participation into two dichotomous categories. The most familiar of these classifications is that of "bosses" and "reformers," as advanced by Merriam and Gosnell, for example.[6] Apparently bosses seek selfish ends such as money or status while reformers have altruistic goals such as particular programs. A related division is made by Samuel Eldersveld in his identification of "power oriented" and "idealistic" participants.[7] By "power oriented" Eldersveld means oriented toward getting votes, toward winning elections. The "idealists" apparently seek nonelectoral rewards such as the satisfaction of an uncompromised program. Although such formulations have theoretical overtones, they are not constructed for the purpose of developing multiple hypotheses. Each category would contain individuals with different incentives.

In his *People and Parties in Politics* John Fenton employs a dichotomous incentive scheme to analyze politics in different American states.[8] In some states (such as Kentucky), he suggests, the dominant incentive for political participation is employment (job-orientation); in others (Michigan, for example), sponsoring public policies seems

4. Robert E. Lane, *Political Life* (Glencoe, The Free Press, 1959), pp. 102 ff.

5. Bernard R. Berelson, Paul F. Lazarsfeld, and William McPhee, *Voting* (Chicago, University of Chicago Press, 1954), pp. 164–65; see also: Roy V. Peel, *The Political Clubs of New York City* (New York, G. P. Putnam's Sons, 1935); Harold F. Gosnell, *Machine Politics: Chicago Model* (Chicago, University of Chicago Press, 1937), pp. 26–68.

6. Charles E. Merriam and Harold Gosnell, *The American Party System* (4th ed. New York, Macmillan, 1949), pp. 202–16; also see Heinz Eulau et al., "Career Perspectives of American State Legislators" in Dwaine Marvick, ed., *Political Decision-makers* (Glencoe, The Free Press, 1961), pp. 242 ff.

7. Samuel J. Eldersveld, *Political Parties: A Behavioral Analysis* (Chicago, Rand McNally, 1964), pp. 222 ff.

8. John H. Fenton, *People and Parties in Politics* (Glenview, Ill., Scott Foresman, 1966).

to be the salient motive for participants (issue-orientation). Fenton goes beyond the descriptive nature of the dichotomy and argues that many contrasts in the different states can be traced to (as causes or effects) the job or issue orientations of the participants, including the role of interest groups, party structure, and governmental performance.

Clark and Wilson propose an incentive approach for the analysis of organizations.[9] They advance three types of incentives: material (tangible), solidary (intangible, but independent of the stated purpose of the organization), and purposive (stated ends of the organization). The writers then speculate about the connections between each of these incentive categories and patterns of organizational behavior.

James Wilson in *The Amateur Democrat* argues that the characteristics of certain Democratic party organizations (the New York Lehman group, the California CDC, the Illinois DFI and IVI) as well as the conflicts between these groups and other party elements can be understood by examining the different incentives present.[10] The former group of participants Wilson identifies as "amateurs," participants seeking policy rewards. The regulars, including most officeholders, are called "professionals" and are assumed to seek nonideological rewards such as status or conviviality, or at least do not seek policy goals at the same level of intensity as the amateurs.

The importance of examining incentives themselves is underscored by studies which suggest that a person's real motives for participating in politics may be unrelated to his ostensible political goals. Leo Lowenthal and Norbert Guterman identify the American agitator as seeking a personal psychological satisfaction unrelated to the solution of social problems he agitates.[11] Lewis Namier interprets mid-

9. Peter B. Clark and James Q. Wilson, "Incentive Systems: A Theory of Organizations," *Administrative Science Quarterly*, 6 (September 1961), 130. For another preliminary discussion of the incentive idea see Frank J. Sorauf, *Political Parties in the Amercan System* (Boston, Little, Brown, 1964), pp. 81–97.

10. James Q. Wilson, *The Amateur Democrat* (Chicago, University of Chicago Press, 1962).

11. Leo Lowenthal and Norbert Guterman, "Portrait of the American Agitator," *The Public Opinion Quarterly, 12* (Fall 1948), 417–29. Other discussions of political motives and their psychological roots appear in Harold D. Lasswell, *Psychopathology and Politics* (New York, Viking Press, 1960) and Lasswell, *Power and Personality* (New York, Viking Press, 1962).

eighteenth-century English politics as revolving about the quest for private rewards:

> Men went there [parliament] "to make a figure", and no more dreamt of a seat in the House in order to benefit humanity than a child dreams of a birthday cake that others may eat it; which is perfectly normal and in no way reprehensible.[12]

Another application of the incentive idea appears in Aaron Wildavsky's study of the 1964 Republican convention.[13] Interviews with convention delegates revealed that a substantial proportion were atypical when matched against the usual American politician. They exhibited a marked interest in seeing that the prevalent American proscriptions about how politicians ought to behave were followed: parties should have different programs; candidates should mean what they say; one should do the right thing, not the popular or expedient thing. These participants were labeled "purists," in keeping with their quest for a pure political style. Their counterparts were the "politicians" whose incentives were directed more toward results (in personal or policy terms) than how these results were arrived at.

The fact that participants with a style incentive were, in unusually large numbers, present at the convention provided an explanation for the jarring incongruity of this event. Such practices as rejecting even token concessions on the formal platform or refusing to balance the ticket with a "liberal" vice-presidential nominee—or indeed, the nomination of an unlikely (but "honest" and "principled") candidate—were all quite at variance with our usual expectations. But if one should ask what is likely to happen in a convention populated by individuals with a style incentive, the pattern of the 1964 Republican convention would be a reasonable prediction.

A clear picture of the incentive concept as advanced in this study appears in James Barber's study of 92 freshmen in the Connecticut legislature.[14] These individuals were divided into four types, based on their willingness to return for another term and upon their level of legislative activity:

12. Lewis Namier, *The Structure of Politics at the Accession of George III* (2d ed. London, Macmillan, 1957), p. 2.

13. Aaron Wildavsky, "The Goldwater Phenomenon: Purists, Politicians, and the Two-Party System," *The Review of Politics, 27* (July 1965), 386–413.

14. James David Barber, *The Lawmakers* (New Haven, Yale University Press, 1965).

1. Lawmakers (high activity, high willingness to return)
2. Spectators (low activity, high willingness to return)
3. Advertisers (high activity, low willingness to return)
4. Reluctants (low activity, low willingness to return).

Having separated the participants in this manner, Barber found, from lengthy, tape-recorded interviews, that each type exhibited a distinct series of attitudes toward legislative life. One of the dimensions that varied for each of the four types was "satisfactions." The Lawmaker's satisfaction lay in producing legislation he desired; the Spectator seemed to seek conviviality; the Advertiser, status; and the Reluctant sought the rewards of "doing a civic duty."

Barber's formulation of these types is explicitly empirical: those legislators with certain activity and willingness-to-return characteristics were also found to have certain satisfactions, attitudes, and so on. But by entering the typology at a different point—incentives—the formulation could be made in theoretical terms. Knowing only the satisfaction (incentive) dimension we could formulate hypotheses about what other characteristics should follow: those with a program incentive (Lawmakers) very likely would be high in activity and high in willingness to return; those with a status incentive (Advertisers) would adopt a show-off pattern of activity; those seeking conviviality (Spectators) would "go along" with party leadership. With incentives the independent variable, one may attempt a predictive theory of legislative behavior.

In this study of Colombian politics I have adopted one specific formulation of the incentive approach. I emphasize at the outset that it is not the only application of incentive theory, but simply one which is useful for the subject matter of this study. I treat incentives as if there were only two possibilities: a status incentive and a program incentive. I say, in effect, that political systems can be treated as if there were only two reasons why individuals participate in politics: to acquire greater status or to effect programs or policies.

Status refers to the prestige participants seek from holding political office. Other terms in this study that are synonymous with status include honor, rank, social position, respect, standing, and prestige. Status is the condition of being considered higher, above, or superior with respect to other members of society in a general, widely recognized sense. It is unspecific and anonymous; it adheres to appearance and position, not to the substance or detailed content of the appearance. The doorman tips his hat for the full professor because the professor has status; whether the professor has advanced or hindered the growth of knowledge in his discipline the doorman does not know, and need not know, to accord him status.

In a sense, then, status is accorded by strangers, by society. Other values, which resemble status, are accorded by friends and colleagues who are in a position to evaluate the content of the appearance. Trust, appreciation, gratitude, admiration, affection, approval—these rewards are given by specific reference groups and are contingent upon the evaluation of some specific behavior of the individual. Thus the stingy, unscrupulous bank president will be neither trusted, admired, nor appreciated. But he will have social status in consequence of his formal position.

Status motivation leads to certain distinctive patterns of behavior. It produces, for example, an emphasis upon "credit-getting" or fame. The important thing is not to achieve but to be credited with achieving, whether one has or not. We should expect—and we find—status-motivated politicians constantly engaging in those activities to which publicity and renown attaches, such as speech-making, and avoiding less visible activities, including the actual formulation of policy and the supervision of its work-a-day implementation. In this respect, the status-motivated politician is the direct opposite of the politician with a program incentive.

A second implication of status motivation is its corrosive effect on friendly personal relations. The desire to appear "higher" and not "lower" impels the individual into competitive personal relationships. He resents those who are above him, such as legislative leaders, and attempts to dispel the impression of submission by acting independently and even obstreperously toward them. With his equals, he is constantly jousting for a position of superiority, of respect. It is only with the abject supplicants that he feels comfortable because they are visible proof of his status. Even here the interaction is not a friendly one since it depends on the constant confirmation of the superior-inferior relationship. The status incentive, therefore, produces a behavioral orientation quite the opposite of the conviviality, or friendship, incentive. The individual whose political satisfactions lie in having friendly relations with others avoids the unpleasant competition for rank. He is cooperative toward those above him, freely acknowledging that their qualifications entitle them to leadership positions. He is courteous toward colleagues and disinclined to elevate himself by pushing others down.

The program incentive describes the satisfactions inherent in working on and toward desired policy objectives. It is important to stress the term "satisfaction." It is misleading to consider the program incentive "altruistic," as if the individual participated in politics because he felt he "ought to." The civic obligation or citizen duty motive—the style incentive—is different from a programmatic one. The style incentive leads people to participate even though they find politics distasteful or alien. Clearly, as suggested by the Goldwater phenomenon, this incentive is likely to be associated with some quite unusual and erratic behavior. And, since in the long run people do only what they enjoy doing, not what they should do, the style incentive would seem to be unstable and temporary.

With a program incentive the individual's satisfactions come from actually working on policies. He enjoys drawing up a bill, examining the budget, and hammering out a workable compromise. In each case, of course, he will have a programmatic goal: getting free lunches for poor schoolchildren, saving the taxpayer's money, having a highway built. The policy goals may be narrow or general, enduring or transitory. They may be ideologically left or right, or divorced from that scale altogether. The program incentive, however, is not the policy goal itself but the satisfactions inherent in working toward it, in achieving it. The incentive lies in actually contributing toward the desired outcome. A program incentive is, in a basic sense, similar to the motivation for pursuing a hobby, for building a model railway or fishing for trout. There is a tangible goal—the railway or the trout—inextricably linked to the motive. But these objects can be purchased in the store; it is the activity of acquiring them that brings the satisfaction.

A word of caution is in order. Ascribing incentives to groups of politicians cannot be done successfully from afar without intimate knowledge of the men and the context in which they behave. Citizens and journalists readily form opinions about the motives of their public officials: politicians are called "idealistic," "power-hungry," "opportunistic," and "ideological." These popular stereotypes are practically worthless as accurate or productive categories for analysis because they are based on careless and superficial observation of behavior. Thus, for example, foreign observers often conclude that the violent, revolutionary oratory of Colombian politicians reflects profound ideological motives; closer examination suggests that this bombastic speechmaking flows largely from the need of status-motivated politicians for publicity. American congressmen are sometimes supposed to have little interest in specific policy outcomes because they compromise and horse-trade on policy matters. Closer analysis produces the opposite conclusion. Because they seek particular policies, program-motivated legislators will compromise in order to obtain part of the policy rather than nothing at all. The status-motivated legislator, not concerned with policy outcomes, is the one who will immobilize the legislative process so that no bill at all is approved. The serious application of incentive analysis, therefore, may easily produce conclusions about the motives of politicians that differ from those in the popular mind.

Limiting attention to only these two incentives, status and program, is the first simplification of incentive theory. The next step is to consider these two incentives as poles on a continuum on which any political system may be located. This continuum is adapted to include the strength of incentives by assuming that the more predominant one incentive is in a system, the stronger it will be (see Figure 1).

The association between the frequency of an incentive in a system and its strength is defended largely on theoretical grounds. The different incentives are seen as mutually competitive, with each constantly tending to displace the other. As one incentive grows increasingly strong we would expect that it will outstrip the other and that virtually all participants will have only this one, stronger, incentive. If, however, the investigator discovered that different participants had different incentives, then he would assume that the dominant incentive was not very strong since it had not clearly outcompeted the other(s).

The formulation of a continuum for the status and program incentives, with the strength of an incentive automatically associated with its predominance greatly simplifies our discussions. Rather than

FIGURE 1

THE STATUS–PROGRAM INCENTIVE CONTINUUM

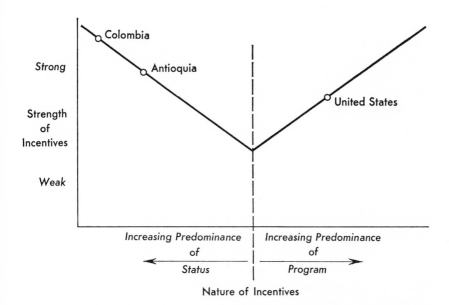

Nature of Incentives

constructing many hypotheses to account for the multitude of possible combinations of the two incentives at different strengths, we need formulate only two hypotheses, one for each end of the continuum. We reason that the closer an intermediate case falls to one or the other end, the more completely the hypothesis constructed for that extreme will apply.

Naturally there must be techniques for measuring or estimating incentives so that we may position different groups of participants on the scale. One possibility is to treat the incentive as a theoretical construct and merely infer its nature and strength from the consequences which are supposed to flow from it. That is, if a series of predictions flowing from an assumption about the dominant incentive in a system prove to be correct, then one may accept the assumption. To a certain extent, I rely implicitly upon the accuracy of predictions to substantiate my judgments about the nature and strength of incentives. However, I formally treat incentives as directly measurable through the use of extended interviews with participants. In such interviews one seeks answers to the questions: Why is this individual in politics? What satisfaction does he seek? Such blunt questions are not particularly useful in the interviews themselves, but there are lines of questioning, discussed in the next chapter, that will provide answers to these questions.

Once one has established the incentive of each respondent, he must decide upon the dominant incentive in the system. According to our formulation, the status or the program incentive should be sufficiently prevalent to enable the investigator to employ the continuum given above. The dominant incentive need not, at this point, be numerically computed, but will be, nevertheless, a rough sort of average. One excludes the cases which do not fall upon the status–program continuum and then balances off the proportion of participants with a status incentive against those with a program incentive. Obviously this method lacks precision, but in dealing with the marked differences in incentives found in the systems we examine it is adequate for our purposes.

A problem arises when considering different levels of political participation. I identify two broad categories of participants: leaders and active followers. Our attention is concentrated primarily on leaders, since these participants appear to be most decisive in shaping the political system. However, active followers also play a critical role in determining certain dimensions of the system, and therefore a knowledge of their incentives is necessary to theorize about these features. For example, it may be that candidates for office (leaders) in a system have a moderate status incentive, but that campaign workers (active followers) have a strong program incentive so that, as the price of their cooperation, they demand that leaders behave in a manner more consistent with their program incentives.

After suffering these pages of theoretical discussion, the reader deserves a preliminary view of the kinds of findings the incentive approach yields. An examination of the Colombian system reveals that the incentive for leaders is status and that this incentive is strong. Colombia may be contrasted with the United States where I judge the dominant incentive is program and of moderate strength. An hypothesis is advanced to explain the strength of the status incentive. This hypothesis identifies three variables which, when all are present, will make status a dominant incentive for leaders in the system: 1) high status-consciousness in the society; 2) high status value of higher political offices; and 3) relatively open recruitment to these higher offices. By "status-consciousness" I mean the importance which members of society attach to an individual's status or social position.

These three variables are present in Colombia. In the United States, although the last two conditions are met, the first—high status-consciousness—is not. Consequently we would expect to find status a strong incentive in Colombia, but not in the United States. In Antioquia, a department within Colombia, status-consciousness is noticeably lower than in the rest of the country. Consistent with our hypothesis, the status incentive appears weaker in Antioquia, and leaders with a program incentive are occasionally encountered. We are thus able to position Colombia, Antioquia, and the United States on the status–program continuum in approximately the manner diagramed in Figure 1.

I extend the analysis by suggesting that most of the other Latin American countries (particularly Peru, Ecuador, Argentina, and Uruguay) fall close to Colombia with status a strong incentive and that many of the European countries (Great Britain, Austria) would lie near the United States with a program incentive of moderate strength. With these observations, we are in a position to employ the incentive concept to generate hypotheses.

We might, for example, be curious about possible differences in the age of entry into politics in the different systems. A knowledge of the different incentives affords a basis for speculation. Status, for those who worry about it, is closely related to career opportunities and success in the eyes of the world. It seems to follow, therefore, that if status is a political incentive, it would appear particularly in younger individuals who are most preoccupied with personal advancement and career success. The program incentive, on the other hand, tends to be an avocational satisfaction, incidental to matters of career. It is less likely to emerge, therefore, in earlier years when the individual is preoccupied with his personal success. Somewhat later, after he has established or at least tested a career, he is more likely, having outgrown the egocentrism of youth, to become interested in the community beyond him. Thus we have the following hypotheses (the numbering corresponds to the order in which the hypotheses appear later in the book):

> *H8. Where the incentive for leaders is status, leaders will enter politics at a relatively early age.*
>
> *H9. Where the incentive for leaders is program, leaders will enter politics at a relatively late age.*

The data indicate that these hypotheses hold for our three cases. A survey of 130 higher Colombian leaders revealed that the median age when they held their first public office was 23 (excluding Antioquia). For the department of Antioquia it was 28. Evidence seems to indicate that the comparable figure for the United States is 30–35.

Another area of interest concerns the differences in policy positions which might exist between leaders of different political parties. Reasoning from a knowledge of incentives, we would expect that where a program incentive predominates, leaders of different parties would hold different policy attitudes. Two mechanisms would account for this condition: (1) individuals with program incentives will, finding the policy dimension salient for themselves, join those parties which are closest to their program goals; (2) within a party where participants hold a program incentive, processes of communication and reinforcement within the party will operate to produce a certain degree of consistency in the policy attitudes of party members. Because policy is important to these participants they will talk about it. Where the status incentive is found, policy positions will not be salient, either in the recruitment process or in patterns of intraparty communication. We may advance the hypotheses:

> *H5. Where status is the incentive for leaders, there will be no differences between the leaders of different parties (or party factions) on program policies.*
>
> *H6. Where program is the incentive for leaders there will be differences between the leaders of different parties on program policies.*

Examination of the findings of several studies reveals that in the United States and Great Britain (program incentive) leaders and active followers of different parties do differ in their positions on a wide range of policy issues. Our survey of Colombian leaders revealed the opposite condition: on the (nonstrategic) policy issues—housing, control of business, protection of labor unions—leaders of the two parties (Liberal and Conservative) did not differ. Further examination shows that the ideology of socioeconomic conservatism is virtually nonexistent among Colombian leaders. In the entire sample of 130 leaders, not one felt the government should do less in housing construction; only six desired both less government control of business and less government protection of labor unions. One conclusion is that the usual left-right terminology (progressive, liberal, conservative, reactionary) often employed by American writers is practically meaningless for Colombia.

A study of the legislature provides another opportunity for the use of the incentive approach. Taking the matter of legislative turnover, for example, we would expect that where a status incentive predominated, members of Congress would come and go quite rapidly. Such participants would seek the status inherent in the title of senator or representative, and having achieved this would move up or out. Running for election to the same house would appear to an individual with a status incentive somewhat like going through college again to get a second Phi Beta Kappa key. The individual with a program incentive gets satisfaction from the job itself, not the title; he is likely to want to return to the legislature to continue to experience the enjoyments of producing policies he favors. Consequently:

H32. In a system where status is the incentive for leaders, legislative turnover will be high.

H33. In a system where program is the incentive for leaders, legislative turnover will be low.

A comparison of the continuity rates of the U.S. House of Representatives with the Colombian House of Representatives (two-year terms in both cases) supports these hypotheses. An examination of the U.S. House in 1958, 1960, and 1962 showed that 85 per cent of the representatives elected in 1958 returned in 1960; 68 per cent of the representatives elected in 1958 were still present in 1962, two terms later. In Colombia a study of legislative continuity since 1923 shows that about 20 per cent of the representatives return for an

immediate second term and about six per cent have three continuous
terms. The above hypotheses would predict (utilizing the continuum
conception of incentives) that Antioquia should have a higher continuity rate than the rest of the country. Studying all the representatives in the period 1923–45 it was possible to construct a continuity
index (average proportion of representatives returning for a second
term out of total number of representatives) for Antioquia and the
two next largest departments, Cundinamarca and Boyacá. For Antioquia the continuity figure was 25.5 per cent; for Cundinamarca and
Boyacá the figures were, respectively, 15.3 and 17.5 per cent.

Beyond the matter of turnover, it is apparent that the difference
in incentives would produce a wide range of contrasts between the
American and Colombian legislatures. The Colombian Congress is
characterized by lack of staff and research facilities, few committee
hearings, delegation of lawmaking to the executive in enabling acts,
inconsistent voting patterns, high abstention in all phases of legislative life, the use of alternates, the absence of norms that prevent
spurious conflicts among legislators and interruptions by observers,
the use of the institution for scandal-mongering and attention-getting. All these traits are implied in the answer to the question: what
would a legislature look like if the members were there to acquire
status and not to make policy?

Incentive theory recognizes that the behavior of political participants in any particular situation is determined both by their incentives and by the structural variables which affect the alternatives
open to them. Thus far we have examined some contrasts between
Colombia and the United States which are explained simply by the
difference in incentives in the two systems. In theorizing about legislative turnover, for example, I have not mentioned a wide range of
structural conditions which could affect turnover. Such conditions
would include election laws, the degree of competition in congressional elections, and the nature of the nominating processes. However, these structural conditions did not differ sufficiently between
the two systems to cause significant differences in turnover. Therefore only the incentive dimension was included in the hypotheses
accounting for differences in legislative turnover in the two countries.
If, however, structural variables do differ significantly in the systems
under analysis, then the investigator must include these differences,
along with differences in incentives, in his hypotheses.

The importance of structural variables as well as incentives is illustrated in the phenomenon of factionalism—that is, the presence, in *general* elections, of competing candidates bearing the same party label. The analysis might begin by assuming that in any political party there will be more than one aspirant seeking the party nomination for at least some offices. What will disappointed aspirants do if they fail to receive the party nomination? They face, it seems, three action alternatives: (1) accept defeat and remain in the party; (2) form a new party (new label) with themselves as candidates; (3) run in general elections under the old party label against the "official" nominee. Which of these alternatives the participants select will depend upon both their incentives and certain structural variables.

If the program incentive is paramount, we should expect disappointed aspirants to elect to remain in the party. Such individuals are likely to see their party as an instrument for effecting certain policies, policies they probably favor. Consequently they are reluctant to weaken the party by forming new parties or factions, even if by so doing they increase their opportunities for winning office. Participants with a status incentive would care nothing for the party as a means of realizing programs or policies. Their objective is simply to get into office. Consequently, if they fail to obtain the party nomination, aspirants with a status incentive will readily form new parties or factions—provided that their opportunities for gaining office with either of these strategies are comparable to the opportunities if they stayed in the "official" party.

Clearly many structural features will affect the attractiveness of the respective alternatives. One is the degree of party identification in the system, that is, the proportion of voters who identify with a party label and are therefore likely to vote for it. Since participants with a status incentive seek only to gain office, they are likely to retain the old, vote-getting labels when party identification is high. The participant with a status incentive needs these votes more than he feels he needs an untarnished image. But if party identification is low, the same participants may form new parties (labels) at no sacrifice, and would do so.

As suggested above, individuals with a program incentive are not prone to break away from their party since they value the party in terms beyond their personal officeholding opportunities. But it may

occasionally happen that breaks occur precisely because participants
do hold a program incentive: they may feel that their program position differs radically from that of the rest of the party. In such a case,
however, we would expect rebels to form a new party, rather than a
faction, even if party identification is high. Rebels with program incentives desire to distinguish themselves from the old party, feeling
that they have a new program. Proud of their difference, they want
voters to know they are different. They are willing to sacrifice the
votes that adhere to the old party label for this purity of image.
Consequently, the relatively infrequent ideological breaks which occur in a system where program incentives predominate will not lead
to factionalism. These conclusions may be presented in hypotheses
which express the importance of both the incentive dimension and
the structural variable (the degree of party identification of the electorate) in determining factionalism:

> *H22. Factionalism will not occur where party identification is
> low.*
>
> *H23. Where party identification of the electorate is high and
> the incentive for leaders is program, factionalism will not be
> prevalent.*
>
> *H24. Where party identification of the electorate is high and
> the incentive for leaders is status, factionalism will be prevalent.*

The evidence seems to support these hypotheses. In Colombia we
suspect that party identification has been high since about the 1850s.
The two parties, Liberal and Conservative, which date from that
period, have been characterized by endemic factionalism. In this
century two presidential candidates bearing the same party label have
run against each other in the general elections of 1904, 1918, 1930,
1942, 1946, and 1962. Twice—in 1930 and 1946—such divisions
cost the majority party the presidency. Most of the other presidential
elections have been characterized by party division in matters of
strategy; e.g. whether to run a candidate, whether to back one of the
other party's nominees. In fact the only presidential election in this
century which was a straight Liberal-Conservative contest was that
of 1922. In local elections, for senators and representatives, multiple
candidacies under the same party label are common. In spite of the
manifest divisions and conflicts within the parties (and the existence

of proportional representation since 1910) no new parties (labels) of significant strength have emerged since the 1850s.

In other countries where status seems to be the incentive, but where party identification, estimated indirectly, appears relatively low—such as Peru or Ecuador—factionalism is not found. Instead we encounter the frequent rise of new parties. Illustrations of recently formed (after 1930) parties of considerable strength include Ecuador's *Alianza Democrática Ecuatoriana, Movimiento Cívico Ecuatoriana,* and *Frente Democrático Nacional* and Peru's *Unión Revolucionaria, Acción Popular,* and *Unión Nacional Odriista.* In countries where the program incentive predominates—the United States, Great Britain—factionalism does not occur to any great extent. Major program policy divisions lead to the formation of new parties: e.g. Republican and Labor.

Antioquia enables us to keep party identification constant and test the incentive component of the hypotheses. I have argued that in Antioquia status is somewhat weaker as an incentive than in the country at large. Consequently, we should expect less factionalism in Antioquia. The lack of Antioqueño support for "nonofficial" presidential candidates and the Antioqueño resistance to national party divisions tend to confirm our expectation.

The importance of both incentives and structure in determining political phenomena is also illustrated in the treatment of the central question raised in the beginning of this chapter: why is political conflict intense in Colombia? Initially, a knowledge of incentives provides certain expectations about the level of conflict. Since incentives are strong, there is a good probability that a relatively high level of conflict will obtain. Participants (including active followers, as I shall show) are willing to make great sacrifices to match the strength of their incentives, and these sacrifices will represent high costs—injuries and deaths. In broad terms the hypothesis that conflict intensity increases as incentives are stronger (on either the status or program side) is consistent with the markedly lower level of political conflict in the United States than in Colombia. It can also be shown that, as expected, Antioquia exhibits a somewhat lower level of political conflict (less involvement in most civil wars, less electoral violence) than characterizes the country as a whole.

But this preliminary hypothesis does not account for certain other variations. The nature and strength of incentives, I believe, are the same in such countries as Ecuador and Peru as in Colombia. While Ecuador and Peru experience greater political violence than the United States, their levels of conflict have been considerably lower than in Colombia. In recent decades Colombia has experienced perhaps a hundred times as many political deaths as these other countries. Furthermore, there are substantial variations in the level of conflict in Colombia at different times. The period 1946–53 was extremely violent; from 1958 to the present there have been relatively few political deaths. An explanation of these differences may be found in the structures through which the incentives of Colombian participants find expression.

The incentive approach, then, focuses both on the satisfactions participants seek and the context that determines which actions will produce these respective satisfactions. A simple illustration is provided in the behavior of a hunter. To predict his actions we first must know which animal he seeks. Then we must know the alternatives open to him—weapons, strategies—and the efficacy of each alternative in bringing back the desired game. We may then predict how he will behave. Essentially, I argue that it is productive in certain cases to treat political phenomena as a function of both incentives and structure.

This statement is not a hypothesis but a research perspective. It stands as an amplification of the traditional approach, which implicitly treats the incentive dimension as a constant for all systems and reasons that changes in certain structures (election laws, constitutions, industrialization, educational systems) will produce changes in behavior. This purely structural approach is productive for the analysis of many problems, particularly if incentives are the same in the systems under analysis. But, as I hope to show in the following pages, the incentives for political participation may differ dramatically from system to system. In such cases the traditional approach of comparing constitutions, topography, or gross national products is bound to be inadequate. Until we know what politicians are seeking in the first place, we cannot predict how they will react to their environment.

CHAPTER 2

THE INCENTIVE FOR LEADERS:

STATUS

Q. *But why should anyone want to go into politics?*
A. *Because it gives one prestige and that helps you in private life. If you are famous, if you make a speech and it appears in the newspapers. . . . Look, a man can do a great work like a doctor making a miraculous operation or an engineer building up an entire suburb through his own efforts: they receive national acclaim; they are famous. But these men are few and far between, and it takes much time to do it that way. Then you see people getting famous because they are in politics, overnight. Then one sees the advantage of being in politics.*

> *From an interview with a fifth-year law student, active in political party affairs (Bogotá, March 2, 1965).*

This examination of the incentives for political participation in Colombia begins with leaders. By "leaders" I mean those participants who hold or actively aspire to the higher public offices listed in Table 2.1.[1] It is convenient to divide the leadership group into two broad levels: "upper leadership" and "lower leadership." The first category identifies the occupants of and aspirants for the more prominent national and departmental positions while the latter comprises individuals holding or seeking the less important local positions. The leadership group also includes the active aspirants for the positions identified in Table 2.1. Although aspirants clearly outnumber incumbents, it is difficult to estimate their number. For the upper leadership positions there may be from 10 to 20 times as many active aspirants as incumbents; for lower leadership positions, perhaps the ratio is five to ten times the number of incumbents. These rough

1. The identification of an "active aspirant" which I have in mind would entail asking an individual's friends something like: "Has (the individual) been interested in becoming a (position)?" "Yes" answers would identify the individual as an active aspirant.

estimates suggest that the entire leadership group might number in the range of 100,000 to 200,000: a massive group, but only a tiny fraction (about one per cent) of the entire population.

TABLE 2.1

Approximate Composition and Size of the
Colombian Leadership Group

Upper Leadership

Ministers, governors, and intendants	40
Supreme Court Justices	20
Councilors of State	10
National agency heads (est.)	250
Departmental agency heads (est.)	216
Senators	98
Alternates	98
Representatives	184
Alternates	184
Departmental deputies	358
Alternates	358
Intendancy deputies	32
Alternates	32
Eight cities of over 150,000:	
Mayors	8
Municipal secretaries (est.)	48
Municipal councilmen (est.)	128
Alternates	128
less overlap in above group (est.)	− 100
Total incumbents	2,092

Lower Leadership

Mayors	853
Municipal secretaries (est.)	1,706
Municipal councilmen	7,524
Alternates	7,524
less overlap in above group (est.)	− 1,000
Total incumbents	16,607
Grand Total, all incumbents	18,699

Sources: Figures not given as estimates have been compiled from: *Factores Colombianos* (Bogotá, Instituto Colombiano de Opinión Pública, 1964), pp. 46–47; Registraduría Nacional del Estado Civil, *Organización y Estadísticas Electorales* (Bogotá, 1965), p. 131.

I distinguish leaders from a second group of participants called "active followers." Active followers are those who do not seek or hold higher public offices but who are politically active: e.g. they attend political meetings or rallies with high frequency, work at election time, or donate money to a party or candidate. Active followers may hold lower public offices (positions in the bureaucracy), but holding office is not one of their defining characteristics.

The terms "leaders" and "active followers" are empirically descriptive of the relationship between the two groups of participants. In Colombia, and most other systems as well, it is the occupants of or aspirants for higher offices (leaders) who organize and direct those who are active in politics but do not seek higher offices (active followers). Obviously, leaders are of utmost importance in shaping the nature of the political system. A knowledge of their incentives, therefore, is the foundation for an analysis of the system. In examining the leadership incentive in Colombia we begin with the question: What conditions would make status the incentive for leaders?

If, in a given society, status is to be a strong incentive for leadership participation, then status itself must have considerable value in that society. There must be a keen awareness of "higher" and "lower" positions, and individuals must be greatly concerned with being seen as "higher" and not "lower." Considerations of rank, title, degree, position, or standing must be prominent in social relationships. This preoccupation with matters of rank I call "status-consciousness." Blalock describes this phenomenon: "the extremely status-conscious person lives and acts as though status considerations are of the utmost importance. They are to him the essence of social interaction." [2] Status-consciousness should not be confused with terms such as "class" or "class consciousness," which refer to other phenomena.

High status-consciousness, then, is necessary if status is to be a strong incentive. Individuals should be acutely concerned with their status and anxious to improve it. However, if this anxiety is to be translated into political participation it must also be true that higher public offices carry considerable status. The achievement of the title of president or representative or mayor should add considerably to one's social position so that individuals seeking status will find it through gaining such offices. If higher public offices carry a moderate or low status value, then highly status-conscious individuals will not seek them.

A third necessary condition for the presence of a strong status

2. H. M. Blalock, Jr., "Status-Consciousness: A Dimensional Analysis," *Social Forces, 37* (March 1959), 243.

incentive is that these higher public offices be relatively open to members of society of medium and low status. It is the gap between the high status of the office and low status of the potential aspirant which gives the status incentive its strength. If they are to become active aspirants to higher public offices, the low status members of society must believe they can obtain these offices. If recruitment to higher political offices were closed so that only a very high status "aristocracy" could hope for these positions, then status as an incentive for participation would be weak. Consequently, there must obtain a relatively open pattern of recruitment to these higher offices. By "relatively open" I do not mean that everyone has an equal chance of obtaining office, but simply that individuals from medium and lower strata have a real chance to reach these positions.

We can formulate an hypothesis expressing the three conditions which, when present concurrently, make status an increasingly strong incentive for leaders in a given system:

> *H1. Status will be an increasingly strong incentive for leadership participation as (1) status-consciousness is higher in the society, (2) the status value of higher political offices is greater, and (3) recruitment to these offices is more open.*

In the following pages we shall explore the degree to which each condition is present in Colombia.

STATUS-CONSCIOUSNESS

Colombians apparently are greatly concerned about status. They worry constantly about being above or below the next man. In many areas of behavior Colombians make conscious, often strenuous, efforts to maintain or improve their status. In titles of address, for example, one notes the impact of status-consciousness. In the blue-collar or *obrero* category, there exists a status distinction based on the title *maestro*. This title is sought by those who have, or claim to have, a certain skill, such as carpenters. The term is flattering, so that the individual who needs something from a blue-collar worker will address him as *maestro*.

Another distinction arises between blue-collar workers and white-collar workers, or more accurately, between those who get classified as *obreros* and those who are *empleados*. There exists an area of ambiguity where there is doubt as to which term might be employed (delivery men, doormen, elevator operators) and in such cases the individual himself will opt for the *empleado* classification whenever possible. In the white-collar category a status distinction commonly arises over the title of *doctor*. In the United States the term doctor is generally reserved for individuals who have obtained university degrees at the highest level. In Colombia the status value of the term makes it a title sought by many who have never even been to a university. One writer observes:

> In Colombia anyone who wears spectacles and speaks with emphasis is *doctor*. A *doctor* can be the chief of a government office, or the person who handles checks in a bank, or a departmental deputy or a celebrity; everybody is a *doctor*. . . . This custom has reached its extreme in Bogotá where there seem to exist only two classes of people: *doctores* and those who . . . want to become *doctores*.[3]

The entire structure and meaning of the Colombian educational system are affected by the pressure for status. In general, education, particularly at the secondary and university level, seems to be valued not so much for what is learned but for the status it provides. "Our peasant," the above writer notes, "dreams not of having his son become useful and well-instructed; instead he wants him to become a *doctor*." [4] The parents, as well as the students, are more interested in the status which comes from *being* a student at a certain institution at a certain level than in what is actually learned. This attitude has, of course, debilitated Colombian education.[5]

The fact that attendance at a university places the individual in a superior status position attracts many to universities, apparently in excess of the demand for university-trained personnel. A study of the

3. Pedro Restrepo Peláez, "La Universidad no Debe Ser una Fábrica de Doctores en Serie," *El Tiempo* (Bogotá), February 28, 1965, Suplemento Semanal, p. 4.
4. Ibid.
5. Fernando Guillén Martínez, *Raíz y Futuro de la Revolución,* (Bogotá, Ediciones Tercer Mundo, 1963), pp. 151 ff; Jorge Hoyos Vásquez, "Diagnóstico de la U," *El Espectador* (Bogotá), June 13, 1965, p. 1F; Gregorio Sánchez Gómez, *Sociología Política Colombiana* (Cali, Sánchez Gómez Hnos., 1943), pp. 82–83; E. Mendoza Varela, "Bachilleres a Granel," *El Tiempo,* June 11, 1965, p. 5.

requirements for high-level personnel needs for the period 1965–68 concluded:

> The supply of personnel in the majority of the specialties will exceed the demand for such personnel in the expansion of production of goods and services (enlargement of existing establishments), even considering attrition due to retirement and death.
>
> This being the case, there will remain a considerable margin of personnel for the initiation of new firms and activities.[6]

The size of this margin is so "considerable" that one may reasonably doubt whether new firms can absorb it. The writer's calculations for the supply and demand in some professions are presented in Table 2.2. The study concluded that there was a clear need for technicians and suggested that they be trained in the universities since "from the point of view of social status, university training will be more attractive to students than the expansion of technical secondary education."[7]

TABLE 2.2

*Projected Supply and Demand for High-level Personnel,
Selected Categories, 1965–1968*

Classification	Total new supply	Total new demand (firm expansion and attrition)	Excess
Architects	836	507	329
Civil engineers	1,116	834	282
Electrical engineers	471	168	303
Electronic engineers	238	117	121
Mechanical engineers	428	319	109
Draftsmen	316	143	173
Agricultural engineers	893	408	485
Industrial engineers	290	124	166
Pharmacists	468	323	145

Source: Instituto Colombiano de Especialización Técnica en el Exterior, "Recursos y Requerimientos de Personal de Alto Nivel" (Bogotá, mimeo, 1965 [?]), p. 82.

6. Instituto Colombiano de Especialización Técnica en el Exterior, *Recursos y Requerimientos de Personal de Alto Nivel* (Bogotá, mimeo, 1965 [?]), p. 81.
7. Ibid., p. 101.

In styles of dress the impact of status-consciousness is clear. Dozens of items from footwear to vests, and of course their cleanliness and state of repair, are status indicators. There is a constant gradation starting with the miserable, rag-shrouded peon toward the bottom, to the well-fed, vest-wearing bank president toward the top of the status scale. Although one might attempt broad divisions into six or seven categories, depending on dress, the fact is that many different points affect the status of individuals wearing the same basic dress: the cut and material of a suit; the tiny fraying at the shirt collar; a little smudge on the tie. Colombians are highly sensitive to these things, both in themselves and in others.

Naturally, dress cannot establish status unless considered in conjunction with other things: where the individual is, who is with him, how he carries himself, whether he appears anxious or self-confident. In general, being alone indicates lower status, since apparently no one else respects the person's company. Standing idly on the street (alone) lowers one's status compared to striding along, supposedly to an office and important responsibilities. Among university students the wearing of a coat and tie reflects the importance of multiple status determinants. The wealthy, higher status students at the Universidad de Los Andes (a private, high tuition institution) are most likely to wear an open shirt, sweater and even blue jeans. The lower status students, such as one finds at the Universidad Libre (a practically free school), almost without exception wear the coat and tie. Other indicators of their social position allow the former students a certain studied informality of dress; the latter group faces the real fear of being taken for what they are: children of lower strata families.

The number of characteristics and behavior patterns that affect status in Colombia is overwhelming. I discovered in the course of living six months with a middle-strata family in Colombia that I impaired my status by oiling a squeaky hinge, by carrying my own suitcase, by teaching the servant girl to read time, by never ringing the servant's bell, by moving my dinnerplate to one side when finished with a course. Needless to say, I did not earn the title of *doctor*. In Colombia status is enhanced by wearing a watch or glasses, by carrying a briefcase or umbrella, by coming late to a meeting, by having visited Europe or the United States. Of course, the more familiar status indicators are also important: type of residence, place of residence, light or dark skin, and family background.

It is true, of course, that some status-consciousness is found in the United States. But, in comparison with Colombia, the importance of status is markedly lower. American university students by the hundreds of thousands take jobs as dishwashers, waiters, or factory workers, unaware of the impact of such behavior on their status. They are unaware of status implications because the society in which they live does not impose these implications on them. The American lawyer will change a flat tire, the doctor will paint the kitchen, the college professor may raise tomatoes. Styles of dress are relatively unimportant in determining status. A new shirt looks "snappy," certain shoes are "comfortable," a person looks "presentable." But Americans are particularly insensitive to implications of "higher" or "lower" as inferred from dress. Social background is often neglected as a status consideration. The bank president is not embarrassed to tell people his father was a blue-collar worker. In dating and marriage, few Americans find that status considerations create a barrier, if, indeed, they pause to examine them at all.

The wide difference between the feeble degree of status-consciousness in the United States and the all-engrossing struggle for status in Colombia is expressed by Gerardo and Alicia Reichel-Dolmatoff in their excellent study of the small Colombian village of Aritama:

> The ultimate goal of life is to be respected (*ser respetado*), and all human activities are essentially oriented toward achieving this end. Leisure, capital, material progress, food, health, or whatever an individual may have made his ambition, are really only means to this single aspiration in life: to be accepted by society; to be free of discrimination, persecution, and ridicule; to be respected.
>
> To be respected means to be accepted as a "civilized" person and to be attributed dignity in spite of skin color and poverty. All inner problems, all psychological tensions, indeed the whole process of individual life develop in this dimension, between the aspired goal of being respected and the ever-present fear of being taken for a backward and poor Indio.
>
> There are minor goals but they are not ends to be achieved

for themselves but are only means for the greater goal. To have a family, to have sons who help in the fields, to have less work and more food, better clothes, to travel, to find a suitable match, were ambitions most frequently stated, but it was always understood that all these minor ambitions had value only insofar as they would contribute to personal prestige.[8]

STATUS VALUE OF POLITICAL OFFICE

Do higher political offices have a high status value in Colombia? To answer this question we prepared and distributed a questionnaire which sought university students' (N=75) evaluations of the social position of different occupations. These questionnaires contained 31 occupations, listed randomly, opposite a seven-position scale of social status. The seven positions, numbered from one to seven, were further identified by terms of progressively decreasing status from "upper-upper" to "lower-lower." The score for each occupation was averaged, producing a mean score which could vary from 1 (highest status) to 7 (lowest status). Details of the survey are presented in Appendix II.

The findings of this survey are presented in Table 2.3. Occupations separated by less than .1 mean score were grouped together since such small differences did not appear to be significant. In this way a condensed status ranking was obtained in which occupations of virtually equivalent status are grouped together. From this table we may conclude that the top national political offices have a high status value. The positions of minister and senator are not only highest on the scale, but are substantially higher in mean score than the next positions. The representative falls somewhat above all the professional categories.

This table, however, cannot be satisfactorily employed to estimate the status of regional or local political offices since the ranking was done by Bogotá students in a Bogotá frame of reference. Unfortunately, residence itself is an important status determinant; living in Bogotá is highest, departmental cities next, and a village lowest.

---

8. Gerardo and Alicia Reichel-Dolmatoff, *The People of Aritama* (London, Routledge and Kegan Paul, 1961), pp. 441–42. Aritama is a pseudonym.

TABLE 2.3

Relative Status Position of 31 Selected Occupations in Colombia
(student evaluations)

Occupation	Simple rank	Condensed rank	Mean score
Ministro (del Gabinete) (cabinet minister)	1	1	1.68
Senador de la República (senator)	2	2	2.04
Industrial (big businessman)	3	3	2.41
Jefe de ventas de gran empresa (Coltejer o Bavaria) (sales manager for big firm)	4	3	2.49
Representante a la Cámera (representative)	5	4	2.52
Arquitecto (architect)	6	5	2.58
Médico (doctor)	7	5	2.62
Profesor Universitario (university professor)	8	5	2.63
Ingeniero (engineer)	9	5	2.65
Odontólogo (dentist)	10	6	2.87
Abogado (lawyer)	11	6	2.92
Hacendado (rancher, hacienda owner)	12	7	3.07
Rentista (rentier)	13	7	3.08
Sacerdote (priest)	14	7	3.10
Diputado a la Asamblea Departamental (departmental deputy)	15	8	3.19
Oficial de la Armada (navy officer)	16	9	3.31
Estudiante Universitario (university student)	17	9	3.34
Comerciante (merchant)	18	9	3.36
Oficial del Ejército (army officer)	19	10	3.59
Periodista (journalist)	20	11	3.72
Funcionario Público (public official)	21	11	3.81
Contador (accountant)	22	12	3.97
Empleado Particular (private firm white-collar worker)	23	13	4.11
Empleado Público (public employee)	24	14	4.25
Oficial de la Policía (police officer)	25	14	4.26
Consejal (municipal councilman)	26	14	4.29
Maestro de Escuela (schoolteacher)	27	15	4.91
Agricultor (small farmer)	28	16	5.34
Carpintero (carpenter)	29	17	6.24
Obrero (blue-collar worker)	30	18	6.56
Campesino (peasant)	31	18	6.65

Consequently any occupation will have a lower status in a village than it would if exercised in Bogotá. Consequently, when Bogotá students rank "departmental deputy" or "municipal councilman," the status given is what people holding these positions would have if they came to Bogotá. This estimate is of little use in determining the status value of the office in the local status framework.

TABLE 2.4

Prestige Position of Occupations in the United States, I

Rank	Occupation
1	U.S. Supreme Court Justice
2	U.S. Ambassador to a foreign country
3	U.S. Cabinet Secretary
4	U.S. Senator
5	Governor of a state
6	College president or chancellor
7	Banker, large city
8	Mayor of city of 500,000 pop.
9	Medical doctor (big city)
10	State prosecuting attorney
11	Captain of ocean-going vessel
12	Criminal lawyer
13	Architect
etc.	

Source: Mapheus Smith, "An Empirical Scale of Prestige Status of Occupations," *American Sociological Review, 8* (1943), 187.

TABLE 2.5

Prestige Position of Occupations in the United States, II

Score	Occupation
96	U.S. Supreme Court Justice
93	Physician
93	State governor
92	Cabinet member in the federal government
92	Diplomat in the U.S. foreign service
90	Mayor of large city
89	College professor
89	Scientist
89	United States Representative
88	Banker
88	Government scientist
87	County judge
87	Head of a department in a state government
87	Minister
86	Architect
86	Chemist
86	Dentist
86	Lawyer
etc.	

Source: National Opinion Research Center, "Jobs and Occupations: A Popular Evaluation," in Reinhard Bendix and Seymour Martin Lipset, *Class, Status and Power* (Glencoe, Free Press, 1960), p. 412.

TABLE 2.6

Prestige Position of Occupations in the Philippines

Rank	Occupation
1	Physician
2	Congressman
3	Lawyer
4	Engineer
5	University professor
6	Priest
etc.	

Source: Edward A. Tiryakian, "The Prestige Evaluation of Occupations in an Underdeveloped Country: The Philippines," *American Journal of Sociology,* *63* (1958), 394.

In Tables 2.4, 2.5, and 2.6 I have presented partial findings of similar studies of occupational standing made in the United States and the Philippines. Differences in method and occupational categories make it difficult to compare these studies with mine; perhaps the only conclusion is that higher public offices carry relatively high status in all countries. If there are national differences in the relative values of such positions it would take more carefully controlled and standardized measures to show them.

RECRUITMENT TO POLITICAL OFFICE

Are the high status political offices open to members of lower strata in Colombia? Can a carpenter become a councilman? Can the son of a schoolteacher become president? Unfortunately, there has been little research done on the social backgrounds of Colombian political leaders. In spite of the absence of data, American scholars have usually assumed that higher public offices are and have been tightly closed to all but a small, self-perpetuating upper tier of high status individuals. The evidence I have collected suggests this assumption is in error.

In recent times three important presidential candidates came from low status social backgrounds: Jorge Eliécer Gaitán, Gabriel Turbay, and Jorge Levya. Earlier we find that Marco Fidel Suárez, president 1919–21, was the illegitimate son of a laundress.[9] Luis A. Robles,

9. Guillén Martínez, *Raíz y Futuro,* p. 155.

a prominent Liberal leader in the late nineteenth century (minister, governor) was extremely dark-skinned, the son of a negro and an Indian.[10] José María Rojas Garrido, president in 1867, was from a "poor and obscure" family.[11] Manual Murillo Toro, president 1864– 66, 1872–74, was of a "modest family." [12] Mariano Ospina Rodríguez, president 1858–60, is cited as being from a "humble origin." [13]

Some men from low social backgrounds have achieved the presidency through the army. Two notable cases are José Antonio Páez of Venezuela and Juan José Flores of Ecuador who separated their respective countries from Gran Colombia (1828, 1830).[14] The Colombian army has been relatively inactive in politics, but twice a man from a nondescript social background has obtained the presidency by means of a military coup; José María Melo in 1854 and Gustavo Rojas Pinilla in 1953.[15]

Colombian politics in the nineteenth century was not, as is sometimes imagined, confined to an aristocratic elite. There were, for example, numerous artisan political societies during the 1840s and 1850s which played an important role. The first president of the reconstituted *Sociedad Democrática de Artesanos* of Bogotá in 1847 was the son of a tailor. In discussing his life history, this man recounted that he had visited with President Santander, had been made an army officer, and later became a mayor. He reported that it was not uncommon for artisans to hold political offices.[16]

Two pieces of quantitative data throw some light upon the social

10. Eduardo Rodríguez Piñeres, *Hechos y Comentarios* (Bogotá, Editorial Sucre, 1956), p. 189.

11. Gustavo Samper Bernal, *Breve Historia Constitucional y Política de Colombia* (Bogotá, Talleres Editoriales de la Litografía Colombia, 1957), p. 109; Milton Puentes, *Historia del Partido Liberal Colombiano* (2d ed. Bogotá, Prag, 1961), p. 249.

12. Samper Bernal, p. 107; Eduardo Rodríguez Piñeres, *El Olimpo Radical* (Bogotá, Librería Voluntad, 1950), pp. 171, 175–76.

13. Juan Manuel Rudas, *Lo que Fué y lo que Es el Partido Conservador* (Barcelona, Imprenta de Juan Tarrall y Cía, 1889), p. 9.

14. David Bushnell, *The Santander Regime in Gran Colombia* (Newark, Del., University of Delaware Press, 1954), p. 250; A. J. Lemos Guzmán, *Obando* (2d ed. Popayán, Editorial Universidad del Cauca, 1959), p. 182.

15. For data on Melo and the coup of 1854 see Pérez, pp. 17 ff.

16. Ambrosio López, *El Desengaño* (Bogotá, Imprenta de Espinosa, 1851), pp. 10–13.

backgrounds of officeholders. The first is a study by the National
Statistics Office on the occupations of political officeholders in 1936.
In Table 2.7 the findings of this study are cross-entered with the
status levels of occupations, as determined in Table 2.3. It was not
stated how the occupational categories were applied, but I suspect
that the respondents identified themselves. Consequently, we may
expect a certain amount of status inflation, for the respondents
would overrate themselves as part of their status-consciousness.
Given the ambiguity of important categories—*industrial, hacendado,
comerciante*—a respondent could hide a decidedly low status background: the peasant sharecropper might call himself *hacendado,*
the popcorn vendor, a *comerciante.*

But even accepting this overstatement of status, Table 2.7 provides a picture of a relatively open recruitment pattern. There is, of
course, a marked overrepresentation of high status occupations (professionals) in the Senate and the House, compared to the frequency
of these occupations in the population. But one also notes the presence of medium and medium-low status occupations—*comerciantes,
empleados, agricultores*—in these bodies. At the level of the departmental assemblies are individuals (9 out of 267) who identify themselves as blue-collar workers (*obreros*).

A crude comparison might be attempted with the United States
by inspecting the Connecticut legislature. The comparison is imperfect since the Colombian departmental assemblies are small (16–
20 members), one-house bodies, while Connecticut has a large, two-
chamber legislature which might be, consequently, less difficult to
enter. We find, however, that in the 1959 session, none of the 36
members of the Connecticut Senate would be classified as *obreros.*
In the 234-member lower house there were only ten blue-collar
workers (seven skilled, three unskilled) as well as six other individuals who might be either self-employed (*comerciantes* in Colombian
terms) or blue-collar workers (two "painters," two "repairmen," a
"cabinetmaker," and an "electrician").[17] This comparison would
suggest that recruitment to political positions is probably no more
closed to lower status individuals in Colombia than it is in the United
States.

A second piece of quantitative data on leadership social backgrounds comes from a survey I conducted on a sample of the upper

17. Compiled from the *Connecticut State Register and Manual 1960,* pp. 104–17.

TABLE 2.7

Occupations of Colombian Officeholders, 1936

Status level in condensed rank units	Occupation	Number of Individuals			
		Senate	House	Departmental assemblies	Town councils
3	Industriales (manufacturers)		3 (3%)	18 (7%)	610 (11%)
5	Médicos (doctors)	4 (7%)	30 (26%)	34 (13%)	187 (4%)
5	Ingenieros (engineers)	4 (7%)	9 (8%)	11 (4%)	78 (1%)
6	Dentistas (dentists)		3 (3%)		47 (1%)
6	Abogados (lawyers)	33 (58%)	38 (33%)	51 (19%)	431 (8%)
7	Hacendados (ranchers)	1 (2%)	3 (3%)	18 (7%)*	902 (17%)*
7	Rentistas (rentiers)			19 (7%)	198 (4%)
9	Estudiantes (students)			12 (4%)	47 (1%)
9	Comerciantes (merchants)	4 (7%)	7 (6%)	43 (16%)	1,788 (34%)
11	Periodistas (journalists)	4 (7%)	7 (6%)	6 (2%)	31 (1%)
12	Agronomistas (agronomists)			3 (1%)	38 (1%)
13–14	Empleados (white-collar workers)		2 (2%)	35 (13%)	293 (6%)
15	Pedagogos (schoolteachers)		2 (2%)	5 (2%)	52 (1%)
16	Agricultores (small farmers)	6 (11%)	5 (4%)	*	*
17	Obreros (blue-collar workers)			9 (3%)	492 (9%)
	Others, unknown	1 (2%)	6 (5%)	3 (1%)	114 (2%)
Totals		57 (100%)	115 (100%)	267 (100%)	5,308 (100%)

*The ocupational category "agricultor" was not used at all for the members of departmental assemblies and city councils. It is reasonable to suppose that many assemblymen and councilmen classified as "hacendados" would have fallen in the "agricultor" category, had it been used.

Source: Dirección Nacional de Estadística, Anuario General de Estadística 1936 (Bogotá, 1937), pp. 519–20.

leadership group (approximately identified in Table 2.1) in 1965. For details of this survey the reader may consult Appendix I. Each respondent was asked to identify the occupation of his father. The results of this question are tabulated in Table 2.8, with the fathers'

TABLE 2.8

Fathers' Occupation, Colombian Upper Leadership Sample

Occupation status (in condensed rank)	Fathers' occupation	Liberals	Conservatives	Total No.	%
2	Ambassador	1		1	1
3	*Industrial*	1		1	1
5	Architect		1	1	1
5	Doctor	2	2	4	3
5	Engineer	1	3	4	3
6	Lawyer	6	13	19	16
7	*Hacendado*	2	1	3	2
7	*Ganadero* (cattle raiser)	2	5	7	6
9	*Comerciante* (and *Negociante*)	16	19	35	29
10	Army officer		2	2	2
11	Journalist	1	2	3	2
11	*Funcionario público*	1	1	2	2
12	Accountant	1		1	1
14	Public employee	3	4	7	6
15	Schoolteacher	1	1	2	2
16	*Agricultor*	10	12	22	18
17	Carpenter (and other skilled blue-collar)	3	1	4	3
18	*Obrero*	2		2	2
	Totals, all known	53	67	120	100
	Unknown, no answer	7	3	10	
	Total, entire sample	60	70	130	

occupations ranked in status, as determined in Table 2.3. Again it is reasonable to expect a certain amount of status inflation as status-conscious individuals seek to avoid the embarrassment of showing low status backgrounds. "No answer" responses probably indicate low status backgrounds. As the table indicates, the bulk of the respondents' fathers had medium or low status occupations. Only one third had fathers at rank 7 (*hacendado*) or above; one third had fathers at rank 14 (public employee) or below. Five per cent of those answering gave their father's occupation as *obrero*.

I conclude that recruitment to political office is relatively open in

Colombia. The son of a blue-collar worker, small farmer, or school-teacher does have a meaningful (but not equal) opportunity to reach top public offices.

A SUMMARY OF THE FINDINGS

I am suggesting, then, that Colombian society is characterized by high status-consciousness, high status value of political office, and a relatively open recruitment to these offices. Moreover, these conditions have apparently existed at least since independence. According to historian Fernando Guillén Martínez:

> The society which arises slowly and with difficulty in the colonial era is a group of exploiters and exploited, forced to coexist in the same territory, in continuous intermixture and without it being possible to maintain the stability of classes or their impermeability. The hereditary continuity of privilege is more apparent than real: what survives in more and more pronounced form is the idea of privilege, not the privilege of a family lineage. And closely tied to privilege is the state, so that the two come to be nothing more than two terms for the same social force.[18]

Other writers have noted the extreme importance of prestige or "honor" in Spanish-American culture. It was the most status-conscious individuals of Spain, some argue, who carried out the conquest and colonization of the New World. The colonies therefore became heavily populated by quasi-, pseudo-, and would-be nobles all struggling for the titles they could not achieve in Spain. The revolution against Spain is also interpreted as a conflict between local-born *creoles* and Spanish appointees for the prestige of governmental positions.[19]

In recounting his memories of colonial life in the Colombian city

18. Guillén Martínez, p. 82.
19. Hugo Latorre Cabal, *La Hispanidad* (Bogotá, Editorial Kelly, 1950), p. 129 and passim; E. Caballero Calderón, *Historia Privada de los Colombianos* (Bogotá, Talleres Antares, 1960), pp. 61–64 and passim; Hugo Velasco A., *Retorno a la Hispanidad* (Bogotá, Editorial Cosmos, 1953), pp. 13–22; Roberto Echeverría Rodríguez, *Los Segundos Libertadores* (Barranquilla, Ediciones Arte, 1950), pp. 41–43; Rufino Blanco-Fombona, *La Evolución Política y Social de Hispano-América* (Madrid, Bernardo Rodríguez, 1911), pp. 23–29; Américo Castro, *The Structure of Spanish History,* trans. Edmund L. King (Princeton, Princeton University Press, 1954), pp. 607–66 and passim.

of Cartagena about 1810, Joaquín Posada Gutiérrez describes a society characterized by both a high consciousness of status and a fluid, ambiguous stratification pattern. He notes, for example, the existence of seven different dance events, each attended by a different strata. But the same lines of division which obtained for the dances were crossed in other events. The divisions and subdivisions were unstable, he points out, and not characterized by impenetrable barriers. He notes the popularity of jewelry, adding, "But do not think that this oriental luxury was reserved to the privileged class; it was used similarly by everyone who could." The use of fake jewelry was common in the lower strata since "to have or not to have has established in human society one difference among differences, and, up to a certain point, *to have* makes one equal to those who have." [20]

These observations about the nature of Colombian society contradict certain views generally accepted in the United States. First, Colombia is *not* characterized by particularly low social mobility, as has been shown with respect to the achievement of top political offices. It may also be seen on an occupational scale, as computed for our sample of upper leadership. I took the respondent's occupation and measured the distance over (or under) his father's occupation in condensed status rank units. The results presented in Table 2.9 show considerable upward mobility for this group. Naturally the figures must be interpreted with caution since the group is atypical of society in general. There is some evidence, also, that on an educational scale mobility is substantial. One study of university students found that only 20.4 per cent of the fathers of the students had had any university education, a fact which justified the writer's conclusion that "the university, in a growing and continuous fashion, is offering means of upward mobility." [21] These findings, albeit fragmentary, contradict such unsubstantiated allegations as Colombia "is a country with extremely low vertical social mobility." [22]

20. Joaquín Posada Gutiérrez, *Memorias Histórico-Políticas* (6 vols. Bogotá, 1951), *3,* 94–95 and passim. See also Jorge Juan and Antonio de Ulloa, *A Voyage to South America,* trans. John Adams (New York, Knopf, 1964), pp. 26–36, 135–46, 193–202.

21. Robert C. Williamson, *El Estudiante Colombiano y sus Actitudes* (Bogotá, Facultad de Sociología, Universidad Nacional de Colombia, 1962), pp. 13, 15.

22. Aaron Lipman, "Social Backgrounds of the Bogotá Entrepreneur," *Journal of Inter-American Studies,* 7 (1965), 228. One writer who argues that mobility is sub-

TABLE 2.9

Social Mobility on an Occupational Scale in Colombia;
Sample of Upper Political Leadership

Status of respondent's occupation compared with the status
of his father's occupation (condensed rank units)*

	−5	−4	−3	−2	−1	0	+1	+2	+3
Liberals	3	2		1	1	6	4	1	9
Conservatives	1	1		3	4	18	3	2	13
Total, both parties	4	3		4	5	24	7	3	22

	+4	+5	+6	+7	+8	+9	+10	+11	Unknown
Liberals	4	1	3	7	1	1	2	3	11
Conservatives	3	2		3	2	1	7	3	4
Total, both parties	7	3	3	10	3	2	9	6	15

Summary totals	Lower status than father	Same as father	Higher status than father
	16 (14%)	24 (21%)	75 (65%)
	Total known cases	Unknown	Sample Total
	115 (100%)	15	130

*See Table 2.3.

Note: Political positions were not treated as occupations. A respondent who happened to be a senator but gave his occupation as "lawyer" (rank 6) and his father's occupation as *"comerciante"* (rank 9) would be classified under the +3 status unit change. The two respondents who gave a political position ("congressman") as the occupation were entered in the unknown column.

Second, Colombia is *not* characterized by "classes," if that term is taken to mean social units within which status is equal, but which are marked off from other segments by significant status distance.[23] Each Colombian is in constant competition with his neighbor for status. At no level does everyone treat each other as equals, free

stantial in Colombia is Gerardo Reichel-Dolmatoff, "Notas sobre la Clase Media en Colombia" in *Tres Estudios sobre la Clase Media en Colombia* (Bogotá, Banco de la República [1955]), p. 51.

23. The term "class" is fraught with confusion; my usage corresponds to that advanced by Walter Goldschmidt, "Social Class in America—A Critical Review," *American Anthropologist, 52* (1950), pp. 483–98.

from considerations of status. Although it may seem, from a distance, that blue-collar workers or peasants form a group of equal-status individuals, the fact is that distinctions and subdivisions are found there, too. The Reichel-Dolmatoffs found in the obscure village of Aritama, all residents of which would be dismissed by Bogotanos as "Indios," the same restless striving for status (respect) as occurs in Bogotá itself. The stratification pattern in Colombia is unbroken by any sharp divisions one could usefully call "class lines"; it comprises no groups of non-status-competitive members one could meaningfully call a "class."

It also seems incorrect to suppose the existence of "classes" in the sense of socioeconomic groups having sharply differentiated worldviews and characterized by a clear sense of identification (class-consciousness). Everyone in Colombia wants to move higher (or at least appear higher), and the meaning of "higher" and "lower" is universal in society. The image of a blue-collar group content with manual labor is mistaken. These individuals are constantly struggling to avoid an *obrero* classification, or at least to see that their sons may avoid it. The peasant dreams that his son may be a *doctor*.[24]

Indeed, the absence of "class" in the above sense would seem to be a requisite for high status-consciousness. The idea of class incorporates the notion that one does not compete with fellow class members for status. Within a class, supposedly, there exists a sense of identification, of being "all in the same boat." Except in unusual cases, individuals in one class would not be concerned with entering other classes, but live securely among their recognized equals. This phenomenon contrasts with high status-consciousness where no one is a recognized equal, where there exists no "we" with which to identify, and where everyone is insecure about status.

24. One of the threads in the confused argument over whether there is or is not a "middle class" in Latin American countries concerns the alleged attitudes of different socioeconomic groups. Some writers have argued that there is no "middle class" because the middle groups have the same values as an "upper class," particularly in disdaining manual labor. This observation is used to support the conclusion that psychologically there are only (?) two classes since those who work manually are supposed, *quite incorrectly,* to see virtue in manual labor. See: Ralph L. Beals, "Social Stratification in Latin America," *The American Journal of Sociology, 58* (January 1953), 333; William S. Stokes, *Latin American Politics* (New York, Thomas Y. Crowell, 1959), p. 23.

Because there appears to be no felt sentiment of class-consciousness in Colombia, I conclude that it is unprofitable and misleading to speak of "classes." [25] For purposes of identifying approximate sections of a smoothly rising stratification curve, the neutral term "strata" is a convenient way to avoid the misleading connotations of "class."

TESTING THE HYPOTHESIS

The available evidence suggests that in Colombia (1) status-consciousness is high, (2) the status value of higher public office is high, and (3) recruitment to these offices is relatively open. According to the hypothesis, then, status should be a strong incentive for leaders. Does the hypothesis fit the facts in Colombia?

My measurement of leadership incentives rests on the use of extended interviews. The object in such interviews was to encourage the respondent to indicate the nature of his satisfactions. For this study, leadership incentives were estimated from about 50 interviews with Colombian leaders, predominantly upper leaders, from seven different departments. Included among the respondents were senators, representatives, departmental deputies, municipal councilmen of big cities, and some higher administrative officials.

In such interviews direct questions such as "Why are you in politics?" are unsatisfactory in revealing incentives because individuals may not be aware of their incentives or, if they are, they may be unable or unwilling to express them clearly. Instead, I employed an indirect method of determining satisfactions from what the respondent talks about and what he knows most about. The assumption is that an individual's attention (interest, knowledge) will focus upon the goals he seeks. In any extended interview, almost regardless of the questions asked, the focus of the respondent's interest will usually be clear. Some useful questions are: What has

25. Guillén Martínez also holds this view, p. 102. Andrew H. Whiteford in his study of the Colombian town of Popayán argues that the three groups, upper, middle, and lower, are "classes," being "real entities." But the substance of his detailed findings seem to refute this thesis for he divides these "real entities" into six levels and repeatedly emphasizes the marginal gradations within and between these levels: *Two Cities of Latin America* (Garden City, Doubleday, 1964), p. 27 and passim.

been happening in the House of Representatives (Senate, council, your department) lately? What was the most important political event of last week (month, year)? Why? What was the X incident all about? What does it mean?

Interviews with Colombian leaders revealed that overwhelmingly they were interested in, concerned about, and knowledgeable on the subject of *obtaining positions*. They were singularly uninterested and uninformed on matters of policy. The episodes and illustrations which respondents mentioned in the interviews concerned the struggle for positions: the fight for congressional seats in Chocó; the intraparty struggle to get on the Liberal directorate of Tolima; the history and tactics of a factionalist's battle to get on the town council of Facatativá; the struggle to unseat a governor in Cundinamarca. These episodes were recounted in strictly strategic terms: who did what *to get a position*. Policy issues or policy decisions were almost never mentioned. Members of congressional committees seemed particularly uninterested in the bills and subject matters of their committees.

Respondents revealed a marked sophistication in their grasp of matters pertaining to obtaining and losing positions. Colombian politicians are, I found, excellent analysts of certain areas of politics: nominations, elections, and electoral strategies. They respond at length and knowledgeably to questions about composing a party list, composing a directorate, the role of a directorate in settling a factional dispute, or the electoral resources of a governor. Colombian leaders are generally shrewd analysts of the strategic implications of constitutional provisions, electoral laws, political alliances, and maneuvers. They are well-versed on these subjects because they think about and discuss them constantly.

The Colombian politician's knowledge of matters affecting office-holding is matched by his ignorance about matters of policy and policymaking. With only a few exceptions, none of the respondents could be considered an expert on matters of policy. The way *not* to learn about such problems as housing, agrarian reform, or industrial development is to ask Colombian politicians. Except for a few, they have no new insights and little information. One finds members of the House budget committee who are unclear or even mistaken about the budgetary process in Congress, who do not know the size of major items in the budget, or even the size of the total budget. A *ponente* (floor manager) of an important bill voted upon two years before could not remember the basic history of the legislation in Congress. In general, congressmen are of little help in tracking down the history of legislation because they forget or never knew which house it started in, what happened in committee, or how it was voted.

In view of the lack of interest in policy matters and the marked interest in positions and position-getting expressed by the respondents, I conclude that it is the position or title itself which they seek. That is, Colombian leaders have a status incentive. Their incentives are not program, style, or conviviality since they do not express the interests that would reveal such incentives: concern with policy, concern with normative behavior, and concern with social interaction, respectively. This conclusion is supported by direct references to motivation made by the respondents. When asked such questions as "Generally speaking, why do people go into politics in Colombia?" the answers were often "honor," "prestige," or "fame" (see excerpt at beginning of the chapter). Although "money" was also mentioned as a motive, it usually appeared as a quick, simple answer which was seldom elaborated in the interviews.

Colombia may be contrasted with the United States where, I believe, the dominant incentive for leaders is program. This conclusion rests, to a certain extent, on my own observation that American leaders are usually interested in and well-informed on matters of governmental policy. However, several studies seem to support this view. One examination of the career perspectives of American state legislators by Eulau and others explicitly touched upon the subject of goals. Although the writers found goals to be mixed, their presentation suggests that the orientation we would describe as a program incentive was most in evidence.[26]

James D. Barber's study of freshmen Connecticut legislators enables us to handle incentives of American leaders in somewhat more quantitative terms. His Lawmakers, as I have already suggested,

26. Eulau et al., "Career Perspectives of American State Legislators," in Marvick, ed., *Political Decision-makers,* pp. 218–63, especially pp. 241–54. See also: Charles L. Clapp, *The Congressman* (Washington, The Brookings Institution, 1963), pp. 420–32.

fit our conception of individuals with a program incentive. He notes, for example, the pronounced tendency of these individuals to direct the interview discussion to specific legislation and policy matters.[27] His group of Advertisers resemble the Colombians: "Advertisers refer to legislation offhandedly, as if the business of the Assembly were someone else's business." [28] The four groups into which Barber divides his 96 freshmen legislators can be identified, albeit cautiously, by their different incentives:

Lawmakers (program)	34%
Spectators (conviviality)	31%
Advertisers (status)	17%
Reluctants (style)	18%

Those with a program incentive do form the largest group.[29] More-over, the Lawmakers would undoubtedly form a greater portion of the entire legislature since they are more willing to return than either Advertisers or Reluctants.

THE STRENGTH OF INCENTIVES

In estimating the strength of incentives from interviews, one seeks indications of the relative value of participation, compared with other things. We might infer weak incentives for Barber's Reluctants and Spectators because their attitude toward their own nomination and election was one of hesitation and almost indifference. They speak as though competing values almost outweighed the attraction of participation. Sometimes respondents will explicitly state values which are stronger than the appeal of participation. Illustrative is this comment of a delegate (a "politician") to the 1964 Republican convention, which appears in Wildavsky's study:

Q. Can the Republicans win?
A. Not unless something happens.
Q. Like what?
A. A white backlash building up if the negroes have a lot of

27. Barber, *The Lawmakers,* p. 164.
28. Ibid., p. 112.
29. Ibid., p. 20.

big demonstrations in the cities; or if Vietnam blew up in our faces. But I'd rather lose than have those things happen. I'd rather lose than have race fights or war.[30]

In interviews with Colombian leaders, I did not find expressions of limits placed on the value of participation. A statement like "I'd rather lose than . . ." would seem incongruous with the attitudes of Colombian leaders toward their participation. With few exceptions, leaders did not speak of their nominations or elections as events met with hesitancy or reluctance. They generally spoke of their nominations as difficult fights into which they jumped boldly. These observations, of course, constitute only fragmentary evidence to support the proposition that incentives are strong in Colombia and of only moderate strength in the United States. Hopefully, future applications of the incentive concept will develop more precise techniques for measuring the strength of incentives along the lines suggested above.

In this study the strength of the dominant incentive is estimated indirectly by assuming that the predominance of the dominant incentive increases as it becomes stronger. By "predominance" I mean the relative frequency with which leaders holding the dominant incentive are encountered. The theory behind this assumption rests upon a competitive conception of incentives.

In any system there are potential participants, each holding different incentives. If none of these incentives is particularly strong, competition is balanced so that in the leadership group one finds some individuals with one incentive and others with a different incentive (e.g. 60 per cent of the leaders with the dominant incentive, 40 per cent with other incentives). But individuals with a particularly strong incentive, being willing to make greater sacrifices, will outcompete and eliminate others holding different incentives of lesser strength, and consequently will be overwhelmingly predominant in the leadership group (e.g. 90 per cent dominant incentive to 10 per cent others). The clear predominance of one incentive, therefore, indicates that it is strong, while a mixture of incentives would indicate that the dominant incentive is of only moderate strength.

30. Wildavsky, "The Goldwater Phenomenon: Purists, Politicians, and the Two-Party System," *The Review of Politics, 27* (July 1965), 397.

I have described the status incentive in Colombia as "strong," because it was so predominant in the sample of leaders I interviewed. In the United States, as indicated in Barber's findings, the program incentive is not so clearly predominant. Consequently I infer that the program incentive is of moderate strength (see Figure 1, Chapter 1).

These conclusions about incentives are consistent with the basic hypothesis advanced above (H1). In Colombia where status-consciousness is high, where higher political positions have a high status value, and where recruitment is relatively open, status is a strong incentive. In the United States where status-consciousness is relatively low (the other two conditions are met), status is not a sufficiently strong incentive to be dominant. Instead, program is the dominant incentive in the United States. This variation in leadership incentives between the two countries is a fundamental difference from which a wide range of specific contrasts flow.

CHAPTER 3

THE INCENTIVE FOR ACTIVE FOLLOWERS:
EMPLOYMENT

Conservative Departmental Directorate
Santander, Colombia
Bucaramanga, March 22, 1965

Mr. E. S. M.

It puzzles me that you refuse to contribute to the treasury of the party to which you belong and to which, if I am not mistaken, you perhaps owe a debt of gratitude for having obtained for you the position you now occupy.

This very day I shall bring this problem of voluntary contributions to the attention of the secretary [of your departmental office]. The payments are being made by the majority of genuine Conservatives, individuals who genuinely deserve positions in the Government and not, like you, who in spite of the fact that the Directorate recommended you for your position, now refuse to contribute to the leadership you are representing in the political division of offices in that agency.

Sincerely,
A. N. Q.
Departmental general secretary

Photostatic copy of a letter published in La República *(Bogotá, March 27, 1965), p. 1.*

Active followers are those individuals who do more than merely vote but who are not aspirants to higher offices. As I have already suggested, active followers are somewhat less important than leaders in shaping the dimensions of politics because they are not in the most decisive positions. Nevertheless, they do play a role. They participate in financial support and electioneering (fixing posters, watching polls, encouraging turnout), enthusiastically join in demonstrations, and act as opinion leaders in their circle of friends and relatives. Leaders, who need this cooperation, may be constrained by their active followers, depending on the incentives of this latter group.

One possibility, for example, is that active followers will have a strong program incentive, requiring leaders with a status incentive to behave in a somewhat program-oriented fashion in order to secure their cooperation. Another possibility is that incentives for active followers are so weak that they will be few in number and nearly apathetic. This condition would probably reduce the likelihood of massive political conflict (riots, clashes) as well as substantially affect styles of electioneering. Neither of these possibilities occurs in Colombia. Instead there are a large number of active followers with a strong incentive, and one which does not cause them to constrain leaders who hold a status incentive.

The incentive for active followers in Colombia is employment. By "employment" I mean paid, non-elective positions in government, excluding the higher administrative posts. This definition describes ordinary bureaucratic positions, as distinct from the top administrative posts (minister, agency head, governor, mayor) which, at least according to Colombian law, are the only positions that should be distributed on a political basis.[1] It is the desire to hold the ordinary bureaucratic positions which motivates most of the active followers in Colombia.

A productive approach to the study of government employment as an incentive focuses upon the supply and demand for government jobs. On the demand side, the fact of greatest importance is that most government jobs are for white-collar or *empleado* personnel. They require such skills as literacy and mathematics, and involve working in an office. In Tables 3.1 and 3.2 I have presented some data on the number of government employees for the three levels of government and for the decentralized institutes. The total number of government jobs was about 262,420 for 1966. Of this total I estimate that about 90 per cent, or about 236,000 are *empleado*

1. Departamento Administrativo del Servicio Civil, *El Servicio Civil y la Carrera Administrativa en Colombia* (Bogotá, Imprenta Nacional, 1961), p. 51.

TABLE 3.1

Number of Permanent Government Employees, 1963

National employees*	82,883
Departmental employees	64,425
Territorial employees	1,357
Municipal employees	38,718
Total	187,383

*Includes only civilian defense personnel.

Source: Departamento Administrativo Nacional de Estadística, *Informe al Congreso Nacional 1964* (Bogotá, Multilith Estadinal, 1964), pp. 58–61.

positions. The predominance of white-collar workers in government jobs makes it necessary to examine the white-collar labor market if we are to understand the employment incentive. What determines the supply of white-collar workers in Colombia?

A first thought might be that the supply of *empleados* would probably lag behind the demand. Economic modernization would cause

TABLE 3.2

Employees of the Decentralized Government Institutes
(projected for 1966)

Institute	Number of employees
Agrarian Reform Institute (INCORA)	1,058
Agricultural Credit Institute (ICA)	715
Housing Institute (ICT)	1,750
Food Supply Institute (INA)	1,597
Worker Apprenticeship Service (SENA)	2,348
Social Security Institute	8,066
National Social Assistance Fund	1,047
National University	3,008
Augustin Codazzi Geographic Institute	1,335
Post Office	2,164
Telephone and Telegraph Corporation	9,100
Radio and Television Institute	470
National Railways	13,711
National Airport Corporation	1,551
National Harbor Corporation	7,056
National Petroleum Corporation (Ecopetrol)	5,686
35 other institutes	6,758
Total, 51 decentralized institutes	67,420

Source: Proyecto Presupuesto de los Establecimientos Públicos Decentralizados (Anexo 1966, Bogotá, 1965).

these better-educated workers to be absorbed faster than the educational system, allowing for lag, could prepare them. Also, blue-collar workers would be relatively slow to adjust their attitudes to the new economic opportunities, to realize as adolescents that staying in school means better pay. This expectation corresponds to the experience in the United States where, it seems, the need for white-collar workers surpasses the supply. One indication of this condition is the substantially higher blue-collar unemployment rates, compared to those of white-collar workers.[2]

But this reasoning ignores the impact of status-consciousness. It assumes that workers entering the labor market as adolescents will remain in the blue-collar category until they clearly perceive the cash value of forgoing wage-earnings for additional years of education. This purely economic calculation is likely to be overridden in a society where status-consciousness is high. White-collar positions will have a status value independent of—or even in opposition to—monetary considerations. Blue-collar workers will try to get themselves, and particularly their sons, into the white-collar category for the status it provides. As long as barriers to mobility into the white-collar category are weak, the movement into that level may be expected to exceed the demand. Stated as a hypothesis:

> *H2. In a society characterized by high status-consciousness and relatively weak barriers to upward social mobility, the supply of white-collar workers will be well in excess of that required by the economic system.*

As observed in the previous chapter, the two conditions of high status-consciousness and upward social mobility seem to exist in Colombia. Testing the hypothesis requires some measure of the economic requirements for white-collar workers in Colombia. As a comparison I employ the United States at a similar stage of economic development, as indicated below. In spite of the imperfect nature of the comparison, the differences discovered are so great that they remain suggestive.

One piece of data comes from an examination of the source of white-collar workers, the educational system. Probably the most

2. In recent years the blue-collar unemployment rate in the United States has been about three times that for white-collar workers; see Bureau of Labor Statistics, *Employment and Earnings, 12* (February 1966), 21.

important mechanism affecting mobility from blue-collar or peasant groups to the white-collar level is education, particularly secondary education. The individual who has had some secondary education in Colombia is very likely to consider himself an *empleado;* and such an individual would be considered eligible for *empleado* positions. If our hypothesis is correct, then, we should expect to find that Colombia has more secondary school students than did the United States at a comparable level of development.

To arrive at this comparison, I have calculated the proportion of secondary school students to total population for each of the two countries in years for which data were available. For the measure of economic development I have used the proportion of workers in the nonagricultural labor force. The two series have been placed on a graph with the proportion of secondary students to total population plotted against the level of economic development. The years in which the stated relationship occurred in each country are given in parentheses on the graph.

Figure 2 shows that at comparable levels of development Colombia has had (and now has) about four times as many secondary students, relative to the size of the population, as the United States. This finding would seem to support the hypothesis advanced above. Naturally there exists reasonable doubt about the comparability of stages of economic development based on the size of the nonagricultural work force—or on any other indicator. But the differences found are so substantial that even a generous allowance for error does not invalidate the contrast.

The implication of Figure 2 is, simply, that perhaps Colombia is *overeducated* at the general secondary level, given its level of economic development. Although usually considered impossible or immoral, this possibility has been cautiously recognized. The 29th session of the Institut International des Civilisations Diférents concluded: *"One ought to be extremely careful in asserting that the number of 'white-collar workers' produced by the educational system can be absorbed by the economy. If a certain equilibrium is not preserved this may be a source of great discontent and even revolutions."* [3]

3. Cited in Robert J. Havighurst, *La Sociedad y la Educación en América Latina* (Buenos Aires, Editorial Universitaria de Buenos Aires, 1962), p. 141 (italics in original).

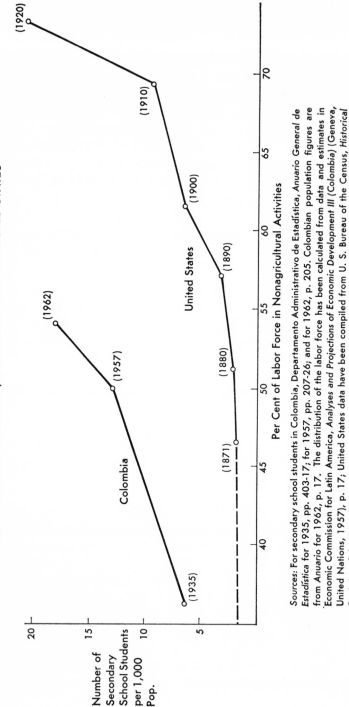

FIGURE 2

RELATIVE SIZE OF THE SECONDARY SCHOOL POPULATION AT SIMILAR LEVELS OF
ECONOMIC DEVELOPMENT, COLOMBIA AND THE UNITED STATES

Per Cent of Labor Force in Nonagricultural Activities

Number of
Secondary
School Students
per 1,000
Pop.

Colombia

United States

(1935) (1871) (1957) (1962)
(1880) (1890) (1900) (1910) (1920)

Sources: For secondary school students in Colombia, Departamento Administrativo de Estadística, Anuario General de
Estadística for 1935, pp. 403-17; for 1957, pp. 207-26; and for 1962, p. 205. Colombian population figures are
from Anuario for 1962, p. 17. The distribution of the labor force has been calculated from data and estimates in
Economic Commission for Latin America, Analyses and Projections of Economic Development III (Colombia) (Geneva,
United Nations, 1957), p. 17; United States data have been compiled from U. S. Bureau of the Census, Historical
Statistics of the United States (Washington, D.C., 1960), pp. 7, 72, 207.

TABLE 3.3

Occupational Composition of the Colombian Labor Force, 1951

Employers	385,943
Independent workers (self-employed)	889,786
Domestic servants	311,001
Empleados	732,875
Obreros	1,238,853
Others	197,151
Total labor force	3,755,609

$$\frac{\text{White-collar workers (Empleados)}}{\text{Blue-collar workers (Obreros)}} = \frac{732,875}{1,238,853} = \frac{5.9 \text{ White-collar workers}}{10 \text{ Blue-collar workers}}$$

Source: Departamento Administrativo Nacional de Estadística, *Censo de Población de Colombia—1951 Resumen,* pp. 140–41.

More direct evidence on the size of the white-collar group compared to the economic requirements may be obtained from census figures on the composition of the labor force. The Colombian figures for the 1951 census are presented in Table 3.3; United States figures for the 1950 census are in Table 3.4. I have tried to make the figures comparable by arranging the American data in categories similar to the Colombian presentation. Calculation of the proportion of white-collar workers to blue-collar workers shows that both countries exhibited about the same ratio (6 white-collar workers to 10 blue-collar workers) at about the same year (1950). This finding is quite striking since, as shown in Figure 3, the white-collar/blue-collar proportion bears a close relationship to economic development, with the relative number of white-collar workers increasing as industrialization proceeds. When placed on the index of economic development (proportion of labor force in nonagricultural activities), in 1951 Colombia had, in proportion to the number of blue-collar workers, about three times as many white-collar workers as the United States at a similar level of economic development (see Figure 3). It would seem, then, that the supply of white-collar workers in Colombia is well in excess of that required by the economic system.

The simple presence of this oversupply of white-collar workers, however, is not sufficient to make government employment an incentive. Those white-collar workers seeking jobs must find that tenure of a government job depends on political participation. If one's

TABLE 3.4

Occupational Composition of the United States Labor Force, 1950
(in thousands)

Equivalent Colombian Classification	U.S. Classification		
	Managers, officials and proprietors	5,155	
	Farmers and farm managers	4,375	
	Service workers, except private household	4,641	
Employers, self-employed, and others	Subtotal		14,171
Domestic servants	Private household workers		1,539
	Professional, technical and kindred workers	5,081	
	Clerical and kindred workers	7,232	
	Sales workers	4,133	
Empleados	Subtotal		16,446
	Craftsmen, foremen and kindred workers	8,350	
	Operatives and kindred workers	12,030	
	Laborers, except farm and mine	3,885	
	Farm laborers and foremen	2,578	
Obreros	Subtotal		26,843
	Total		58,999

$$\frac{\text{White-collar workers}}{\text{Blue-collar workers}} = \frac{16,446}{26,843} = \frac{6.1 \text{ White-collar workers}}{10 \text{ Blue-collar workers}}$$

Source: U. S. Bureau of the Census, *Historical Statistics of the United States* (Washington, D. C., 1960), p. 74.

political participation does not affect his chances of holding a government job—as under a rigorous civil service system—then those who want employment will not enter politics in search of it. Therefore, if employment *is to be an incentive, political participation must be a requisite for government employment;* that is, the patronage system must prevail.

When will a patronage system obtain? When there is a high degree of competition for government jobs. The patronage system is, after

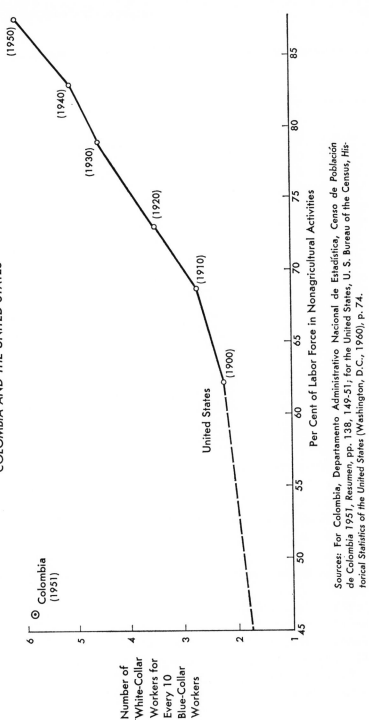

FIGURE 3

RELATIVE SIZE OF THE WHITE-COLLAR GROUP COMPARED TO THE BLUE-COLLAR GROUP,
COLOMBIA AND THE UNITED STATES

Number of
White-Collar
Workers for
Every 10
Blue-Collar
Workers

⊙ Colombia
(1951)

United States

(1900)
(1910)
(1920)
(1930)
(1940)
(1950)

Per Cent of Labor Force in Nonagricultural Activities

Sources: For Colombia, Departamento Administrativo Nacional de Estadística, Censo de Población
de Colombia 1951, Resumen, pp. 138, 149-51; for the United States, U. S. Bureau of the Census, Historical Statistics of the United States (Washington, D.C., 1960), p. 74.

all, supported or abolished by leaders. If by using the patronage system leaders are more successful in getting into office than without it, then we may expect them to defend and employ this system. The utility of the patronage system to the aspirants for elective office (leaders) will reflect a balance between the number of voters who want it (employment-seekers and their friends) and the number of voters who oppose it (those who do not seek employment and who are aware of the disadvantages of a patronage system). The most important variable which affects this balance is the amount of unemployment in the group aspiring to government jobs. As unemployment rises there will be more voters in favor of the patronage system. When unemployment is high, leaders may build up considerable support from among the ranks of job-seekers and thereby out-compete other leaders who do not cultivate this kind of support. The patronage system is a response to the demands of a sizable group seeking government employment—that is, the unemployed white-collar workers not already absorbed by government. In summary:

> H3. In a society characterized by an oversupply of white-collar workers, not taken up by government, political participation will be a requisite for government employment (widespread use of the patronage system), and employment will be a strong incentive for political participation (active followers).

The phrase "not taken up by government" in the hypothesis is important because by absorbing all the unemployed white-collar workers, the government could end job competition. This competition spurs people to participate. Those without jobs participate (get votes for leaders) to obtain jobs; those with jobs must, therefore, participate to keep their jobs against this competition. Thus the patronage system prevails. But absorb all the unemployed white-collar workers into government, and participation cannot be made a condition of employment. Aspiring leaders would have no one to whom they might offer employment in return for electoral assistance. Consequently no one finds it useful to defend the patronage system and a civil service arrangement may be easily established.

This absorption of the oversupply of white-collar workers by government is a real possibility. It has happened, I believe, in Uruguay where, relative to the size of the population, one finds four to five times as many public employees as in Colombia. Consistent with our hypothesis, a civil service system is found in Uruguay—at least to the extent that government employees have permanent tenure and therefore need not participate to retain their employment.[4]

The decline of the patronage system in the United States is, I think, consistent with the hypothesis. There was no mass of unemployed white-collar workers whose political participation was, or could be, a critical electoral force. Leaders could renounce and oppose the patronage system at relatively low risk. As the disadvantages of the spoils system became apparent (e.g. the assassination of President Garfield by a disappointed office-seeker), political leaders could safely oppose it. Certain pockets of unemployment, particularly the big eastern cities, did sustain patronage systems. But in general the relatively feeble demand for government employment deprived the patronage system of its political utility and leaders could surrender it rather easily or, indeed, silently forget and disuse it.[5]

Does the hypothesis (H3) fit Colombia? There is, as suggested above, an oversupply of white-collar workers. Has the government absorbed this oversupply? There are several indications that it has not. One suggestive piece of evidence lies in the observation that when changes in party control of the government took place (1930, 1946) most of the public employees, observers agree, were replaced by partisans of the victorious party. This replacement process was spread out over a period of several years and may not have touched everyone. But the considerable turnover does suggest that the complement of actual and potential public employees substantially exceeded the number of positions, perhaps by a factor of two.

Party leaders who must face job seekers directly are unanimous

4. Philip B. Taylor, *Government and Politics in Uruguay* (New Orleans, Tulane Studies in Political Science, 1960), pp. 99–100. In 1956 Uruguay had a population of about 2.6 million and 157,500 government employees. In the same year Colombia had about 160,000 government employees (including decentralized institutes) and a population of about 12.9 million.

5. For an analysis of the patronage system in the United States see the three articles by Frank J. Sorauf: "Patronage and Party," *Midwest Journal of Political Science, 3* (May 1959), 115–26; "State Patronage in a Rural County," *American Political Science Review, 50* (1956), 1046–56; "Silent Revolution in Patronage," *Public Administration Review, 20* (Winter 1960), 28–34.

in their perceptions of a tremendous pressure for employment and the impact of this force on political organizations. One secretary of a big-city municipal party directorate noted: "Before an election one finds a cloud of people drifting into the party office: one or two, then three or four each day as the election gets closer. These people are unemployed individuals who hope to get jobs after the election."

An indication of the number of employment seekers may be had by examining the number of "recommendations" issued by party executive committees at the national, departmental, or municipal level. These recommendations are simply letters given to job-hunters stating that the individual is a member in good standing of the party and desires to work in certain named agencies. Depending on the particular practice of the directorate, these recommendations may be given automatically to anyone who asks for them and purchases a party membership card, or only to those individuals explicitly approved by a member of the directorate. Usually such recommendations are not sufficient to obtain employment; they are hunting licenses given to those with no direct connections with important administrators. However, they give an indication of the size of the group of office-seekers.

In Table 3.5 I have tabulated the number of recommendations given by the Liberal directorate of Bogotá in the period January–April 1965. This directorate follows an open recommendation policy, giving letters to all those who ask for them and pay the party membership fee. A calculation of the number of recommendations given

TABLE 3.5

Recommendations for Government Jobs Given by the Liberal Party Bogotá Municipal Directorate, January–April 1965

	Number of days	Number of recommendations
January 11–31	21	92
February 1–28	28	138
March 1–31	31	130
April 1-26	26	95
Totals	106	455

Average per day (including Sundays and holidays) = 4.3

Note: Figures courtesy of Ricardo Baquero, secretary of the Liberal Directorate of Bogotá.

in a two-year period (disregarding the probable increase in the rate at which such recommendations are given around election time) yields the total of 3,140 recommendations, and, by inference, the same number of job-seekers. The number of positions which these individuals would theoretically compete for, Liberal-held positions in the Bogotá administration, was 3,703 in 1963.[6] This comparison suggests that the number of job-seekers is approximately equal to the number of actual office-holders.

The estimate of one unemployed office-seeker for every government employee can be seen as too small or too large, depending on how one interprets this Bogotá experience. I prefer to adopt a somewhat more conservative estimate of about two unemployed for every three employees. This ratio would give us about 175,000 unemployed office-seekers in the nation. Consequently the condition stipulated by the hypothesis—oversupply of white-collar workers not taken up by government—is present in Colombia.

That the patronage system obtains in Colombia seems beyond doubt. To obtain an appointment to a government job one must belong to a political party (faction) and usually be further supported by a prominent leader. Public employees are required, in most cases, to contribute a small amount to the campaign funds of their respective parties. One party secretary explained this practice:

> We require public employees to donate to the party because it is the party which supports them. You know the terrible unemployment we have and the pressures this brings into government. Consequently the isolated employee is constantly threatened and without the backing we give him, he would not be able to survive. It's only fair that in return for this support, the employee assist the party.

In spite of much attention given to its disadvantages and many attempts to prevent it, the patronage system prevails in Colombia. If a civil service system could be established by laws alone, Colombia would have one several times over. Most recent "reforms" include a constitutional amendment of 1957; a congressional law (19 of 1958) giving general guidelines for administrative reform; a series of executive decrees (550 of 1960, 1732 of 1960, 1679 of 1960);

6. *El Espectador,* September 15, 1963, p. 1.

and the establishment of the Administrative Department of Civil Service (DASC) in 1960. But, in fact, these measures have scarcely touched the patronage system.

One problem is getting national employees classified under "administrative career" and thus covered by the civil service idea. In 1965 only about four per cent of national jobs were classified under administrative career. But even these positions (about 2,500) are not actually under the civil service since the ministers and agency heads usually circumvent the Department of Civil Service. They repeatedly reject the approved applicants the DASC sends to them, exhausting the supply; or they appoint temporary employees of their own choosing since "temporary" employees do not need civil service approval. Congressmen are generally opposed to the DASC as a waste of money and most seem to favor its abolishment. Officials of the Department of Civil Service realize that their agency was created by executive decree (of well-meaning President Alberto Lleras) and would not have been approved in Congress.[7] This department is an excellent illustration of an agency existing in a hostile environment, pathetically going through the motions of giving examinations and publishing pamphlets on how the civil service system works.

In the process of exploring the hypothesis I have, I believe, presented enough evidence to show that employment is an important incentive for political participation. Most of the holders of government jobs participate, at least to the extent of donating money, to hold their jobs. Aspirants seeking positions come to party committees or political leaders and are willing to participate in exchange for employment. A typical illustration of the employment incentive at work is found in this episode I witnessed at one of the party directorates of Bogotá. Late one afternoon an elderly lady came in accompanied by a young man, a relative of hers. She addressed the directorate secretary in energetic terms:

> W: Roberto [a pseudonym], you've got to help me. I have this boy here who's got a family to support and has no work. What can he do? We went to the DAS [an expanding special

7. Information in this paragraph is based largely on an interview with Guillermo Valencia Ibáñez, sub-director of the Departamento Administrativo del Servicio Civil, and Alonso Ortiz Lozano, director of the División Registro y Control, DASC (Bogotá, April 20, 1965).

security agency] and they gave us the run-around—and you know that place is full of *corbatas* [people who get paid without working]. This boy is willing to work hard.

ROBERTO: Well, I don't know . . . I really don't have any say in these matters.

W: Look, I've been a worker for the party all my life. If the party isn't going to take care of its people, then who will? Come on, Roberto, don't be an oligarch. I thought you were a friend of the masses. This boy has his second year of secondary, what can we do for him?

After some delay, the young man was issued a party card and given a letter of recommendation. But this was not the last I saw of the pair. The next evening the party's presidential candidate was holding a rally in a Bogotá suburb. At the door of the meeting hall I noticed the same woman and her charge, energetically greeting those who entered and busily attending to details of the rally. Thus the pattern came full circle: from unemployment, to the party, to active participation.

It is inaccurate to ignore completely the participation of blue-collar workers in Colombian politics. There are about 30,000 *obrero* jobs in government and it appears that many of these positions are held through political participation. In May 1965 I witnessed a meeting of some leaders of the railroad workers' union in the department of Valle with a member of the Cali (Valle) city council. The purpose of this consultation was to devise a strategy to oppose the calculated dismissal of those workers on the state-run railway identified with a certain political group. Apparently these workers were being discharged to make room for others identified with another political group. On the lowest level one finds that blue-collar workers and riff-raff are hired by the parties to carry signs, to distribute handbills, or just to attend demonstrations. However, compared to the role of white-collar workers, blue-collar participation at the active follower level is not large.

The importance of the employment incentive in Colombia may be established by computing the size of the group of active followers participating in response to this incentive. We have already mentioned the approximately 175,000 unemployed individuals seeking government jobs, almost all of whom will make active attempts to obtain positions. Of the 262,420 government employees, most, but not all, will be politically active to retain their jobs. Some (such as veterinarians or electric company engineers) will have a particular skill which serves to shelter them from competition; to some extent unions of public employees make it inexpedient for a political leader to discharge personnel and this protects employees from being coerced into participation. I estimate that perhaps two thirds of the total number of public employees, or about 175,000 are politically active, certainly to the extent of contributing money to a candidate or party faction. This brings the total number of active followers responding to the employment incentive to about 350,000.

To put this figure in perspective we might speculate about the electoral impact of the active followers. They are predominantly white-collar, relatively alert, and relatively influential. Their electoral impact would greatly exceed that of a similar number of peasants or blue-collar workers. Colombian leaders considered that one active follower (*seguidor*) could produce perhaps ten votes from among his family, relatives and friends. Even taking a more conservative estimate of six votes for each active follower (five besides himself), we find that active followers would sway about 2,100,000 votes. The total potential electorate in 1964 was 6,135,628; the total number of voters, 2,261,190.[8] What opportunity would there be, then, for a leader who ran on a platform of abolishing the patronage system *and really meant it?*

A knowledge of the incentive for active followers in Colombia enables us to understand the relationship between participants and leaders. As I shall show in the following chapters, the status incentive is associated with nonideological, opportunistic patterns of behavior. Leaders who seek the status of public office are not concerned with defending particular policies or following particular principles. How would active followers respond to the opportunism of status-motivated leaders?

Let us suppose, first, that active followers have a program incentive, that they are participating to effect programs they prefer. Such

8. Registraduría Nacional del Estado Civil, *Organización y Estadísticas Electorales* (Bogotá, 1964), p. 190.

people would find the opportunism of status-motivated leaders repulsive. They would be inclined to oppose them or at least constrain them to behave in a more program-oriented fashion. In the United States there seem to be many program-motivated active followers (Young Republicans, Republican Women, League of Women Voters, "amateur Democrats") who reinforce the program incentive of leaders.

If active followers with a program incentive were numerous in Colombia, leaders would be somewhat constrained in responding to their status incentive. In order to gain the support of such active followers, Colombian leaders would have to moderate their amoral opportunism and defend specific programs with some consistency. But Colombian active followers do not have a program incentive; their incentive is employment. As long as a leader wins and provides employment for them, they do not care which policies, if any, he espouses.

INCENTIVES AND POLITICAL CONFLICT

With the analytical material now advanced it is possible to essay a preliminary explanation for the relatively high level of political conflict in Colombia. The existence of a large group of active followers seeking an objective of great importance to them might well increase the likelihood of substantial political violence. They have enough at stake—employment—to be willing to take energetic action. They are sufficiently numerous (over 300,000) to create an extensive conflagration if properly stimulated. But will they be mobilized and directed into combat?

The answer depends heavily upon the leadership situation. Leaders, the aspirants to higher offices, are the ones who assemble political organizations, who construct justifications and focus ideals. Leaders inform and agitate; indeed, they usually instruct their followers in the measures they are to carry out. What if, for example, leaders are only weakly interested in winning office and therefore have little desire to incite active followers? Or what if the supply of leaders is so limited that not even two (competing) political organizations can be formed? In such cases, even though white-collar unemployment is high and employment is a strong incentive for active followers, we would not expect to find a particularly violent politics.

But Colombia has no problem of tepid leadership in limited supply. The strength of the status incentive causes individuals to aspire to higher governmental positions in numbers vastly exceeding the opportunities. Local leaders estimate that in a town of about 20,000 inhabitants there will be five to ten times as many aspirants for the city council as seats available. In the 1964 elections for national representatives there were 1,200 legally registered candidates for 184 seats, or about a 7:1 ratio.[9] These registered candidacies represent only a part of the supply, since many other active aspirants would have withdrawn at earlier stages.

This picture contrasts with American politics where many offices at the state and local level are hardly sought after, and even difficult to fill. Barber notes, for example, that in many small Connecticut towns the "major problem for the local party committee [is] . . . simply finding some minimally acceptable person to allow his name to be put on the ballot." [10] The authors of *Voting* found a similar condition prevailing for some positions in Elmira, New York.[11]

It is the combination of strongly motivated leaders *and* followers, then, that makes extensive political violence a clear possibility:

> *H4. When incentives for political participants are strong, intense political conflict is probable.*

This hypothesis itself is not particularly interesting, but may be restated in broader form:

> *H4a. In a society characterized by (1) high status-consciousness, (2) high status value of higher political offices, (3) relatively open recruitment to these offices, and (4) weak barriers to upward social mobility, intense political conflict is probable.*

This restatement simplifies certain steps in our analysis (see Figure 4), and is, I believe, a useful generalization to keep in mind. It

9. *El Tiempo* (Bogotá), March 10, 1964, p. 1.
10. Barber, *The Lawmakers*, pp. 26–27.
11. Berelson et al., *Voting*, p. 165. Robert Dahl notes apathy at the active follower level in New Haven: *Who Governs?* (New Haven, Yale University Press, 1961), p. 179.

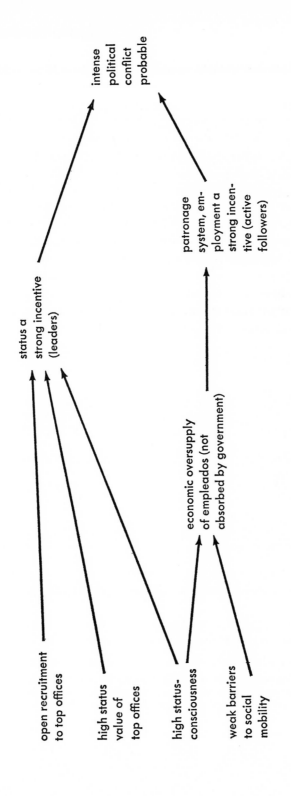

FIGURE 4

ANALYSIS OF INCENTIVES IN COLOMBIA, OUTLINE

suggests that certain social conditions—which may be found in many countries—are at the bottom of a rather violent, explosive pattern of politics. It should be emphasized that the hypothesis (H4a) can do no more than orient one's expectations, because it does not consider the structural variables that would affect the patterns of conflict. In later chapters I examine these structural variables to understand more precisely the mechanisms of Colombian political violence.

The characterization of incentives in Colombian politics as private and "selfish" does not contradict the conclusion generally held by Colombians. Citizens, scholars, and even the participants are usually agreed that the driving force of Colombian politics is *egoismo,* or selfishness.[12] To express the political phenomena associated with private political rewards, Colombians have developed a number of colorful terms:

manzanillo—an individual who participates in politics for purely selfish reasons; he has no interest in politics beyond the private rewards which flow from it.

lagarto ("lizard")—an individual who seeks to ingratiate himself with leaders of stature in order to gain employment or other personal benefits.

corbata ("necktie")—a paid public job for which the employee does no work.

politiquería—political maneuvering designed to produce a greater share of bureaucratic and leadership positions for a group or clique, maneuvering devoid of policy-making intentions.

The wording of the Colombian constitution also suggests a pervasive concern with the distribution of personal rewards. Specific

12. "A thirst for prominence and a thirst for money . . . seem to be the motives which drive and move the men who today enter or are pushed into public life over the well-trod path of that militant policy that anything is justified in reaching one's objects. Naturally such a phenomenon cannot be anything but the expression of a materialistic conception of politics itself, which subordinates all societal ends to personal convenience, all altruistic motives to selfishness and all spiritual goals to inferior biological needs." Sánchez Gómez, *Sociología Política Colombiana,* p. 84. Also see: Guillén Martínez, *Raíz y Futuro,* pp. 134–39; E. Caballero Calderón, *Historia Privada de los Colombianos,* pp. 107–11; José Gutiérrez, *La Revolución Contra el Miedo* (Bogotá, Tercer Mundo, 1964), pp. 85–100.

attempts to control abuses of employment appear in fourteen articles.[13] Attempts to control abuses in the handling of government funds appear in twelve articles.[14] One finds such instructive clauses as Article 105:

> The individuals of either house of Congress represent the entire nation and must vote consulting only the ideals of justice and the common welfare.

Article 63, in effect, prohibits *corbatas·*

> There shall not be in Colombia any employment which has no functions described in law or administrative regulation

The stipulation that holders of various high administrative offices must leave their jobs six months before an election if they intend to run for elective office (Articles 108, 111, 129) reflects the fear of constitution-makers that high officials would establish *maquinaria* (machines) by appointing supporters to jobs in the critical pre-election period. In sum, a total of 27 articles are aimed at preventing practices which directly involve the distribution of personal rewards.

The focus of this analysis has been the phenomenon of political participation and the variables which explain it. Our interest has been drawn to leaders and active followers who, acting in response to their incentives, shape the nature of the political system. An exploration of the incentives for political participation in Colombia has led to the conclusion that the roots of political conflict lie in certain social conditions (stipulated in hypothesis H4a) which have prevailed since independence. These conditions give rise to a copious supply of energetic leaders seeking status and a mass of superfluous white-collar workers seeking government employment.

It is important to note that the analysis disregards a variable usually considered to be of great importance in politics: the degree of economic development. In my view a country may be developed or underdeveloped without such conditions having a direct impact on the incentives discussed and therefore on politics in a country like Colombia. Nor will the rate of economic development, within realistic limits, directly affect these incentives. Indirect effects of economic

13. Articles 61, 62, 63, 66, 67, 108, 109, 110, 111, 129, 140, 160, 174, 201.
14. Articles 36, 42, 59, 64, 78, 112, 113, 142, 190, 207, 210, 213.

modernization on the variables affecting the incentives described are difficult to discern. The apparent persistence of the status incentive in Colombia for over 100 years, in spite of substantial economic changes, dims my expectations of finding a clear connection between economic development and the incentives I have identified.

Some writers have presented an interpretation of politics in underdeveloped countries which resembles this analysis, but in inverted form. The low level of economic development, they contend, leaves few opportunities for white-collar and professional groups in private industry so they must turn to politics and government.[15] Thus the supply of educated individuals is taken as given, and a backward economy is held responsible. I feel this interpretation is basically in error.

The critical question is: Why should there be an overproduction of "intellectuals" in advance of the economy? Such a condition is certainly not a necessary one. Moreover, this overproduction is not a new or modern phenomenon. José María Samper, writing in 1881 gave the same explanation for movement into Colombian politics in those days: the backward economy could not absorb educated personnel.[16] The American economy in 1800 or 1850 could not have absorbed many educated personnel either, but there were relatively few to absorb. I argue that high status-consciousness (which did not obtain in the United States) and weak barriers to upward mobility lie at the bottom of this oversupply of white-collar workers.

The implication of the economic development interpretation is that with some more economic development the oversupply of educated personnel will disappear. But this hope is illusory. High status-consciousness will drive more and more people into the white-collar group as development proceeds. Even if the government should resist further increases in public secondary school enrollment, the movement would not be halted. An increasing number of blue-collar workers, growing more affluent with economic progress, will send their children to private secondary schools.

15. See Merle Kling, "Toward a Theory of Power and Political Instability in Latin America," *Western Political Quarterly*, 9 (March 1956), 21–35; Myron Weiner, *The Politics of Scarcity* (Chicago, University of Chicago Press, 1962), pp. 158 ff., 183.

16. José María Samper, *Historia de Una Alma* (first published 1881, Bogotá, Editorial Kelly, 1946), *1*, 205.

However, the elimination of the employment incentive for active followers, even if achieved in one form or another, would solve only part of the problem. There would still remain the copious supply of leaders responding to a strong status incentive.

CHAPTER 4

LEADERSHIP INCENTIVES AND
POLICY ATTITUDES

1959

In Colombia it is an obvious fact that Liberals and Conservatives are not separated by irreconcilable ideological and philosophical differences as was the case in the last century. They have ended up growing closer together until their ideological boundaries are now meshed and there exists only the plain and simple distinction of label.

> Jorge Cárdenas García, El Frente Nacional y los Partidos Políticos *(Tunja, Imprenta Departamental, 1958), p. 80.*

1873

Nowadays [the two great parties] exhibit neither consensus on strategies nor complete agreement on programs, either as national or local parties.

One cannot see the clear predominance of either ideals or philosophies in our parties. . . . Each sub-group orients itself in a different direction; everywhere one finds contradictions, antagonisms, and petty rivalries . . . and on almost the entire political scene one observes a deplorable lack of logic, of criteria, and of strategy.

> José María Samper, Los Partidos en Colombia *(Bogotá, Imprenta de Echeverría Hermanos, 1873), pp. 135–36.*

Do the century-old Colombian parties, Liberal and Conservative, have different programs? This question has, of course, been discussed by many Colombian writers.[1] Unfortunately, most of the conclusions

1. See: Guillén Martínez, *Raíz y Futuro de la Revolución*, pp. 139–43; Gonzalo Restrepo Jaramillo, *El Pensamiento Conservador* (Medellín, Tipografía Bedout, 1936), pp. 56–120; Guillermo Salamanca, *Los Partidos en Colombia* (Bogotá, Editorial "El Voto Nacional," 1961), pp. 153–205, 265–96; Puentes, *Historia del*

about party differences are based on little evidence and are frequently expressed in vague, equivocal terms. As illustrated in our introductory quotations, the carelessness with which the problem is treated may lead to "good old days" speculations which contradict each other. A writer in 1959 sees the nineteenth century as the age of ideological conflict between the parties. But a writer in the nineteenth century deplores the lack of principles and philosophies in his day and, in turn, looks back to yet earlier days when ideological divisions allegedly existed.

Before attacking this problem, it is important to clarify it and formulate some hypotheses. We may begin by speculating about the mechanisms which produce or prevent the development of distinct party positions. One process might involve recruitment: persons desiring to participate in politics would select the party closest to their own policy attitudes and, in so doing, would further enhance the distinctiveness of the respective parties. In an established party system, however, relatively little recruitment will occur in this manner. Most potential participants would, from childhood, already be identified with party labels and would naturally participate in the party they already considered "theirs."

Nevertheless, recruitment processes could still operate to produce distinctiveness in the parties through an extensive reinforcing cycle, briefly outlined in the following steps. (1) In a certain historical context a party projects an image (feeble at first) of favoring social group A. (2) In response to this image some members of that social group identify with the party. (3) When members of group A decide to participate in politics, they will, in reflection of their party identification, go disproportionately to this party. (4) Once in the party we assume they will voice pro-A sentiments and thus add this position to the intraparty communication which, we assume, will be taking place on policy matters. (5) Given the well-known tendency of group members to adopt homogeneous attitudes toward matters

Partido Liberal, pp. 17–22; Julio Londoño, *Nación en Crisis* (Bogotá, Biblioteca de Autores Contemporaneos, 1955), pp. 53–74; Ofelia Uribe de Acosta, *Una Voz Insurgente* (Bogotá, Editorial Guadalupe, 1963), pp. 159–86; Eduardo Santa, *Sociología Política de Colombia* (Bogotá, Tercer Mundo, 1964), pp. 47–55; Sánchez Gómez, *Sociología Política Colombiana*, pp. 3–11; Gutiérrez, *La Revolución contra el Miedo*, pp. 79–83; Mario Laserna, *Estado Fuerte o Caudillo* (Bogotá, Ediciones Mito, 1961), pp. 52 ff.

of importance to the group, we should expect a more prominent pro-A position to emerge within the party as a whole. This position, in turn, strengthens the party's pro-A image, more members of group A become identified, and so the cycle is reinforced. In this way the party will come to hold a distinctive policy position.

This reasoning, however, ignores a critical variable: incentives. It assumes that when members of group A enter politics they retain and, more importantly, voice their pro-A sentiments. It assumes that party leaders do communicate about policy matters, that policy positions are sufficiently prominent in party life to enable the process of reinforcement to operate. These assumptions are probably justified if the incentive for participation is program. Such an incentive implies an interest in policy matters, and a concern with the policy position taken by other party leaders.

But if the incentive is status, the mechanism suggested is unlikely to operate. Individuals from group A are entering politics for status and are not concerned with defending group A or any other group. Within a party where status is the incentive, communication on policy matters will be unimportant, vague, contradictory. The whole theory of communication and psychological reinforcement within a group rests on the assumption that the matter on which reinforcement is to take place is salient enough to receive attention, important enough to cause discomfort to those who deviate from the group.

Consequently, in a system where status is the incentive, the mechanisms producing party distinctiveness on policies would not operate. Even if the party should momentarily project a pro-A image, and even if identification and recruitment operated as expected, the cycle would be broken at that point. The processes of communication and reinforcement would fail to operate and the party would lose its distinctive image on the issue.

A preliminary expectation, then, would be that distinctive policy positions would exist between leaders of different parties where there is a program incentive, but not where a status incentive is dominant. This conclusion, however, overlooks the possibility that some issues necessarily affect the relative power positions of the parties. An example of such a policy would be an electoral reform which enhances the influence of voters in a certain region—who happened to belong predominantly to one party. Other parties could be expected to oppose such a reform, regardless of the nature of incentives, simply to maintain their officeholding possibilities.

This kind of issue may be called "strategic." A strategic issue or policy is one which necessarily and in a predetermined fashion alters the power distribution between the parties, *regardless of which party supports it.* Strategic issues contrast with "program" issues which do not have necessary or predetermined effects on relative party strength. One way to distinguish between the two kinds of issues is to ask: If both (all) parties supported putting the policy into effect, would any certain change take place in the relative power positions of the parties? If the answer is yes, that policy is a strategic issue.

Labor union leaders in the United States, for example, are disproportionately identified with the Democratic party. If trade unions were accorded greater representation in Congress, Republicans would be disadvantaged, since a disproportionate number of the trade union representatives would be members of the Democratic party. The Republicans would still lose, even if they supported the measure. If the proposal is, however, to raise minimum wages and the Republican party supports the proposal as fully as the Democratic party, we should expect no alteration in the relative power positions of the parties. Those benefiting from the measure (blue-collar workers) are disproportionately identified with the Democratic party, but this identification would not be altered if both parties took the same position. The matter of trade union representation would be a strategic issue, while the minimum wage would be a program issue.

Stands taken on program issues may, of course, produce an alteration in the relative power position between the parties, but this alteration is not *necessary* or *predetermined.* Whether a party gains from taking a position on a program issue depends upon whether the idea is popular, what position the other parties take, and to which party the voters ascribe responsibility for the measure.

Leaders with a status incentive are keenly aware of strategic issues. They are clearly interested in winning office and consequently would be sensitive to any measures that affected officeholding opportunities for their party (or faction). Whether leaders have a status or program incentive, we may expect them to think about, talk about, and take stands on strategic issues, since these matters affect their ability to realize policies (program incentive) or to gain office (status incentive). The speculations advanced thus far may be summarized:

> *H5. Where status is the incentive for leaders, there will be no differences between the leaders of different parties (or party factions) on program policies.*

> *H6. Where program is the incentive for leaders, there will be differences between the leaders of different parties on program policies.*

> *H7. In any system (status or program incentive) there will be differences between leaders of different parties on strategic policies.*

To test these hypotheses I conducted a survey of Colombian leaders in which they were given a questionnaire containing multiple-choice answers to policy questions. This procedure is not the only way to measure party issue-positions, but is, I feel, the most reliable. To infer party positions from actions or speeches, one must not only bring all such actions to a common denominator for purposes of comparison, but, in addition, somehow subtract the situational and strategic content of the action from the underlying attitudinal component. For example, a strong opponent of government housing may vote for an extreme pro-housing amendment to a bill because he knows it will cause the bill to fail. With leaders who have a status incentive, the strategic impact of actions would practically obliterate underlying policy preferences. A "yes" vote would most likely mean that the faction to which the individual belonged felt its officeholding opportunities would be served by passing the measure; it would give little indication of the private policy preference of the individual.[2]

2. In measuring historical differences between factions or parties, one must necessarily employ actions to indicate policy positions, removing, of course, the strategic implications of the actions. One would seek to learn if the parties ever held positions which conflicted with strategic advantage, and if a party or faction ever voiced, firmly and for a long time, a position which had no strategic implication for it. My examination of nineteenth-century Colombian politics suggests that the hypotheses do apply to this period. Unfortunately, a full documentation of this conclusion by tracing the history of issues and the behavior of parties (factions) is beyond the scope of this study. My preliminary findings, however, are: (1) the dramatic issues, particularly clericalism and federalism, were ones of clear strategic content. Shifting factions tended to adopt the position on these issues which accorded

A short questionnaire containing policy attitude questions was distributed during 1965 to a sample of 130 Colombian leaders (upper leaders, as defined in Chapter 2). The sample includes leaders from seven different departments representative of the geographical and cultural diversity of the country. Leaders of the two Conservative factions *(Ospinista* and *Lauro-alzatista),* some independent Conservatives, and the major Liberal faction *(Oficialista)* were included. Unfortunately limitations of time made it impossible to include leaders of the small Liberal faction (the *Movimiento Revolucionario Liberal,* which received 17 per cent of the votes in the 1964 elections). A new third party, the *Alianza Nacional Popular,* which obtained 14 per cent of the votes in 1964, also was not included. Our comparisons are confined therefore to differences between the Officialist *(Oficialista)* Liberals and the Conservatives, and within the Conservatives, between the above-mentioned factions. The reader may consult Appendix I for further details of the survey and a translated copy of the questionnaire.

The survey questionnaire contained six questions on important political issues, matters much discussed and clearly recognized as related to government action. Among the questions were four concerning attitudes toward program policies: the government's role in housing construction, in the control of private industry, and in the protection of labor unions, and the government's foreign policy orientation. These are program issues because government policy on these issues could change without there being any predetermined change in the relative strength of the parties.

Two issues of a strategic nature were selected: the size of the army and the influence of the church in the government. These are strategic policies because they have affected the power distribution between the parties. The partisan position of the army has a long history. One may go back to the civil wars of 1895 and 1899–1902 when Liberal revolutionaries were engaged in an open military strug-

---

with their strategic interests; and (2) on matters such as ending slavery, tariffs, fiscal policy, educational policy, and foreign policy, conflicts were sporadic and no party or faction held, for any substantial length of time, a position that firmly and visibly contrasted with that of another party or faction. Some investigations suggest I may be overstating the case, however; see David Bushnell, "Two Stages in Colombian Tariff Policy: The Radical Era and the Return to Protection (1861–1885)," *Inter-American Economic Affairs,* 9 (Spring 1956), 3–23.

gle with the Conservative government's army. Until 1930 the Conservatives controlled the government and tended to place and promote Conservative-identified officers in the army. After the Liberals came to power in 1930 they turned toward building a partisan police force since apparently they could not successfully penetrate the Conservative army.[3]

In the period following the Conservative return to power in 1946 the army was increasingly employed to prevent rioting, armed attacks, and guerrilla activity. Unavoidably, therefore, it played a pro-Conservative, anti-Liberal role, sustaining the incumbents while injuring the Liberals. Although the Liberals were initially happy with the army coup of 1953 against Conservative Laureano Gómez, it soon turned out that they were excluded from adequate participation in the Rojas regime and ended up, by about 1955, opposing the army again. Although in the period 1958–65 the army appeared not to menace the Liberal position, it is reasonable to suppose that a policy orientation built up over such a long time will continue for some time after the reasons which gave rise to it have disappeared. The Liberals, then, should be somewhat more anti-army than the Conservatives, for strategic reasons.

The strategic relationship between the Catholic Church and the political parties is somewhat more complex. Priests are influential; they can sway votes. In a system where elections are important—and they have been important in Colombia—clerical support becomes a useful political resource for party leaders. Unless priests have a powerful commitment to the non-temporal sphere, they are likely to be enticed into using their influence in the political arena. But if the priests support one candidate, then his opponent must side against the clerics.

It is important to notice that elections constitute a critical link in the process whereby priests are brought into partisan politics. If leadership transfer is decided mainly by military force, then politicians have little use for clerical support and the church will play a reduced role in political matters. It is no accident that in Colombia, which saw an unusually large number of meaningful elections in the

3. See Rafael Azula Barrera, *De la Revolución al Orden Nuevo* (Bogotá, Editorial Kelly, 1956), pp. 83–85; Carlos Galvis Gómez, *Por Qué Cayó López,* (Bogotá, Editorial ABC, 1946).

nineteenth century, the church was most thoroughly embroiled in partisan politics. In nations which lived largely by the military coup in that period—Ecuador, Peru—the church figured much less prominently on the political scene.

The involvement of the clergy in Colombian politics dates back to at least the 1820s.[4] Until about 1842–50, clerical partisanship was fluid and contradictory, following the loose, shifting nature of the political groupings. But the rise of party labels in the 1840s provided the basis for a more enduring alignment of the clergy. In 1850 Liberal President José Hilario López, supported by some ecclesiastical officials, expelled the Jesuits from Colombia, apparently for pro-Conservative political meddling.[5] Other Catholic groups were untouched and some even supported the move, but the die was being cast: the Liberal party label was becoming increasingly identified with anticlericalism. Conservative president Mariano Ospina Rodríguez brought the Jesuits back again in 1858 and thus further sharpened the pro-clerical image of the Conservatives.

In 1860–61 the Liberals waged a revolution against the Conservative government of Ospina, led by Tomás Cipriano de Mosquera, who had himself only recently adopted the Liberal label. When Mosquera was victorious he set about punishing the clerical allies of Ospina. To the constitutional convention of Rionegro (1863) president-elect Mosquera submitted a most illuminating law which included the following articles:

Article 1: The aforementioned Archbishop of Bogotá and the Bishops of Antioquia, Cartagena, Panamá, Pamplona, and Pasto, and the Vicar-general shall be expelled from Colombia; and in no way shall their authority . . . be recognized in the United States of Colombia.

Article 6: The national government recognizes the Bishop of Popayán and all the Catholic officials who have supported and

4. See Bushnell, *The Santander Regime in Gran Colombia,* pp. 195–248.

5. José María Samper notes that the Jesuits "were considered the most powerful auxiliary of the tremendous opposition which the Conservative party was making against the government." *Historia de una Alma, 1,* 230. See also Diego Montaña Cuéllar, *Colombia País Formal y País Real* (Buenos Aires, Editorial Platina, 1963), p. 80; José Manuel Restrepo, *Historia de la Nueva Granada,* Vol. 1: 1832–45 (Bogotá, Editorial Cromos, 1952), Vol. 2: 1845–54 (Bogotá, Editorial el Catolicismo, 1963), *1,* 149–53; Puentes, pp. 158–59.

respected the supreme authority of the country as citizens worthy of the protection of the government; and consequently they are permitted to exercise their ministry with absolute liberty.

Article 7: From the national treasury the Bishop of Popayán shall be given two hundred pesos monthly income, in order that he may live independently.[6]

This proposal, incidentally, was defeated (32–23) by the all-Liberal convention as too antireligious.[7]

Notice that the proposal does not represent an ideological anti-Catholic position: clerical enemies are punished, but clerical friends are rewarded (during the civil war, the Bishop of Popayán had given Mosquera a loan of 52,000 pesos to meet military expenses).[8] Catholic clergy were being attacked by the Liberals not because the Liberals had any ideological commitment to anti-Catholicism, but because the clergy was interfering with their officeholding opportunities.

The subsequent presidency of Mosquera (1863–64) set a sufficiently anticlerical tone (including expropriation of church property) to complete the identification of the Liberal label with anticlericalism and, conversely, the Conservative label with pro-clericalism. This identification has been reinforced and continued for 100 years down to the present. Most priests are identified with the Conservative label. It is an enduring identification which cannot be broken either by an order of the higher clergy or a Liberal attempt to appease Catholics. Consequently, any measure that would increase the influence of the Church would, de facto, increase the influence of those bearing the Conservative label and necessarily weaken the Liberals. The influence of the Church in the government is a strategic issue, and therefore, by our hypothesis (H7), the parties should differ on it.

In Table 4.1 the answers to five of the policy questions are tabulated in their original form. To simplify the handling of these and subsequent findings, I have assigned numerical values to each of the five positions thus: 1=much more, 2=more, 3=same, 4=less, 5=much less. This scaling enables us to compute a mean party posi-

6. In Ramón Correa, *La Convención de Rionegro* (Bogotá, Imprenta Nacional, 1937), pp. 248–49.

7. Ibid., p. 250.

8. Pérez, *25 Años de Historia Colombiana*, p. 111.

TABLE 4.1

Responses of Party Leaders to Policy Questions

1. In housing construction do you believe the government should do

	Liberals	Conservatives
much more	50	54
more	10	12
the same as now	–	3
less	–	–
much less	–	–
no answer	–	1
total	60	70

2. Do you believe the government ought to control private industry

	Liberals	Conservatives
much more	16	20
more	20	21
the same as now	10	5
less	9	17
much less	2	5
no answer	3	2
total	60	70

3. In the legal protection of trade unions do you believe the government ought to do

	Liberals	Conservatives
much more	17	15
more	22	23
the same as now	18	18
less	2	11
much less	–	2
no answer	1	1
total	60	70

4. Do you believe the army should be

	Liberals	Conservatives
greatly increased	1	4
increased	1	11
the same as it is	22	30
reduced	23	16
greatly reduced	11	9
no answer	2	–
total	60	70

5. Do you believe the influence of the Church in government should be

	Liberals	Conservatives
much more	1	7
more	–	2
the same as now	11	37
less	12	13
much less	33	8
no answer	3	3
total	60	70

tion (disregarding the "no answer" responses) which is much easier to grasp and manipulate than the entire five-position presentation. The respective computations of mean party positions are presented in Table 4.2, along with the standard deviations from each mean. The standard deviations give a measure of the degree of intra-party consensus on each issue, ranging from about .6 (very high agreement) to 1.1 or more (very low agreement).

TABLE 4.2

Mean Party Positions on Policy Questions

| | Liberals | | Conservatives | | | statistical |
	mean position	standard deviation	mean position	standard deviation	difference in means	significance of difference
Housing construction	1.17	.373	1.26	.529	.09	NS*
Control of private industry	2.32	1.14	2.50	1.33	.18	NS*
Protection of labor unions	2.09	.850	2.45	1.08	.36	.05
Size of army	3.73	.846	3.22	1.04	.51	.01
Church influence in government	4.34	.906	3.20	1.05	1.14	.001

*Not significant at the .1 level.

The application of these findings to the hypotheses requires some standards for accepting a conclusion of "the parties are different." Statistical significance has been computed using the student's "t" test (difference of means), applying a two-tailed test throughout. A level of significance of .1 was adopted so that any difference of means entered as not significant (NS) could have happened by chance in more than 10 times out of 100 samples chosen.[9] A significance level of .01, for example, means that the difference in means of the two parties would be produced by chance in only one out of 100 samples.

9. The adoption of the low (.1) level of significance is prompted by two considerations. The first three issues, by hypothesis, should show no difference between the parties. That is, we wish to accept the null hypothesis rather than reject it, as is usually the case in such demonstrations. Consequently, the adoption of a demanding level of significance, e.g. .01, would make it quite easy to assert that no difference (beyond chance) obtains and thus would validate our hypothesis (H5). Technically for issues four and five (army and church) we should raise the level of significance (to .01 perhaps) and use a one-tailed test, since we have predicted a difference and the direction of that difference. Taking such a one-tailed test would increase the level of significance of these last findings from .01 to .005 and from .001 to .0005, respectively. Such changes in levels of significance and the number of tails chosen are unnecessarily complicated for a preliminary study of this nature. Also, in view of the small samples, it is better to retain the low level of significance (.1) throughout so that suggestive findings are not discarded.

In addition to the criterion of statistical significance, there is another concept, that of "importance" of a difference. The judgment of importance must be made in the context to which the differences apply. For example, we might measure the heights of two men and find that one is 1/16 of an inch taller than the other. Whether this difference is important depends upon the context to which the difference applies. If the two men are astronauts who must fit into a space capsule, the difference might be important; but for most purposes the men could be regarded as the same in height.

In our five-position scale the maximum difference that could obtain between the mean positions of the two parties is four units (5 minus 1). In practice such a difference would be extremely unlikely given the usual tendency toward the scattering of answers in such questionnaires. But a difference of two units, produced, for example, by one party having a mean position of "more" (2) and the other having a position of "less" (4) would be possible and would represent "extreme cleavage." A difference of one unit is less dramatic, but would nevertheless represent an "important" difference. As the difference in means declines below this point its importance decreases until, at about .5 units in the difference between the means, party differences become "unimportant," even if statistically significant.

An inspection of Table 4.2 reveals hypotheses H5 and H7 to be substantially correct. They predicted that where status is the incentive for leaders (Colombia), party leaders would not differ on program issues but would differ on strategic issues. On the program issue of government construction of housing there is no difference between the parties. Both are agreed that the government should do "much more." As indicated by the very low standard deviations, consensus within each party on the matter is very high. On the program issue of governmental control of private industry, the parties are not different; both favor moderately increased government control. The high standard deviations indicate that within the parties consensus on this issue is quite low.

On the program issue of government protection of labor unions a statistically significant difference appears (at the .05 level): the Liberals are slightly more pro-labor than the Conservatives. But the difference in mean position is only .36 units and does not, therefore, acquire "importance."

On the strategic issue of the size of the army, the difference between the parties is somewhat greater (.51 units, significant at the .01 level). The Conservatives are just barely in favor of a smaller army; the Liberals, moderately in favor of reduction of army size. It is on the strategic issue of the influence of the Church in government that the only important difference between the parties obtains. The difference in mean position is 1.14 with the Conservatives barely anti-church and the Liberals strongly anti-church.

Another question asked in the survey concerned foreign policy attitudes. Unfortunately the question turned out to be too complicated for some respondents and incomplete for others, as indicated by a relatively high number of "no answer" responses. Nevertheless, with appropriate caution, we may inspect the results of this question, presented in Table 4.3. Foreign policy orientation, in this context, is a program issue, not affecting the relative strength of the parties.[10]

TABLE 4.3

Responses of Party Leaders to Foreign Policy Question

Which foreign policy do you believe would be best to advance the economic development of Colombia?

	Liberals		Conservatives	
	No.	%	No.	%
a. Depend more on the United States and the Alliance for Progress	6	10	15	21
b. Depend more on exports to Europe and the United States	28	47	36	51
c. Depend more on the United Nations and its agencies	3	5	2	3
d. Depend more on the rest of the Latin American countries and the Latin-American Free Trade Association	15	25	9	13
no answer*	8	13	8	11
Total	60	100	70	100**

*Those respondents giving multiple answers are included in the "no answer" figure.

**Does not add because of rounding.

10. "Anti-Americanism" would be a strategic issue between government supporters and opposition, since American dollars are useful to incumbents. In this question, however, anti-Americanism is tapped only partially, and the respondents were almost entirely government supporters of varying degrees of fidelity. It seems probable that if the vigorous opposition groups (MRL and ANAPO) had been included, the "dependence on the U.S." answer would have been shunned by them.

The distribution of answers by party reveals no fundamental difference. About half of each party emphasized exports. The light tendency of Liberals to look toward other Latin American countries and the United Nations, while Conservatives look toward the United States reached only the .1 level of significance (using a chi-square test, excluding the "no answer" responses and combining the "U.N." and "Latin American countries" responses).

Our hypothesis is constructed to apply not only to parties but to factions of parties: organizations which bear the same label but compete with each other in general elections. In the sample we have a sufficient number of Ospinista and Lauro-alzatista Conservatives to attempt a measurement of policy differences between these two factions. The Ospinista Conservatives are followers of ex-president Mariano Ospina (1946–50), the formation of this faction dating to about 1951. The Laureanista faction included followers of ex-president Laureano Gómez (1950–53). Since the split in the early 1950s, the two factions have usually opposed each other, with partial lulls in the 1962 and 1964 elections. In 1965 they were bitterly opposed. In 1960 another Conservative leader, Gilberto Alzate, died. His followers, known as Alzatistas, went largely to the Laureanista faction and a formal unification of Laureanistas and Alzatistas was achieved in 1964. Consequently the faction was generally known in 1965 as the Lauro-alzatista Conservatives, although it was predominantly composed of Laureanistas led by Laureano Gómez and, after his death in 1965, by his son, Alvaro Gómez.

As before, the program issues remain housing, private industry, and labor; the questions of army size and church influence are strategic matters. The army, in the coup of 1953, deposed Laureano Gómez, and consequently he and his followers might be expected to harbor a certain antagonism toward that institution, even twelve years later. For many years Gómez had been sparring with the Catholic hierarchy; although I cannot identify the first break between Gómez and the clergy, it seems clear that the gap was fostered by similar mechanisms as operated to engender the Liberal-Conservative church split. Once Gómez began to feel that the high clergy was not supporting him adequately against other Conservatives, he attacked the churchmen and further reduced his chance of support.

In 1942 when the Liberal government was consummating a revised concordat with the Vatican, Gómez attacked the new treaty as a sellout of Catholic interests. Since the Colombian archbishop and the Pope had approved the new concordat, it seems clear that this attack was strategic.[11] Attempting to gain the political support of lower clergy and devout Catholics, Gómez insinuated the incredible: the Pope was unmindful of the interests of true Catholicism! Another clash between Gómez and the hierarchy followed the 1953 coup when Gómez expressed his bitterness toward them for supporting the coup of General Gustavo Rojas Pinilla against him.[12] The tension between Gómez and the hierarchy was reflected in the conspicuous absence of high church officials at his funeral in 1965.

Table 4.4 presents the issue positions of the two factions. On the three program issues there are no differences. On the strategic issue of army size, the Lauro-alzatistas are mildly anti-army while the Ospinistas are weakly pro-army, a difference of .56 units. On

TABLE 4.4

Mean Positions of the Two Conservative Factions on Policy Questions

	Mean Position			statistical significance of difference in means
	Lauro-alzatistas (n=27)	Ospinistas (n=34)	difference in means	
Housing construction	1.22	1.36	.14	NS
Control of private industry	2.38	2.60	.22	NS
Protection of labor unions	2.44	2.41	.03	NS
Size of army	3.41	2.85	.56	.05
Church influence in government	3.35	3.09	.26	NS

the church issue, the difference in mean scores is not statistically significant and we must conclude that no difference obtains. The comparison of the two factions, then, tends to support the hypotheses: there were no differences between the factions on program issues; on one strategic issue there was a mildly important difference, but on the other there was no difference.

The conclusion that Colombian parties and factions represent no

11. Robert H. Dix, *Colombia: The Political Dimensions of Change* (New Haven, Yale University Press, 1967), p. 310.

12. Some of these attacks and counterattacks are contained in *Dos Actitudes Frente a la Jerarquía* (Bogotá, 1956).

clear ideological or policy differences, except on strategic matters, is probably an unwelcome one for most Colombian politicians. The usual claim is that parties have profound differences in *doctrina* or philosophy, even though they do not differ on substantive policy matters.[13] I believe that this argument is largely a scholastic obfuscation made by party historians to convince themselves that so much fighting and conflict must surely have roots in some great issue of principle. I attempted, however, to explore a possible difference in the philosophical orientations of the parties by a question designed to reveal the areas of leadership interest: "What do you think is the most serious problem facing Colombia?" Presumably the answers would reflect different philosophical orientations toward policies and the world. The answers are tabulated (verbatim) and grouped into broad categories in Table 4.5.

Certainly no dramatic contrasts emerge between the leaders of the two parties. Over half of both groups look to the socioeconomic sphere (most, in significantly vague terms). About the same proportion in each party mention political problems. There is slightly more Conservative than Liberal interest in the moral and communism areas, perhaps the result of closer Conservative contact with the Catholic Church position. On balance, I am not inclined to relinquish my skepticism about the existence of profound Liberal-Conservative philosophical differences.

The data collected in the survey may be rearranged to throw some light on possible differences in the attitudes of different generations of party leaders. It might be thought that the newer generation of leaders had different policy attitudes, that they represented some kind of "new movement" in ideological orientation. In Table 4.6 each party sample is divided into older (over 40) and younger (40 and under) age groups, and the mean issue positions are computed for each of the four groups. Only two statistically significant differences appear: the younger Conservatives are in favor of "more" govern-

13. "One could say that the Conservatives have sought to govern with dogmas and the Liberals, with principles. It is here where the substantial ideological difference between the two parties is found." Sánchez Gómez, p. 8. Restrepo Jaramillo points out that the two parties have not differed on acceptance of democratic norms, economic issues, federalism, individual freedoms, female suffrage, and free trade, but nevertheless "the political parties are separated by an ideological abyss and defend or attack transcendental antagonistic principles." *El Pensamiento Conservador*, pp. 71, 87, 94–100.

TABLE 4.5

Areas of Leadership Interest

Verbatim responses to the question: What do you think is the
most serious problem facing Colombia?

Response	Number of times mentioned	
	Liberals	*Conservatives*
SOCIOECONOMIC GROUP		
economic	11	16
socioeconomic	7	4
social	3	1
economic underdevelopment	6	2
lack of jobs—unemployment	6	8
poverty (of the people)	1	1
education		2
need for technical education	1	
economic and fiscal chaos		1
need for investment		1
excessive birthrate—population explosion	1	1
underproduction	1	1
agrarian		1
capital flight		1
need for better organization of production		1
economic instability	1	
monoculture of coffee	1	
scarcity of foreign exchange	1	
high cost of living	1	
lack of industries	1	
monetary instability	1	
malnutrition	1	
lack of housing	1	
misery	1	
Total, Socioeconomic group	46 (68%)	41 (51%)
POLITICAL GROUP		
political	1	4
leadership disunity	1	3
misgovernment (*desgobierno*)	3	
lack of energetic government		2
politiquería	2	
lack of government planning		1
lack of leadership	1	
crisis of leadership responsibility		1
need for administrative organization		1
presidential succession		1
ineffective political system	1	
disorganization of the political parties	1	
lack of political education		1
Total, Political group	10 (15%)	14 (17%)

Response	Number of times mentioned	
	Liberals	*Conservatives*
CRIME-VIOLENCE GROUP		
La Violencia*	3	8
personal insecurity (from crime)	3	1
banditry		1
impunity of criminals	1	1
public order		1
Total, Crime-Violence group	7 (10%)	12 (15%)
MORAL-MORALE GROUP		
moral		2
lack of faith in ourselves	1	1
lack of mutual trust and solidarity		2
defeatism		1
lack of popular trust in the leadership classes	1	
popular apathy		1
lack of honesty and industry of many Colombians		1
Total, Moral-Morale group	2 (3%)	8 (10%)
COMMUNISM-SUBVERSION GROUP		
communism		4
communist infiltration		2
the campaign against democracy	1	
Total, Communism-Subversion group	1 (1%)	6 (7%)
OTHER RESPONSES		
all the same	1	
the crisis of the system	1	
Total responses	68 (100%)	81 (100%)

The total number of responses exceeds the number of respondents (70 Conservatives, 60 Liberals) since those making two responses were counted twice.

*La violencia (literally, "violence") is a general term which in 1965 was used to refer to banditry, kidnappings, and homicides, particularly in rural areas.

ment control of private industry, while the over 40 group has a mean position of "same." This generational difference is not found on the Liberal side, however; in fact, the young Conservatives are slightly more in favor of governmental control than either young or old Liberals. On the Liberal side the only difference produced between the two groups was on the church question, with the young Liberals being somewhat more anti-church than the over-40 group. With the apparent exception of a shift in the Conservative party toward favoring more government control of private industry, there appears to be no important gap on issue positions between the younger and older Colombian leaders.

TABLE 4.6

Leadership Positions on Policy Questions, Younger and Older Age Groups

	Liberals			Conservatives		
	40 and under (n=23)	over 40 (n=37)	SS*	40 and under (n=41)	over 40 (n=29)	SS*
Housing construction	1.13	1.19	NS	1.27	1.24	NS
Control of private industry	2.26	2.35	NS	2.12	3.03	.01
Protection of labor unions	2.00	2.14	NS	2.32	2.62	NS
Size of army	3.78	3.69	NS	3.34	3.03	NS
Church influence in government	4.68	4.12	.02	3.30	3.04	NS

*SS = statistical significance of the difference in mean position, older party leaders compared with younger leaders in the same party. NS means not significant at the .1 level.

A note of caution might be inserted here regarding the interpretation of the findings presented thus far. I have shown only the policy attitudes of leaders as expressed in responses to the questionnaire. I have said nothing about when or whether these attitudes would affect behavior. It would be unwise to reason that because expressed attitudes on issues differ, the attitudes will be translated into policy when a given party obtains power. Such reasoning would be particularly defective when applied to leaders with a status incentive. If their opportunities for advancing their own personal position conflict with their issue attitudes—as frequently will be the case—the behavior of status-oriented leaders will reflect these opportunities and not their policy preferences.

LEFT AND RIGHT

The picture given thus far corresponds to our hypotheses H5 and H7: Colombian parties (and factions) do not differ on program issues; they do tend to differ on strategic issues. Unfortunately the strategic issues selected were of a somewhat diffuse, distant nature. If I had chosen matters of immediate concern to the politicians, such as (in 1965) the desirability of holding the 1966 presidential elections before, instead of after, the congressional elections, then we would have seen a dramatic example of cleavage. The Lauro-alzatistas opposed the candidacy of Liberal Carlos Lleras and realized that if presidential elections came first he would be elected and then shape congressional elections in his favor and to their disadvantage. If congressional elections were held first, the Lauro-alzatistas might gain enough strength to jeopardize the Lleras candidacy. Consequently they opposed an early presidential election. The Ospinista Conservatives, allied with Lleras, naturally took the opposite position since early presidential elections would be beneficial to them. If a question on this matter had been presented in the survey, it very likely would have revealed a cleavage between these two Conservative factions as great as the scale permitted.

The findings about the almost complete absence of program cleavage in Colombian politics contradict the usual picture presented by scholars and journalists. That picture is one of ideological rainbows: reactionaries, rightists, moderate conservatives, progressive leftists, and so on.[14] The Laureanista Conservatives, for example, are customarily dubbed "rightists." In view of the findings in Table 4.4, this label is completely misleading. In fact, noting the actual issue-positions of the parties, it appears that on program matters both factions of the Conservatives and the Officialist Liberals have a "leftist" stance, even though governmental policy in Colombia is already strongly biased toward interventionism and social welfare measures.

To illustrate this point, I manipulated the sample to uncover the presence of "socioeconomic conservatism" among Colombian leaders. By "socioeconomic conservatism" I mean a basic attitude against a larger government role in economic and social life. If this attitude existed among Colombian leaders, there would presumably be a significant number who, on the questionnaire, evidenced a desire for

14. See, for example, Kenneth F. Johnson, "Political Radicalism in Colombia: Electoral Dynamics of 1962 and 1964," *Journal of Inter-American Studies, 7* (1965), 15–26; "Colombian Rightists Gain Heavily in Voting," *The Washington Post,* March 22, 1966, p. A16.

less government control of business, less government protection of labor unions, *and* less of a government role in housing construction. Breaking down the respondents along these lines, it was found that out of the entire sample of 130 leaders of both parties, there were only five "moderate conservatives" (four Conservatives and one Liberal), leaders who, although they selected a "more" answer for the housing question, chose "less" or "much less" answers for both the control of private industry and protection of labor unions questions. Since no one in the entire sample answered "less" to the housing question, we had to be content with a "same" answer as the conservative response to that question. In the entire sample there was only one individual who desired "less" on both the control of private industry and protection of unions, and the "same" on housing construction— a "true conservative."

Significantly enough, this one true conservative (a member of the Conservative departmental directorate for Antioquia) had little in common with the usual stereotype of the conservative Latin American politician as a wealthy businessman or aristocratic landholder. He was a simple Antioqueño merchant who, with his brother, personally ran a stall in one of the central markets of Medellín selling rice, soap, and sugar to housewives.

In thinking about Colombian politics, then, we must discard labels of "left" and "right," of "progressive reformers" and "regressive reactionaries." These labels do not identify or explain the major political cleavages.

THE AMERICAN CASE

The analysis of the relationship between incentives and differences between party leaders on issue positions predicted that where a program incentive is dominant the leaders will differ on program issues (H6). In the United States, I have argued, program is the dominant incentive for leaders. Do American party leaders hold different program policy positions? Fortunately, there is an excellent study of this question by Herbert McClosky, Paul J. Hoffman, and Rosemary O'Hara, after which, in fact, my own survey was patterned.[15] They

15. "Issue Conflict and Consensus among Party Leaders and Followers," *American Political Science Review, 54* (1960), 406–27.

asked American party leaders to express their attitudes toward 24 policy areas, all of which were program issues in our sense.[16] The investigators found that out of the 24 issues selected, important differences between Republican and Democratic leaders obtained on 15 issues (including government role in housing, regulation of business, and regulation of labor unions); statistically significant but smaller differences were found on eight other issues; and on only one (defense spending) was there no difference.[17] It does appear, then, that the American case is consistent with the hypothesis: where the incentive is program, differences do exist between leaders of different parties on program policies.[18]

16. The leaders selected were delegates and alternates to the Republican and Democratic national conventions. Strictly speaking, many of these individuals would not be leaders by our definition, but "active followers." However, the correspondence with the Colombian sample is sufficiently close for our purposes.

17. The authors did not employ criteria of importance. I have, after inspecting the variations possible in the scale, decided that a difference in "support ratios" of about .18 or greater roughly corresponds to our measure of an "important" difference.

18. I have not attempted to incorporate "active followers" into the analysis since I have no satisfactory data for Colombian active followers. The direction such theory-building would take is perhaps clear by now: the employment incentive would also be associated with lack of interest in program policies and produce no difference between the parties. I suspect that program is the dominant incentive for U.S. and British active followers. This speculation is consistent with the frequent observations of program differences between active followers in these countries; see: Eldersveld, *Political Parties: A Behavioral Analysis*, pp. 184 ff.; Dwaine Marvick and Charles Nixon, "Recruitment Contrasts in Rival Campaign Groups," in Marvick, ed., *Political Decision-Makers*, pp. 211–14; Leon P. Epstein, "British M. P.'s and their Local Parties," *American Political Science Review*, 54 (1960), 374–90; Richard Rose, "The Political Ideas of English Party Activists," *American Political Science Review*, 56 (1962), 360–71.

CHAPTER 5

THE DEVIANT CASE:
ANTIOQUIA

I remember how my father, born in Antioquia, used to tell of his surprise when, having recently arrived in Bogotá as a law student, he noticed that those people not belonging to the lowest social classes shunned all manual labor; while he remembered that the Antioqueño blacksmiths used to leave hammer and forge in the afternoon and mingle with the most notable people in every town on a complete social basis, a pattern unknown in the rest of the country.

> Fernando Guillén Martínez, Raíz y Futuro de la Revolución *(Bogotá, Ediciones Tercer Mundo, 1963), p. 62.*

The inhabitants of the Colombian department of Antioquia differ from other Colombians. The Antioqueños themselves, and outsiders, have long recognized the contrast. The precise nature of the Antioqueño distinctiveness, however, has not been clearly identified. It is often remarked that these people are self-confident, industrious, proud of being Antioqueños; indeed, that they resemble North Americans.[1] The Antioqueño proclivity for commercial and industrial activity is well-known; in Antioquia economic development began earlier and has proceeded further than in all other parts of Colombia.[2] Among other distinctive features, Antioquia is generally recog-

---

1. Guillén Martínez, pp. 57–62; E. Caballero Calderón, *Historia Privada de los Colombianos,* pp. 99–104; *El Pueblo Antioqueño* (Medellín, Universidad de Antioquia, 1942); James J. Parsons, *Antioqueño Colonization in Western Colombia* (Berkeley, University of California Press, 1949), pp. 1 ff.

2. See Everett E. Hagen, *On the Theory of Social Change* (Homewood, Ill., The Dorsey Press, 1962), pp. 353–79. Hagen's interpretation of Antioqueño economic progress is somewhat misleading. He characterizes the Antioqueños as a despised minority who "smart under" (p. 377) the attitudes of other Colombians toward them as outsiders and have therefore sought to prove their worth through success in economic activities. This interpretation suggests that Antioqueños are highly

nized as the best-governed department in Colombia—although, paradoxically, Antioqueños are not known as "politicians."

When I first began research in Colombia, I tended to ignore the supposed cultural differences in Antioquia. I was, at that time, seeking an analysis which focused on political institutions and in which basic social variables would play little part. But as the inquiry led back to incentives and then to status-consciousness, Antioquia began to take on significance.

Shortly after I arrived in Medellín, the capital of Antioquia, I began to realize what was so special about the Antioqueños: they were less status-conscious than other Colombians.[3] One indication of this difference was the ease with which I could get party leaders to respond to the survey questionnaire. In other departments I had encountered the most frustrating obstacles: leaders would feign to be too busy and promise to answer the next day. At later, agreed-upon times they would still not have answered. They would have me wait in their offices indefinitely until they arrived or became "unoccupied." Since the questionnaire was only one page long and could be answered in less than three minutes, this procrastination had little to do with time considerations.

It became increasingly apparent that these many postponements and broken promises hinged upon attempts to enhance status, for the leaders evidenced little objection to the idea of the questionnaire itself, nor to the questions on it. By procrastinating in answering the questionnaire, the leaders were apparently attempting to demonstrate their importance, to seem waited-upon and sought-after. In Antioquia the problems of delay were much less acute. Only a few leaders adopted a fully evasive status-enhancement routine. Many answered immediately; others, when they promised to have the questionnaire answered at a certain time, usually kept their word.

I also noticed that in general Antioqueños were more punctual, both in personal contacts and for meetings. This pattern also reflects

status-conscious, greatly worried about what other Colombians think about them. I would argue the reverse: it was precisely the Antioqueño *disregard* for status considerations which led to their activity in the economic sphere.

3. A search for the source of this lower status-consciousness is beyond the aims of this study. A preliminary guess might point to the influx of Basque immigrants. In Spain Basques are recognized for their lower status-consciousness. See Parsons, p. 2.

lower status-consciousness. People come late to demonstrate their higher status, to show they should be waited-upon. If everyone is attempting to enhance his status, then all will come late and meetings will begin late. In Bogotá a meeting of a party executive committee will regularly begin over an hour and a half late; in Antioquia the one party executive meeting I observed began only fifteen minutes late.

In other spheres Antioqueños demonstrate less status-consciousness than other Colombians. They are more casual about dress, willing to take off their coats and roll up their shirt-sleeves. As indicated by the opening quotation, they are less concerned with the status implications of manual work. The usual picture of the Antioqueño as self-confident is consistent with lower status-consciousness. The highly status-conscious individual is always anxious, fearing that any action or word might impair his status. The person who is less status-conscious is more secure in his behavior toward others, less afraid of the status implications of his actions.

If status-consciousness is lower in Antioquia than in the rest of Colombia, by hypothesis we should expect status to be less prominent as an incentive for leaders (the other conditions obtaining):

> *H1. Status will be an increasingly strong incentive for leadership participation as (1) status-consciousness is higher in the society, (2) the status value of higher politicial offices is greater, and (3) recruitment to these offices is more open.*

In our formulation of the status-program continuum, the decline of the status incentive is associated with the increased presence of the program incentive. Although my evidence about the incentives of Antioqueño leaders is incomplete, based on extended interviews with only eight leaders, I encountered two striking cases.

One interview was with a Liberal councilman of Medellín, an engineer, 50 years old, and a member of the departmental boards of electric production and community road-building. The interview began in his office in the late morning. While exchanging pleasantries, I noticed an electric power station on a far-away hill and remarked upon it. Immediately the respondent launched upon an extensive discussion of that station, when it was built, what its production was, and then to a full survey of electric production in the department: hydro-electric capacity of the river system, total production three years ago, production at date, projected needs and capacities, years of completion of different projects, financing and rates— in short, a thorough examination of the problem.

The interview continued through lunch at a local restaurant. The subject matter: road construction through local self-help. Again I was given a lengthy disquisition on the problem: methods of financing, confiscation of lands, upkeep, miles built per year, dollars per mile, costs to property owners. Then the subject shifted to housing construction: cost per unit, cost per square meter, typical family budget, proportion of family budget spent on housing, years for repayment, interest rates. In vain I tried to elicit information about party nominations, getting on the directorate, and factionalism within the party. He either ignored these questions or treated them distantly and briefly as incidental matters to which he had paid little attention.

Initially I was disappointed with this interview since, despite its length (three hours), I had learned so little about the machinery of politics. But upon reflection, I began to grasp the stunning incongruity of this individual when placed against the many other leaders I had interviewed. I had uncovered a most unusual case: a Colombian leader with a clear program incentive.

In another interview with an Antioqueño, I found, in less dramatic form, a similar program orientation. He was a Liberal member of the House of Representatives and a member of the House Budget Committee. At 66 he was almost certainly the oldest member of the House (this fact has theoretical significance, see below). In the interview he expressed concern with the problem of malnutrition, citing the per capita caloric intake and what it ought to be and digressing on this matter for some time. Unlike other budget committee members I had interviewed, he had considerable knowledge about the various expenditures of government. As in the interview noted above, the respondent was unable to give detailed answers to questions about nominations or elections.

Ascribing a modal incentive to Antioqueño leaders is clearly an uncertain task with only this premlinary data at hand. The respondent in the first interview threw some light on the matter:

RESPONDENT: I am in politics to get things done, to advance the development of the region.

Q: How many others are there like you, on the Liberal (departmental) directorate?

R: Well, I would say it's about even. There are seven or eight of us who want to do things. When we take an office it's to get projects put through. Then there are about seven or eight who are mainly interested in the positions themselves and favors.

I am inclined to believe, however, that the balance is not quite even between those with a program incentive and those with a status incentive. Both the interviews and briefer contacts with Antioqueño leaders have led me to decide, quite tentatively, that the dominant incentive is still status.

The ascription of less strength to the status incentive in Antioquia is not based on the interview responses. Instead I have employed the competitive conception of incentives introduced earlier. I assume that leaders with different incentives are in competition with each other. If the status incentive is very strong, individuals with this incentive will outcompete leaders with other (weaker) incentives. Therefore, one will find only leaders with a status incentive in the leadership group. If some leaders with a program incentive are found (as in Antioquia), then the status incentive must be weaker than in another system (the rest of Colombia) where such leaders are not encountered. We may cautiously conclude, then, that as predicted by hypothesis H1, the lower status-consciousness in Antioquia does produce a status incentive of less strength than in the rest of the country (see Figure 1, Chapter 1).

POLITICAL CONFLICT

In Chapter 3 I summarized the analysis of incentives in a general hypothesis about the intensity of conflict in a system:

H4a. In a society characterized by (1) high status-consciousness, (2) high status value of higher political offices, (3) relatively open recruitment to these offices, and (4) weak barriers to upward social mobility, intense political conflict is probable.

Although status-consciousness is lower in Antioquia, the other conditions—2, 3, and 4—appear to be substantially the same as in the rest of the country. If the hypothesis is correct, then, we should expect to find a lower level of political conflict in Antioquia. I have not documented for Antioquia all the steps in the analysis behind this hypothesis, particularly those concerning active followers, but we may at least see if the overall conclusion holds.

A test of the hypothesis was somewhat hampered by the fact that Antioquia is a part of the larger political system and would therefore be affected by conflicts generated outside the department. Nevertheless, it is possible to make some approximate comparisons. Most observers and politicians both in Antioquia and in the rest of Colombia seem to agree that politics in Antioquia is "more serene," "less agitated," than in the rest of the country. This characteristic was also present in earlier times. In the period 1831–40, when most of the rest of the country was violently agitated by political struggles, Antioquia remained remarkably calm.[4] In the civil war of 1860–61, Liberal leader Pascual Bravo found the Antioqueños annoyingly uninterested in the conflict, and criticized their "materialism" which blinded them to the "ideals" at stake in the conflict.[5]

A quantitative indication of a lower level of political conflict in Antioquia can be developed by a content analysis technique. In the election campaign of 1921–22, there was considerable violence. The Liberals were competing openly against the Conservatives for the presidency, then held by the Conservatives. The Liberals lost, they claimed, because of intimidation, violence, and fraud. To substantiate their claim, they published a lengthy work which contains, among other things, a 240-page, department-by-department compilation of telegrams and newspaper clippings pertaining to violence employed against the Liberals: clashes, arrests, intimidation of voters, and harassment of Liberal candidates. Perhaps the editors of this book devoted space to each department proportional to the amount of electoral violence which occurred, but more probably they simply emptied out their files and included everything.

In either case, the space (number of pages) devoted to each department would serve as a rough index of the actual amount of violence. There might be some distortions: an overstatement for the department of Cundinamarca where Bogotá is located since news

---

4. Jorge Ospina Londoño, *Pascual Bravo—Los Partidos Políticos en Colombia* (Medellín, Imprenta Universidad, 1938), p. 37.

5. Ibid., p. 160.

from there would more easily reach the national directorate office; and an understatement of violence for the very backward, rural departments, particularly Huila and Cauca, where communication would be poor and proportionately more events would go unrecorded. Since the number of instances of violence would be a function of the number of people in a department, I have adjusted each department's figure to its population. The number of pages devoted to each department was multiplied by Pa/Pd, where Pd is the population of the department and Pa is the population of Antioquia. In this way population size is eliminated and we have, in effect, a per capita index of electoral violence, as shown in Table 5.1.

TABLE 5.1

Departmental Comparisons of Electoral Violence, 1921–22

Department	Number of pages*	Population**	Per capita index of electoral violence
1. Atlántico	19	135,792	115
2. Norte de Santander	32	239,235	110
3. Cundinamarca	99	812,036	100
4. Tolima	34	328,812	85
5. Valle	20	271,633	61
6. Bolívar	25	457,111	45
7. Magdalena	11	211,395	43
8. Boyacá	27	657,167	34
9. Santander	20	509,161	32
10. Nariño	12	340,765	29
11. Cauca	7	238,779	24
12. Caldas	12	428,137	23
13. Huila	5	183,337	22
14. Antioquia	17	823,226	17

Los Partidos Políticos en Colombia (Bogotá, Aguila Negra Editorial, 1922), pp. 55–394.

**Data for census of 1918 in *Anuario de Estadística General 1931* (Bogotá, Imprenta Nacional, 1934), p. 4.

In the ranking of the departments in order of decreasing violence, Antioquia does fall at the bottom, as expected.[6] It is worth noting in

6. This finding is apparently contradicted by the amount of violence in Antioquia during 1949–58. Guzmán et al., *La Violencia en Colombia, 1,* 291, estimated that Antioquia suffered about 10,000 deaths, or more than most other departments.

passing that Caldas, which also falls low on the list, is geographically contiguous with Antioquia and was the recipient of much Antioqueño migration in earlier years.

In other elections similar observations about less fraud and violence in Antioquia have been made. An observer of the elections of 1896, for example, noted that intimidation and fraud were extreme throughout the country, with the exception of Antioquia where the opposition Liberals were rather fairly treated (indeed, winning two seats in the House of Representatives in a strongly Conservative department).[7] The hypothesis relating status-consciousness to the level of political conflict (H4a) is borne out in Antioquia. In this department where status-consciousness is lower than in the rest of the country, the intensity of political conflict also is lower.[8]

RECRUITMENT AND RETIREMENT AGES

The experience in Antioquia may be employed to test other hypotheses in which incentives are the independent variable. This devi-

---

Although the data are unreliable, it seems clear that Antioquia did have about the average per capita incidence of *la violencia*. As argued in Chapter 8, political conflict did provide the necessary context and stimulus, but *la violencia* was a bundle of secondary and tertiary effects of the political context combined with numerous social and geographical conditions. These secondary effects include such simple criminal activities as homicide, banditry, and aimless guerrilla activity. Whether or not the political stimulus led to a large number of deaths, therefore, depended heavily upon conditions in the local region including, perhaps, the size, nature, and density of farm holdings, the amount of geographic mobility, and the physical terrain. We note, of course, that *la violencia* was a rural, not urban, phenomenon. Also, some departments, such as Atlántico and Nariño saw virtually no guerrilla activity. But it was in Nariño that the first strictly political clashes occurred in 1946. Cundinamarca saw relatively little violence—but we certainly would not judge that political conflict was low there in view of the Bogotazo.

The number of deaths attributed to *la violencia,* therefore, is an invalid measure of interdepartmental levels of political violence. Intervening variables obscure the effect of moderate departmental variations in the level of political conflict on the overall death rate.

7. Eduardo Rodríguez Piñeres, *Diez Años de Política Liberal, 1892–1902* (Bogotá, Librería Colombiana, 1945), p. 33.

8. Another deviant system in Latin America which is remarkably similar to Antioquia in many respects is Costa Rica, where status-consciousness is much lower and, among other political contrasts with neighboring countries, the intensity of conflict has been lower. See James L. Busey, *Notes on Costa Rican Democracy* (Boulder, University of Colorado Press, 1962).

ant case is useful, for example, in analyzing leadership recruitment and retirement ages. It is possible to reason from a knowledge of incentives to hypotheses that predict variations in these ages in different systems.

In a system where status is the incentive for leaders we would expect a man to enter politics at an early age. Status is valued for what it will do for him, for its effects on his career and life chances. It is when the individual is starting out in life that he feels the need for status most acutely; for him status and success go together. It is the young who seek success most fervently, and if status is linked to success, it will be the young who drive hardest for status. The "status-or-failure" perspective of the law student presented at the beginning of Chapter 2 illustrates the youthful attitude toward status and career success.

The program incentive would seem to work in an entirely different manner. It is detached from matters of success and career. It is not likely to emerge as a man approaches adulthood, but somewhat later in life, after he has considered and chosen a vocation—and perhaps found it unfulfilling. In late adolescence and early adulthood the individual is preoccupied with himself and his own future. He is not likely to exhibit an interest in matters of general community concern. At a later age perspectives would shift from personal to community needs and issues of public policy. These reflections may be summarized:

> *H8. Where the incentive for leaders is status, leaders will enter politics at a relatively early age.*

> *H9. Where the incentive for leaders is program, leaders will enter politics at a relatively late age.*

In passing we might offer an obvious corollary:

> *H8a. Where the incentive for leaders is status, university students will be highly active in politics.*

Although Colombian student-politicians are customarily described as "forces for democracy," the hypothesis suggests that any relationship between university students and democracy is largely coincidental. It should not be supposed, incidentally, that student political activity in Colombia is in any way new or unusual. Students were quite active, for example, in the many political societies in existence around 1850, including the Filotémica, the Democrática, and the Escuela Republicana (see Chapter 6).

To test these hypotheses I used the survey of 130 leaders already mentioned. The respondents were asked to name their age when they held their first public office (not party position).[9] If our hypotheses are correct, the respondents, excluding those from Antioquia, should have a low entry age, while in Antioquia the age at first public office should be somewhat higher.

The findings did conform to these expectations. For the Colombian sample (excluding Antioquia) the median age for holding first public office was 23 (N=89). For Antioquia it was 28, although this finding must be treated with caution in view of the small sample (N=16).[10] To complete the picture I have calculated, from data given by Donald R. Matthews, that the median age of U.S. senators when they hold their first public office is about 31.[11] Reasoning that to go to the top of the (legislative) political ladder U.S. senators probably entered politics earlier than state legislators or big city councilmen, we might suspect that a strictly comparable sample for the Colombian data would have given a somewhat higher median age of entry, perhaps about 35.

Hypotheses about retirement ages can be constructed along the lines developed above. The individual seeking status from participation is likely to feel a diminishing need for *more* status as he grows older. The youthful perspective of high success and career advancement is gradually replaced by a desire to live out one's life in comfort, to rest on one's laurels. Consequently we would expect status-motivated leaders to retire from politics at a relatively early age.

The implication of the program incentive would be different. This incentive is largely detached from career interests, but rests on the

9. The sample contained persons (19% of the sample) who, although they were members of departmental or big-city party executive committees (directorates), had not held a public office. They were not included in this tabulation.

10. A different presentation of the data, however, yields the same conclusion: only 37% of the Antioqueños had held their first office before the age of 27; 76% of the non-Antioquia sample had held their first office before age 27.

11. *U.S. Senators and Their World* (Chapel Hill, University of North Carolina Press, 1960), p. 50. Matthews grouped these ages in ten-year blocs. I have interpolated to arrive at the median year.

positive satisfaction resulting from actually working on policy and enacting programs. There is no reason to believe that this satisfaction will decline with age, any more than the satisfactions of fishing or ham radio decline as a person grows older. Consequently:

> *H10. Where the incentive for leaders is status, leaders will retire from politics at a relatively early age.*
>
> *H11. Where the incentive for leaders is program, leaders will retire from politics at a relatively late age.*

Unfortunately, I cannot test these hypotheses directly since calculation of retirement ages requires information which active leaders could not provide. Nevertheless, by inspecting the age distribution of present leaders, we may form some conclusions about the age at which retirement is taking place in the system. If there are comparatively few leaders in the older age groups, we may assume that retirement is occurring at a relatively early age.

One of the striking features of Colombian politics is the youth of even prominent leaders. In the House of Representatives, for example, the age of the typical member appears to be about 40; men over 60 are extremely rare. This contrasts with the United States House of Representatives, a body of men whose typical age lies between 55–60. The survey of Colombian leaders enables us to document the dearth of older leaders more precisely. In the non-Antioquia sample (n=108) only 48 per cent of the leaders were over 40, 19 per cent were over 50, and 4 per cent over 60. In the Antioquia sample there was a suggestion of somewhat older leadership: 64 per cent of the respondents in this sample (n=22) were over 40.

These findings may be compared to the American experience. The data given by Matthews for U.S. senators show that about 95 per cent are over 40, 72 per cent over 50, and 33 per cent are over 60.[12] Senators are not, of course, fully comparable with our Colombian sample. However, numerous studies of state legislators in the U.S. have shown their median age to be in the range of 49–52.[13] That is, about 50 per cent of American state legislators are over 50 years old, compared to the figure of 19 per cent in Colombia.

12. Ibid., computed from the table on p. 14.
13. See Frank J. Sorauf, *Party and Representation* (New York, Atherton Press, 1963), pp. 66–67.

In view of these findings we may conclude, as predicted by hypotheses H10 and H11, that American politicians retire at a later age than their Colombian counterparts. The general impact of the status incentive, then, is to produce a younger leadership, entering earlier and leaving earlier. As the status incentive weakens, and the program incentive emerges somewhat, the pattern shifts toward later entrance and later retirement, as suggested by the findings for Antioquia (see Table 5.2).

TABLE 5.2

Recruitment Ages and Present Age Profiles of Leaders:
Colombia, Antioquia, and the United States

	Median age at first public office	Present age of leaders: proportion of leaders who are*		
		over 60	over 50	over 40
Colombia (except Antioquia)	23 (n=89)	4%	19%	48% (n=108)
Antioquia	28 (n=16)	(9%)**	(23%)**	64% (n=22)
United States	31–35	15%–33%	50%–72%	66%–95%

*columns are cumulative
**too few cases to be significant

The inquiry up to this point has defined the nature of incentives and produced a few preliminary hypotheses relating them to the political system. Before turning to an examination of the mechanics of Colombian politics, however, I must attempt definition and explanation of some critical structural features in the system. This examination takes us somewhat far afield but leads to an understanding of fundamental institutions, including party identification, the military coup, and the pattern of intense political conflict which I call a "defensive feud."

PART TWO

STRUCTURES IN THE
POLITICAL ENVIRONMENT

CHAPTER 6

THE RISE OF POLITICAL PARTIES
IN COLOMBIA

The great majority of the artisans of Bogotá had been, up to that time [1847–48], supporters of the incumbents, or rather, available material to serve as soldiers and voters for the Conservative leaders and capitalists, and the clergy. How could they be drawn away from this influence and placed on the side of the Liberals? It was thought that the best way to achieve this object was to flatter . . . their self-esteem with the prospect of becoming . . . a political and social force by means of the permanent association of their dispersed elements. For this reason the society was named Artisans' Democratic.

> *Jose María Samper,* Historia de una Alma *(Bogotá, Editorial Kelly, 1946),* 1, 218.

In Colombia the military has played a relatively minor role in political life, and large, permanent political parties have existed there for a long time. In these two respects Colombia differs from states like Ecuador and Peru where the military has played a much more pronounced role and where permanent parties have not existed.

These preliminary observations suggest that perhaps there is an association between the military role and the party system in a Latin American country. It might not be merely an accident that Colombia has had a relatively inactive military *and* large, permanent parties. A necessary association, I believe, does obtain, and in this chapter and the next I shall attempt to trace out some of the connections. The first step is to seek an explanation for the early appearance of permanent parties in Colombia.

For our analysis a party is a collection of participants bearing a distinct label, the overt purpose of which is to capture governmental positions for its members. A faction is a group of participants bearing the same label as another group but which competes for office with that group in general elections. Thus the emphasis of this definition is upon labels. Each group bearing a different label is a party; participants competing in general elections under the same label are factions of that party label. Included as factions are groups bearing different complete labels, but having the same root label. For example, participants bearing the labels Conservador, Liberal, Alianza Nacional Popular are each parties since they have distinct labels. But groups known as Liberal oficialista, Movimiento Revolucionario Liberal, Movimiento Independiente Liberal, Movimiento de Regeneración Liberal, and Acción Liberal are all factions of the Liberal party since they bear the same root label but compete in general elections with other groups bearing the label "Liberal."

Although this emphasis on labels may at first appear superficial, a label-oriented definition of a political party is actually quite significant and extremely useful. To understand this, we must consider the phenomenon of *party identification*. In many countries the electorate is identified with various political party labels. That is, some high proportion of voters (about 75 per cent in the United States, somewhat higher in Great Britain) will consider themselves as belonging to a political camp, placing themselves under one or another party label. Once established, party identification tends to be stable over time. As might be expected, those individuals who identify with a political party label usually vote for that party. Rather than making an autonomous, unbiased choice at each election, the identified voter makes his perceptions of issues and candidates consistent with his preexisting party identification. Consequently party identification, insofar as it exists, is an extremely important determinant of the voting choice.[1]

With these facts in mind, the connection between permanent parties and party identification becomes clear. Politicians who know

1. The conclusions in this paragraph are drawn from many studies of voting behavior, including: Paul F. Lazarsfeld, Bernard Berelson, and Hazel Gaudet, *The People's Choice* (2d ed. New York, Columbia University Press, 1948); Berelson, Lazarsfeld, and McPhee, *Voting;* Angus Campbell, Philip E. Converse, Warren E. Miller, and Donald E. Stokes, *The American Voter* (New York, John Wiley and Sons, 1960); R. S. Milne and H. C. Mackenzie, *Marginal Seat 1955* (London, The Hansard Society, 1958); Mark Berney, A. P. Gray, and R. H. Pear, *How People Vote* (London, Routledge and Kegan Paul, 1956).

that a substantial proportion of the electorate is identified with certain party labels may be expected to employ these labels year after year. To advance a new label is to waste votes. Where party identification is high, therefore, we would find that the same parties remain on the political scene and that no new parties (labels) arise to replace them.[2] But if party identification is low, so that few voters are attached to existing labels, politicians may readily employ new labels to identify themselves and their organizations at no sacrifice. Consequently where voters' party identification is low, we could expect parties (labels) to come and go.[3]

An explanation for the early rise of permanent political parties in Colombia, then, must identify the mechanisms which gave rise to widespread party identification at an early date. Beginning with an electorate which is not identified with party labels, the most natural means whereby people may acquire party identification is through the activities of popular electoral organizations. Aspiring politicians, in an effort to broaden their electoral support, may be expected to set up various types of political organizations designed to draw voters into their camp. And, of course, these leaders will adopt labels to identify themselves and their followers. Membership and participation in electoral clubs in support of a given party label would seem to provide, in the initial stages, a mechanism for promoting party identification.

But if leaders are to found electoral organizations, the votes of potential members must be important in the political system. Politicians are unlikely to expend great efforts to organize an electorate into voting blocs if the blocs play no role in matters of leadership selection. There are two general conditions which discourage leaders from organizing the electorate: an extremely small electorate or the perversion of elections through fraud or violence. The first condition characterized the United States and Great Britain at earlier times, and many writers have noted the association between the expansion

2. I am making the assumption that a status incentive prevails. If the incentive of leaders is program, this hypothesis would not apply, as I shall show in Chap. 9.

3. This hypothesis has been advanced by Philip Converse and Georges Dupeux, "Politicization of the Electorate in France and the United States," *Public Opinion Quarterly*, 26 (Spring 1962), 1–23. They found that a relatively lower degree of party identification in France (about 45 per cent of the electorate) was associated with the abrupt rise and decline of new parties.

of the electorate and the rise of party organizations in these countries.[4]

A highly restricted electorate, however, is only one condition which might discourage leaders from establishing mass party organizations. The perversion of elections is another, and one which is more relevant for Latin American countries. If elections are undermined by frauds, cancellation, or annulment, then obviously citizen votes are of relatively little importance. If 10,000 votes are never felt in leadership selection, owing to the disuse or abuse of elections, then politicians will not be prompted to form organizations to gather these votes.

Pushing the analysis further back, then, under what conditions will electoral abuse be most prevalent? The first answer to this question points to the strength of incentives. As winning becomes more important (stronger incentives) then electoral fraud is more likely. Frauds in the election of president of the local stamp club, for example, are unlikely because no one is sufficiently eager to win that office. That is, the incentives for being president of the stamp club are likely to be weak. This consideration of incentives would explain the broad contrast between the amount of Anglo-American electoral abuse and the extent of such practices in Latin American countries. But we must look more closely to explain contrasts in the amount of electoral abuse in different Latin American countries in the nineteenth century where, I suggest, incentives were quite strong generally.

In a context where incentives are strong, it is evident that participants will not treat the matter of leadership transfer lightly. An election is not, after all, an absolute decision. An absolute decision rests upon force, and elections will be accepted only if all participants feel that settling the matter by force is too costly or too uncertain. In the United States elections have almost always decided matters of relatively minor importance to Americans. As a consequence, except

4. "The larger the electorate, the more elaborate will be the party organization" is the hypothesis as advanced by William Goodman, *The Two-Party System in the United States* (3d ed. Princeton, D. Van Nostrand, 1964), p. 59; E. E. Schattschneider, *Party Government* (New York, Holt, Rinehart and Winston, 1942), pp. 47–50; R. T. McKenzie, *British Political Parties* (New York, St. Martin's Press, 1963), pp. 1–10; Robert E. Lane, *Political Life* (Glencoe, The Free Press, 1959), pp. 8–40.

in rare cases like "bloody Kansas," it has not been worth it to attempt massive fraud or violence to undermine an electoral decision.

But suppose that an election were to decide something of great importance to Americans. Suppose that the United Nations were to conduct a worldwide election to name the country which would rule the world. The Soviet Union and the United States are candidates. The Soviet Union wins. In such a case no amount of "civic education" and no supposed "allegiance to democratic norms" would lead Americans to accept this decision. We would deny the validity of the one man, one vote principle; the elections would be considered unconstitutional or nonconstitutional; fraud would be alleged. Our attitude would be, in effect, that the question of world hegemony is too important to be decided by an election because we have too much to lose. By keeping in mind this illustration we may grasp the perspectives of participants in so many Latin American elections.

It seems probable, as noted above, that in a system where incentives are strong, force or the threat of force is an extremely important element of the electoral context. The pivotal group in this situation will be the organization capable of holding the monopoly of force in society, the military. By effecting a coup against an incumbent the military could bypass the electoral process. Or the military could defend an incumbent against his enemies while he carried out a fraudulent maneuver to keep himself or his group in office. The pattern which would emerge is one of leadership transfer through coups and leadership continuity through fraud or easily controlled indirect elections by the national congress or an ad hoc constitutional convention.

There is nothing in this pattern, incidentally, which requires the military to be united or to play an "unpopular" role. The coup situation could be generated by a wave of popular agitation against a "tyrannical, unconstitutional dictator," perhaps even while the incumbent was perpetrating a fraud. The military itself could disagree on the desirability of a coup, thus producing an intra-military struggle which one side or the other would win with bluff or even blood. In any case elections would seldom be meaningful instruments of leadership change.

But what if the military segment is so small that armed civilians may defeat it? What if it does not hold the monopoly of force in society? The coup-fraud pattern is undermined. The incumbent cannot be removed by a coup because the incumbent and his allies could raise sufficient forces to defeat the army. But *if the incumbent effects an electoral fraud he cannot rely upon the military to defend him either.* Thus the military is removed from the political scene, not playing a critical role either in sustaining an incumbent or in removing him.

How then is leadership transferred? There are two possibilities. Opposition forces, not being able to rely upon the military to work their desires, may launch a revolution. They raise an army of partisans, the incumbent raises an army of partisans and the matter is decided on the battlefield. Needless to say the civil war method of leadership transfer is costly. But more important, it is uncertain. The participants can seldom foresee the outcome of such a war, calculating as they must in terms of potential armies and probable alliances. Assuming that civilian groups are numerous, no one leader or faction can safely defy all the rest. As a consequence leaders will be wary of the civil war method of leadership transfer and attempt, instead, to reach an implicit bargain on the acceptance of elections. The incumbent is threatened with a civil war if he attempts to continue in office beyond the legal date. If he tries to control the elections in favor of one candidate, all the other forces may join together against him. Opposition groups, assuming that the incumbent is following established legal norms, will be hesitant to attempt a civil war because they are not assured of full support and complete unity in such an effort.

This is not to say, however, that fraud or civil war are impossible. The incumbents, if they are reasonably united, may strongly bias elections in their favor. Opposition forces may then feel that they have no hope to gain office except through force. But our expectation is that quite frequently incumbents will not be united so that elections prove to be reasonably fair, or rather, that the biases in the electoral context will be distributed more or less equally. Consequently, when by its relatively small size the military is removed from the scene, elections become important instruments for leadership transfer. This is so not because force is removed from the context, but because the fluid, dispersed nature of civilian political groups frequently prevents anyone from obtaining the monopoly of force.

This brief outline of the connection between military size and party development greatly simplifies the mechanisms involved while neglecting many qualifications and ramifications. But it does identify, I believe, some basic relationships. Arranging the analysis in chronological form, we have the following hypotheses:

> *H12. In those Latin American countries where the military was relatively small after independence, meaningful elections were frequent.*
>
> *H13. In those Latin American countries where the military was relatively large after independence, meaningful elections were infrequent.*[5]
>
> *H14. In countries where meaningful elections are frequent, mass electoral organizations will be formed on a large scale.*
>
> *H15. In countries where meaningful elections are infrequent, mass electoral organizations will not be formed on a large scale.*
>
> *H16. The formation of electoral organizations on a large scale will produce a high degree of party identification so that major, permanent political parties will exist.*
>
> *H17. The absence of electoral organizations on a large scale will produce a (continued) condition of low party identification so that major, permanent political parties will not exist.*

MILITARY SIZE AND ELECTIONS

In testing the hypotheses presented above I shall examine only three countries—Colombia, Ecuador, and Peru. Ideally, of course, the analysis should be applied to all Latin American countries in order to test the supposed relationships and, in all probability, to modify and qualify the hypotheses, but that study would require an entire volume. The first step is to determine the relative size of the military organization in each of the three countries following independence.

After its independence in 1824, Peru seems to have had an army of considerable size. In 1828, just prior to the brief Peru-Colombia

5. The phrase "Latin American countries . . . after independence" is a simplified way of identifying variables common to the cases under discussion. These conditions include: strong incentives for political participation; a nontotalitarian political environment; low party identification; and a primitive state of military technology and organization which made military strength against civilians closely dependent on numbers of men.

war, a reliable source reports that Peru had a regular army of 9,200.[6] A Colombian source places the number of Peruvian troops brought to the front (March 1829) at between 8,500 and 9,500, and reports that after the battle of Tarquí losses reduced the troops on this front to between 6,000 and 7,000.[7] Another source notes that a preliminary draft of a treaty with Bolivia stipulated the reduction of the Peruvian army to 6,000, indicating that the actual size was above this figure.[8] Later figures for army size given by the *Statesman's Year Book,* a source of uncertain value on these matters, are 16,008 for 1864,[9] and 13,200 for 1870.[10] These sources seem to indicate that Peru had a regular army of about 8,000 immediately following independence and that the size of this force increased somewhat during the decades that followed.

The army of Ecuador, when that country broke away from Gran Colombia in 1830, was composed of diverse elements. The backbone of this force was apparently the former Colombian Army of the South which was led by General Juan José Flores and became Ecuador's when Flores established this new country. In 1829 the size of this force was reported to be 6,000.[11] Another source places the size of Flores's forces at the time of separation at 2,000.[12] In the

6. Carlos Dellepiane, *Historia Militar del Perú* (2 vols. Lima, Imprenta Gil, 1931), *1,* 311–12.

7. José Manuel Restrepo, *Dario Político y Militar* (4 vols. Bogotá, Imprenta Nacional, 1954), *2,* 14. Restrepo contradicts himself slightly in stating, in another work, that the number of Peruvian troops in the Peruvian-Colombian war was 8,400: José Manuel Restrepo, *Historia de la Revolución de la República de Colombia* (8 vols. Bogotá, 1945), *7,* 177.

8. Jorge Basadre, *Historia de la República 1822–1899* (Lima, 1939), p. 88. In a detailed study of the war with Bolivia in 1841 we find that the number of Peruvian troops dispatched to the front to initiate the invasion was 4,120. The total size of the Peruvian force, augmented by some temporary recruiting, was over 6,800. It seems probable that the entire regular army was not brought to the front; see Estado Mayor General del Ejército, Quinta Sección, *Campaña de Goyeneche en el Alto Perú, 1811; Guerra con Bolivia, 1841* (Lima, 1931), pp. 65–67, 78.

9. *The Statesman's Year Book* (London, Macmillan, 1865), p. 579.

10. Ibid. (1872), p. 550. Another source places the size of the army at 12,000 in 1872 but reports that Civilista President Manuel Pardo reduced its "nominal strength" to 4,500. That there was a movement to reduce the size of the army at that time seems clear, but I should doubt that, in fact, such a dramatic reduction as indicated above was achieved. Clements R. Markham, *A History of Peru* (Chicago, Charles H. Sergel, 1892), p. 380.

11. Restrepo, *Historia de la Revolución, 7,* 176–77, 182.

12. José Le Gouhir y Rodas, *Historia de la República del Ecuador* (Quito, Editorial Equatoriana, 1935), *1,* 267.

battle of Miñarica in 1835, fought between two segments of the Ecuadorean Army and apparently not involving all military forces, 3,000 troops are reported to have participated.[13] Much later, in 1876, the size of the Ecuadorean army is placed at 7,000.[14] I would fix the size of the Ecuadorean military after separation from Colombia at between 4,000 and 6,000.

Table 6.1 shows the size of the Colombian military in selected years for the period 1831–99. In general, the reported size (R) is less than the legal size (L) as established by Congress, apparently because the military budget was not adequate to sustain the full complement. The fluctuations in the size correspond to a threatened international war (1832) and periods of civil war (1840–41 and 1852). The military budget for the period 1832–44 was, in absolute terms, remarkably constant indicating that fluctuations in the size of the military establishment must have been relatively superficial.[15] From the evidence presented in Table 6.1, the size of the Colombian military in this period can be fixed at about 3,000 men.

The figures on military size must be translated into relative terms to arrive at an indication of the balance between potential civilian forces and the regular army. The Colombian population was slightly larger than Peru's and over twice as large as Ecuador's in this period.[16] Moreover, both Ecuador and Peru, with their high proportions of politically inert Indian population, would have had a relatively small reservoir of civilians available for military activity. Colombia had more towns and cities from which civilian armies

13. Alfredo Pareja Diezcanseco, *Historia del Ecuador* (2 vols. Quito, Casa de la Cultura Ecuatoriana, 1958), *2*, 27.

14. M. A. Jurado R., "El Capitán General Ignacio de Veintemilla," *Boletín del Centro de Investigaciones Históricas 1930–31*, p. 49.

15. Restrepo, *Historia de la Nueva Granada, 1*, 372.

16. In the census of 1876 Peru had a population of 2,673,075: Markham, p. 377. In the census of 1851 Colombia had 2,243,730, and the census of 1864 gave a population of 2,694,487: Juan Luis de Lannoy and Gustavo Pérez, *Estructuras Demográficas y Sociales de Colombia* (Bogotá, Centro de Investigaciones Sociales, 1961), p. 21. It seems, then, that Peru had a population about four fifths the size of Colombia. The Census of 1825 gave Colombia (what was to become Colombia) a population of 1,373,110 and Ecuador 524,477: Restrepo, *Historia de la Revolución, 7*, 301. Restrepo himself gives a different figure for Colombia in this census in another work (1,223,938—yet the separate departmental figures he presents and sums to produce this figure actually add to 1,491,538): *Historia de la Nueva Granada, 1*, 4.

TABLE 6.1

Size of Colombian Regular Military Establishment,
1831–1899 (selected years)

Year	Size	
1831	2,300 (L)	
1832	3,880 (L)	6,000 (L)
1833	3,320 (L)	
1834	3,320 (L)	
1837	3,330 (L)	
1839	2,925 (L)	
1840	3,330 (L)	
1841	5,000 (L)	
1842	5,000 (L)	4,882 (R)
1843	5,000 (L)	3,928 (R)
1844	3,400 (L)	3,197 (R)
1846	3,100 (R)	
1848	1,500 (L)	
1851	1,331 (R)	
1852	4,648 (R)	
1853	1,500 (L)	
1854	800 (L)	
1858	511 (R)	
1875	3,000 (L)	
1899	8,000 (R)	

L = legal size established by Congress
R = reported size, as reported by Minister of War or other source

With the exception of 1858 and 1899, figures include a small number of navy personnel.

Sources: José Manuel Restrepo, *Historia de la Nueva Granada* (Bogotá, Editorial Cromos, Editorial el Catolicismo, 1952, 1963), *1,* 13, 36, 61, 130, 145, 354, 364, 370, 372; *2,* 13, 29, 81, 140, 178, 217, 277, 310; Restrepo, *Historia de la Revolución de la República de Colombia* (8 vols. Bogotá, 1945), *8,* 314; Gustavo Arboleda, *Historia Contemporanea de Colombia* (6 vols. Cali, 1935), *5,* 491; Antonio Pérez Aguirre, *25 Años de Historia Colombiana 1853 a 1878* (Bogotá, Editorial Sucre, 1959), p. 350; Jorge Martínez Landínez, *Historia Militar de Colombia* (Bogotá, Editorial Iqueima, 1956), *1,* 260.

could be raised.[17] Relative to the size of the population, then, the armed forces of Peru and Ecuador were about three times as large as Colombia's. When the size of the politically active populations in

17. At the end of the civil war of 1860–61 the victorious Liberals reportedly had an army of about 20,000, see: Samper Bernal, *Breve Historia Constitucional y Política de Colombia,* p. 99. In the battle of Palonegro, a major encounter in the civil war of 1899–1902, the Liberals had a force of 6,342 and the Conservatives, about 22,000; see Jorge Martínez Landínez, *Historia Militar de Colombia* (Bogotá, Editorial Iqueima, 1956), *1,* 333–34. These figures give a rough impression of the magnitude of potential civilian military strength.

these countries is considered, the relative position of the Colombian military was even weaker.

The explanation for the small Colombian military establishment in 1831 lies, I believe, in the pattern of the war of independence.[18] The first region to be liberated in the northern portion of South America was Colombia at Boyacá in 1819. The war movement then swept eastward to Venezuela and southward to Ecuador and Peru. When the revolution ended in 1825, the armed forces of the movement, estimated at about 25,000,[19] were not in the central region, the part soon to become Colombia. The troops were mainly in Venezuela, southern Colombia, and Peru. Before the battle of Ayacucho in Peru (December 1824) the Colombian contingent numbered 7,869, including officers and sick.[20] In 1827 there were various contingents of Colombian troops in Bolivia (Alto Peru) as well as the Colombian Third Division in Lima. Although most of this latter unit reportedly left Peru in 1827, its members seem to have progressed only as far as Guayaquil and Loja in Ecuador.[21]

I have already mentioned the Colombian Army of the South which became Ecuador's when Flores established this new nation in 1830. Depending on how one views the matter, possession of this army might have been too high a price to pay for sovereignty. One writer notes that Ecuador "separated from Colombia; but it remained with Flores and his army, the worst inhabitants of Colombia." [22]

THE USE OF ELECTIONS

Following the hypothesis given above (H13), we should expect to find that since the military was relatively large in Peru and Ecua-

18. The small size of the Colombian military has also been noted by J. Leon Helguera, "The Changing Role of the Military in Colombia," *Journal of Inter-American Studies, 3* (1961), 351–58. The explanations he offers for the weakness of the army in Colombia (the defeat of the army by civilians in 1830, the exile of military men in the same year, and the failure of the 1833 coup attempt) seem largely circular since these events illustrate the weakness of the military in the first place.

19. Bushnell, *The Santander Regime in Gran Colombia,* p. 249.

20. Carlos Cortes Vargas, *Participación de Colombia en la Libertad del Perú* (3 vols. Bogotá, Estado Mayor General, n.d.), *2,* 230.

21. Dellepiane, *Historia Militar del Perú,* pp. 293–94, 298.

22. Robert Andrade, *Historia del Ecuador* (7 vols. Guayaquil, Reed and Reed, n.d.), *6,* 2,248.

dor after independence, meaningful elections were relatively infrequent. The experience in Peru is summed up by historian Jorge Basadre. He considers the elections of 1851

> the first time that Peru was to attempt a genuine presidential election, since previously the president of the Republic had been selected by congressional vote (1827), by a military coup later legalized by an election of form (1829, 1839, 1845), or *de facto* by a military coup without any legal ratification (1835, 1836, 1842, and 1843).[23]

Even in this 1851 case, however, I would hesitate to call the election meaningful. The government candidate, Echenique, won, there was reportedly considerable fraud, and the total number of voters was only 4,250.[24]

The first meaningful presidential election in Peru was apparently that of 1872. This election was unusual in several respects. First, the winner, Manuel Pardo, was not the government favorite. Secondly, although Pardo eventually did take office, a coup and a counter-coup transpired before he did so. On July 22, 1872, the four Gutiérrez brothers, highly placed in the military, effected a coup to prevent Pardo from taking office. Incumbent president José Balta was imprisoned and then murdered. But a few days later, the army troops stationed at Callao effected a popularly supported coup against the Gutiérrez brothers and in favor of Pardo. After a brief period with a military chief executive, Pardo took office on August 2, 1872.[25]

In Ecuador the experience seems to have been similar. Historian Alfredo Pareja calls the elections of 1875 "the first free elections which the Republic had." [26] However, the winner, Antonio Borrero, was deposed only one year later by a military coup led by General Ignacio de Veintemilla who subsequently occupied the presidency for seven years, until 1883.[27] The elections of 1875 had been, in

23. Basadre, p. 213.

24. Ibid., p. 219; Carlos Zavala Oyague, *Historia del Perú* (Lima, Imprenta Torres Aguirre, 1951), p. 283.

25. Zavala, pp. 309–11; Markham, pp. 372–73; Carlos Wiesse, *Resumen de Historia del Perú* (3d ed. Lima, Galland E. Rosay, 1899), pp. 161–62.

26. Pareja, 2, 188.

27. Ibid., p. 200.

turn, the outcome of a bloody, stand-off battle within the military in deposing García Moreno. García Moreno himself had come to office in a military coup which forestalled the elections of 1869.[28] In 1864 the government candidate obtained 21,000 votes against 8,000 for the opposition candidate in elections judged to be fraudulent.[29] In earlier times, 1830–60, military coups and intramilitary battles fully dominated the scene, undermining the possibility of a popular, competitive presidential election.

The Colombian pattern contrasted sharply with the experience in Peru and Ecuador. Significantly enough, the new nation of Colombia in 1830, then separate from Ecuador as well as Venezuela, began its life with the suppression of a military coup. In August 1830, Generals Florentino Jiménez and Rafael Urdaneta, acting in a confused political situation and with some popular support, effected a coup against President Joaquín Mosquera and Vice-President Domingo Caicedo. But the outcome demonstrated that the military was not strong enough to sustain a regime against ad hoc irregular forces. José Hilario López, José María Obando, and Juan N. Moreno each organized forces to combat Urdaneta and forced his capitulation less than a year later.[30]

A constitution for Nueva Granada (Colombia) was drawn up and promulgated in 1832. From that date to 1860 elections were regularly employed to change leadership, with the exception of the coup of 1854 and its defeat by civilians. In most cases the elections, held every four years for president and every two years for vice-president and Congress, were quite competitive. In three presidential elections the incumbent group(s) lost (1836, 1848, 1855), in three other presidential elections the vote was extremely close or divided so that no candidate obtained a majority (1840, 1844, 1858). The two presidential elections that were won handily (1832, Santander; 1852, Obando) are better attributed to the preeminence of the individuals at the moment than to extensive fraud. In addition to the presidential elections there were vice-presidential and congressional elections

28. Ibid., pp. 164 ff.
29. Ibid., p. 157.
30. Lemos Guzmán, *Obando*, pp. 198 ff; Samper Bernal, *Breve Historia*, pp. 32–36. Ibid., p. 36, reports that López led an army of 5,000 into Bogotá against Urdaneta.

every two years. Although there was some fraud by the incumbents in many of these elections, opposition groups almost always made a substantial showing and usually won considerable representation.[31]

It is difficult to determine the size of the electorate in these early years since under the constitution of 1832 elections were indirect, through an electoral college. The constitution of 1853, which also expanded the electorate, provided for direct elections. In the September 1853 elections for attorney general (*procurador*) and supreme court justices the total number of votes, excluding those for minor candidates, is reported to have been 384,067.[32] In these elections, incidentally, the Conservatives won handily, even though the presidency was occupied by a Liberal (Obando). In the presidential election of 1858 there were 210,480 votes.[33] These facts support the thesis that in Colombia, where the military was relatively small after independence, elections were frequent and meaningful.

The subordinate position of the military in Colombia is well illustrated in the coups of 1854 and 1867. On April 17, 1854, army general José María Melo effected a military coup, first against Congress and then, when incumbent president José María Obando refused to be the figurehead of the regime, against the executive. Melo received considerable support in Bogotá, particularly from artisans of the Sociedad Democrática who armed themselves to defend him. Outstanding leaders of both parties fled to the provinces, organized armies of their own, and crushed Melo seven months later.[34] This event illustrates the proposition I have already advanced, that the Colombian army was not strong enough to dominate the political scene. It also points to another proposition: unequivocal moves of usurpation by one individual would inevitably fail. The reason is that

31. The most detailed account of these elections is given by Restrepo, *Historia de la Nueva Granada,* 1, 34, 75, 96, 118, 139–40, 179, 225–26, 345–46, 354, 378, 381–82; 2, 40, 56, 89, 100 ff., 145, 159, 163, 237–38, 261, 303. See also Puentes, *Historia del Partido Liberal Colombiano,* pp. 105–06, 115, 143, 146, 180, 195.

32. Restrepo, 2, 303; Angel y Rufino José Cuervo, *Vida de Rufino Cuervo y Noticias de su Epoca* (2 vols. Bogotá, Biblioteca Popular de Cultura Colombiana, 1946), 2, 278. The figures in this latter source omit the Liberal votes for some minor candidates and thus give a total vote of about 15,000 less than the above figure.

33. Pérez, *25 Años de Historia Colombiana,* p. 57.

34. Ibid., pp. 12–24; Puentes, pp. 177–80; Roberto Echeverría Rodríguez, *Los Segundos Libertadores* (Barranquilla, Ediciones Arte, 1950).

an attempt to establish a dictatorship was interpreted by other politicians as an attempt to exclude them. Although little agreement could be found on the question of who should rule, consensus was readily achieved on the point that no one should rule exclusively or indefinitely.

In 1867 Liberal President Mosquera violated this norm against usurpation. Beleaguered by an implacable opposition and a hostile Congress, Mosquera arbitrarily dissolved Congress, and arrested a number of prominent political leaders. Almost immediately a civil war was in the making as provincial leaders organized armies to combat Mosquera. This time, however, political leaders prevailed upon the army to take action. Mosquera was quickly deposed in a bloodless coup which was received favorably by virtually all political groups, including, particularly, the main faction of the Liberals (known as "radicales").[35] Colombia had, then, only three military coups in the nineteenth century. Two (1830, 1854) illustrate the inability of the army to sustain a regime against civilian forces and the third (1867) was a convenient substitute for a civil war which would almost certainly have achieved the same object: the removal of a potential dictator.

It should not be thought, however, that apart from these disruptions of the constitutional order politics among civilians was calm and restrained. Elections were events of enormous importance to all participants. The different groups were keenly interested in winning and profoundly apprehensive about losing. This pressure gave rise to a tendency toward fraud. The fraud was not of the overt, dramatic variety: extension of the presidential term, cancellation of elections, or refusal to relinquish office to the victor. Such steps were not employed because they would quickly galvanize the opposition into a civil war. But inevitably the incumbent group, through its control of appointments and employment, tended to bias elections in its favor. This bias, or "creeping fraud," was beyond the control of any one individual. At hundreds of points in the system—through a police chief here, a mayor there—the incumbents gradually gained majority control of the electorate. Furthermore, this control increased as each electoral victory placed in the hands of the winners even more instruments with which to reinforce their electoral strength.

35. Pérez, pp. 260–74; Rodríguez, *El Olimpo Radical,* pp. 75–83.

One conclusion of this pattern of creeping fraud could be civil war. The opposition group(s) could come to the conclusion that they would remain in a minority position indefinitely unless they fought their way back into power. The civil wars of 1839–41, and 1851 were both, it seems, examples of this pattern. In the first case the (incipient) Liberals were in the opposition; in the second, the Conservatives fought incumbent Liberals. In both instances the incumbents were victorious. The civil war of 1860–61 also follows this pattern, although it appears that the provocation of the opposition Liberals was somewhat more obvious. The incumbent Conservatives approved an election law which, because it gave Conservatives majorities on all the electoral commissions, obviously disadvantaged the Liberals.[36] In this war, perhaps because of the more blatant provocation, the opposition was successful and incumbent Conservative Ospina was defeated. This civil war of 1860–61 was the only one in which a constitutionally elected president was deposed by a civilian revolution. All the other civilian revolts were defeated by the incumbents (1839–41, 1851, 1876, 1885, 1895, and 1899–1902).

The pattern of creeping fraud, however, never succeeded in fully undermining the electoral process because the incumbents could only occasionally agree upon a slate of candidates. The division and competition within the ruling segment produced a highly pluralistic context for most elections, and in this environment opposition groups could frequently compete directly or through alliances. Thus, the division of the ruling party was actually the more common termination of creeping fraud. If the opposition won, it would take office primarily because the "incumbents" were so divided that they could not take concerted action. In the 1848 elections, for example, Conservative President Mosquera had to deliver the government to victorious presidential candidate José Hilario López, a Liberal, because no other practicable alternative existed. In this election the Conservatives divided into three groups, each with a presidential candidate. Mosquera could not remain in office himself without causing all candidates to unite against him. Nor could he give the presidency to one of the losing Conservatives, since the others, as well as López, would have been justifiably furious.

Of course, when a civil war was fought, the losers could expect to be discriminated against immediately following their defeat. But

36. Pérez, p. 94.

the inevitable divisions in the ruling party enabled them to reenter the electoral scene in a relatively short time in local elections, in alliances with dissident factions of the ruling party, or directly with their own presidential candidate. Consequently, in spite of the tendency toward fraud and the civil wars, Colombian elections were meaningful instruments of leadership transfer. The military was too small to decide matters of leadership transfer, and the fluidity and factionalism of civilian groups made it difficult for any one segment to obtain the balance of force.

THE RISE OF ELECTORAL ORGANIZATIONS

We have already posited that where elections are used with frequency to decide leadership transfer, politicians will form organizations to win voters to their side. Without such elections there would be little purpose for electoral activities of this nature and mass organizations would not be formed. The experience in the three countries appears to conform to these expectations.

In Peru the first electoral organization was apparently the *Club Progresista,* formed in 1851. Apparently its purpose was to gather support for Domingo Elías in the presidential elections of that year, elections which proved to be, as noted above, fraudulent.[37] This organization was apparently quite small, existed only in Lima, and disappeared forever after this date. In the 1872 elections, mentioned above, a *Partido Civil* was founded to back the candidacy of Manuel Pardo.[38] The *civilista* label does reappear in later times, although I find no indication that the *civilista* group ever had an extensive, mass organization.

In Ecuador electoral organizations seem to have been equally unimportant in these early years. A political society called *El Quiteño Libre,* founded in Quito in 1833, apparently consisted of a small number of intellectuals who were in opposition to the Flores regime. Flores exiled members of this club and it disappeared from the political scene.[39] A similar political club, the *Sociedad Filotécnica,* was

37. Basadre, *Historia,* pp. 215–19.
38. "The 'Partido Civil' ought to be considered as the first attempt at a modern political organization made in our country." Zavala, p. 311.
39. Pareja, *2,* 21; J. Gonzalo Orellana, *Resumen Histórico del Ecuador* (2 vols. Quito, 1948), *1,* 20–21.

formed in Quito in 1844.[40] Again it seems to have had a small membership of university students and it never again appears on the political scene. In the election of 1864 a *Club Liberal* was founded to back an opposition candidate; it was declared illegal by the government, whose candidate won the election by a wide margin.[41] This organization, however, appears to have been much more an electoral society than the earlier ones and might be classified as a first attempt at a mass electoral organization.

In the half-century following independence, then, neither Peru nor Ecuador saw the formation of popular electoral organizations on a large scale. The few attempts that were made to found such organizations were apparently confined to the capital cities, had relatively small membership, and did not exhibit even minimal temporal continuity.

In Colombia considerable attention was given to the formation of mass electoral organizations. In 1838, in preparation for the off-year election for vice-president, two competing electoral societies were formed—the *Sociedad Democrática de Artesanos* and the *Sociedad Católica (Sociedad Popular)*—not only in Bogotá but in other cities as well.[42] At first these two sets of societies did not exist continuously nor did a national organization of each exist. Rather, they were reactivated from time to time by local politicians for vote-getting purposes. In about 1845 we note that aspiring leader Rafael Núñez joined the local *Sociedad Democrática* in the town of Cartagena, indicating the national scope of these clubs at that time.[43] Another source mentions the founding of political organizations in many parts of the country around 1845.[44]

During the period 1847–54 the two societies, *Democrática* and *Popular,* existed continuously and were very active. The *Sociedad Democrática de Artesanos* was refounded in October 1847, ostensibly to protest the lowering of tariffs, but practically to form an

40. Oscar Efren Reyes, *Breve Historia General del Ecuador* (2 vols. Quito, 1957), *2,* 526; Julio C. Troncoso, *Odio y Sangre* (Quito, 1958), p. 32.

41. Pareja, *2,* 157–58.

42. Restrepo, *Historia de la Nueva Granada, 1,* 139; Angel y Rufino José Cuervo, *2,* 124.

43. Indalecio Liévano Aguirre, *Rafael Núñez* (Bogotá, Segundo Festival del Libro Colombiano [1944]), p. 32.

44. Cuervo, *2,* 124.

electoral base for the Liberals (see the quoted material at the beginning of this chapter).[45] In reaction to the spurt of activity on the part of the Liberals, the Conservatives rejuvenated the *Sociedad Popular* of Bogotá somewhat later.[46] Both of these organizations, the Democratic and Popular societies, were national in scope and apparently had a considerable membership.[47] Although students had been participating in these two societies, special clubs were established for intellectuals in 1850: the *Escuela Republicana* of the Liberals (September 25) and the *Sociedad Filotémica* of the Conservatives (October 28).[48] Although the Republicana appeared in other parts of the country, these societies were largely confined to Bogotá. Their importance as mass electoral organizations was much less than that of the Democratic and Popular societies.

Tracing the development of the party labels is a task of enormous complexity and one which I shall not attempt here. The term "Liberal" has been a political label at least since the 1830s, but having been adopted by most politicians, it did not clearly distinguish one group from another. The moment of final clarification came, apparently, just prior to the election of 1848 when the incumbents adopted the Conservative label[49]—whether arbitrarily, or because it was the next most popular term after "Liberal," is not clear. Following 1848 the two party labels were fully established as terms identifying leaders and voters.

45. Ambrosio López (first president of the refounded *Democrática*), *El Desengaño* (Bogotá, Imprenta de Espinosa, 1851), p. 15; Emeterio Heredia, *Contestación al Cuaderno Titulado "El Desengaño"* (Bogotá, Imprenta Morales y Cía, 1851), pp. 23–24. A number of sources (Puentes, p. 147; Samper, *Historia de Una Alma, 1*, 218) suggest that the *Democrática* was refounded in 1848, not 1847. The evidence of the two contemporary members of this society indicate this observation to be in error.

46. Posada, *Memorias Histórico-Políticas, 6*, 197; Restrepo, *Historia de la Nueva Granada, 2*, 134, places the date of the founding of the *Sociedad Popular* as December 17, 1849.

47. Posada, *6*, 197 ff. Posada notes (p. 253) that at a gala meeting of the *Popular* in 1850 in Bogotá there were over 1,000 members present including "many" artisans and farmers. See also Restrepo, *Historia de la Nueva Granada, 2*, 134, 167–70; Samper, *1*, 217–20.

48. Restrepo, *2*, 163; Posada, *6*, 255.

49. Cuervo, *2*, 116; Restrepo, *2*, 76; José Joaquín Guerra, *Estudios Históricos* (Bogotá, Biblioteca Popular de Cultura Colombiana, 1952), p. 108.

ELECTORAL ORGANIZATIONS AND PERMANENT PARTIES

The final pair of hypotheses (H16 and H17) expresses a relationship between the widespread formation of electoral organizations and the development of a high degree of party identification. The degree of party identification, in turn, determines the extent to which large, permanent political parties will be found. Because we cannot determine party identification of past generations directly, we must assume the relationship between the presence of this condition and the permanence of parties.

The experience in Peru is broadly consistent with hypothesis H17: none of the nineteenth-century parties exists on the contemporary scene. A number of labels were advanced by different leaders toward the end of the last century, but none of them remained prominent beyond the Leguía regime (1919–30). Among them were the *Constitucional, Demócrata, Liberal,* and *Civil* parties.[50] In view of their disappearance I would conclude that widespread popular identification was not achieved.

In Ecuador two nineteenth-century political labels, *Liberal* and *Conservador,* have existed down to the modern era. Inspection of the electoral scene since 1933 indicates, however, that these two labels do not dominate the scene. The electoral groupings which arise in Ecuador are temporary alliances or movements that form around a likely presidential candidate, and are composed of leaders bearing different party labels as well as "independent" figures. It is the presidential candidate that identifies the group and not the party label. Illustrations of such successful alliances include the *Alianza Demo-*

50. Zavala, *Historia del Perú,* pp. 311–42; Wiesse, *Resumen de Historia del Perú,* pp. 179–81; Pedro Davalos y Lisson, *Diez Años de Historia Contemporanea 1899–1908* (Lima, Librería Gil, 1930), pp. 83–130; Toto Giurato, *Perú Milenario* (3 vols. Lima, Editorial "Ecos," 1947), *3,* 835–50. Giurato mentions (*3,* 877) the existence of a Partido Civil in 1931, but it seems clear that this organization was little more than a minuscule group of leaders, completely overshadowed by two new organizations, the *Unión Revolucionaria* of Luis Sánchez Cerro and the APRA. Wiesse (pp. 145, 146) mentions a *partido conservador* and a *partido liberal* as existing around 1851. These must have been ephemeral groupings indeed since other historians do not mention them. I find no mention of the Conservative label at any other time; a Liberal party appeared briefly around 1902–04 (Davalos y Lisson, pp. 88, 108).

crática Ecuatoriana which formed around José María Velasco Ibarra in the 1944 presidential elections, the *Movimiento Cívico Ecuatoriana* of Galo Plaza in 1948, and the *Frente Democrático Nacional* in the 1956 elections. It is instructive to note that these alliances are only as strong as the presidential candidate. In 1944 the ADN won handily with Velasco Ibarra; in 1952, without Velasco, the ADN got about six per cent of the votes.[51]

This pattern of fragmentary electoral groupings would suggest that the party labels themselves, Liberal and Conservative, as well as Socialist, Radical, Christian Democrat, and Falangist, do not attract large numbers of votes. If they did, leaders would run on these labels rather than behind prominent presidential candidates in temporary electoral movements. The election of 1952 further illustrates this point because it was a rare case of a contest fought mainly along party lines, with one independent, Velasco, in the race. The results were as follows:

Velasco Ibarra (independent)	150,000
Alarcón Falconí (Conservative)	118,000
Chiriboga Villagómez (Liberal)	70,000
Alianza Democrática	20,000 [52]

This outcome supports the conclusion that party identification is relatively low in Ecuador. Indeed, the spectacular political career of Velasco, an independent, seems to demonstrate that it is the man, not the party, which counts in Ecuador. Four times, running in different ad hoc alliances, Velasco has triumphed in elections: 1933, 1944, 1952, and 1961.[53] Consequently, although the Liberal and Conservative parties have exhibited a certain degree of permanence, they cannot be considered major parties in the sense of dominating the political scene to the exclusion of other labels.

In Colombia the Liberal and Conservative labels have dominated the political scene almost completely from about 1848 to the present. Apparently the energetic and extensive activities of the electoral organizations, particularly in the period 1847 to 1854, aligned a sub-

51. Pareja, *2*, 448–54, 460–61.
52. Ibid., *2*, 460–61.
53. The information contained in these two paragraphs is drawn from Pareja, *2*, 415–64.

stantial proportion of the electorate behind the two labels. An early indication of their strength might be gleaned from the presidential elections of 1857. There were three candidates: Mariano Ospina Rodríguez, Conservative; Manuel Murillo Toro, Liberal; and ex-president Tomás Cipriano de Mosquera. Mosquera, formerly a Conservative, founded a new party of his own called the Partido Nacional.[54] Although one source suggests that this grouping was simply a faction of the Conservative party, it did have a new label and was therefore a separate party under our definition.[55]

We might suppose that Mosquera, a prominent ex-president, would have done quite well in this election against less prominent opponents, but in fact he was roundly defeated:

Ospina (Conservative)	97,271
Murillo (Liberal)	80,171
Mosquera (Nacional)	33,038 [56]

A lesson such as this was not lost on politicians. It became clear that for vote-getting purposes one of the two party labels was necessary for quick success. The leader who chose to found a new party and run under that label was placing himself in a disadvantageous position. Although many divisions and conflicts arose within each party, even producing competing candidacies, leaders did not relinquish the basic party label. Although factions frequently had nicknames (gólgotas, draconianos, radicales, históricos, doctrinarios) these titles were not used alone to identify candidates before the electorate. For this purpose leaders retained the labels "Liberal" and "Conservative."

On numerous occasions leaders from both parties entered into various kinds of alliances, but almost always without losing their partisan identity. The Unión Republicana, founded in 1909 as a front against the Reyes regime, illustrates the fate of those who took a new party label too seriously. The first and only president to call

54. Samper Bernal, Breve Historia, p. 83; Puentes, Historia del Partido Liberal, p. 195.

55. Pérez, 25 Años, pp. 56–57. Puentes (p. 195) reports that several Liberal leaders, including Obando and López, supported Mosquera, so the view that the Partido Nacional was merely a Conservative faction would be mistaken on the grounds of its membership composition.

56. Pérez, p. 57.

himself a "Republican" was Carlos E. Restrepo (1910–14), a Conservative elected in the constitutional convention of 1910 with the support of some Liberal delegates. When the popular elections came in 1914, those who called themselves Republicans were roundly defeated in the congressional elections [57] and lost the presidency by an enormous margin:

Concha (Conservative)	205,439
Esguerra (Republican)	23,564 [58]

Colombia, then, has seen the existence of large, permanent political parties, dating back to about 1848. It would be difficult to account for dominance and permanence of these party labels unless we assumed that popular identification with them was quite high during this period.

In this chapter I have attempted to define and explain some basic contrasts in the nineteenth-century experience of Colombia and two other Latin American countries. I have found two distinct patterns: one is characterized by a relatively small military after independence, the frequent use of elections, and the rise of major, permanent political parties; the other features a relatively large military organization, the infrequent use of elections, and the absence of major, permanent parties.

This analysis has been cast in extremely simplified form. No doubt further examination of the problems discussed here will lead to qualifications and corrections of the argument advanced. The claims which can be made for the theory as presented above are that it is broadly consistent with a limited range of data and that it identifies variables and relationships likely to be important in a more comprehensive theory of party development in the nineteenth-century Latin American context. The analysis does, at least partially, explain why, as Colombia entered the modern era, party labels were so well established. The presence of these established parties becomes an independent variable of critical importance in the subsequent analysis of the patterns of conflict in the modern period.

57. Rodríguez, *Hechos y Comentarios,* pp. 268–96, especially p. 292.
58. Instituto Colombiano de Opinión Pública, *Factores Colombianos* (Bogotá, 1964), p. 73. The Liberals did not present a candidate of their own.

CHAPTER 7

THE PARTY SYSTEM AND
MILITARY INTERVENTION

The mechanical fulfillment of the function of praetorian guard for any government, no matter how blameless it might be—and none is absolutely so—awakes in the consciousness of the [military] officer the insidious temptation to consider himself as having the right to judge and weigh the capacity or morality of those whose sleep he guards without rest, including those—almost never lacking—who are, with or without reason, the targets for the severe criticism of the opposition.

Arturo Bray, Militares y Civiles *(Buenos Aires, 1958), p. 130.*

In the preceding chapter I traced a relationship between the political role of the military and the development of party identification. Only where the armed forces were small, I argued, could they be effectively excluded from the political scene, so that competitive elections, mass electoral organizations, and permanent parties might come into being. Underlying this analysis was the assumption that powerful forces in these countries draw the military into politics. In this chapter I shall examine the nature of these forces in an attempt to explain military intervention in Latin American politics today.

It is apparent that we cannot assume that the size of the army is still what limits its role. While this assumption may be useful for analyzing the nineteenth-century experience, it becomes inadequate when applied to the twentieth century. Today, owing to the advances in military technology, size no longer determines the army's relative power position against civilians. On a strict fire-power basis a modern army cannot be defeated by civilian forces many times its size.[1]

1. The phenomenon of guerrilla war does, it is true, represent a special case of civilian-military war and one in which small numbers of civilians may ultimately gain their object over the military. In practice, however, the guerrillas do not overpower the military with force, but demoralize and undermine it.

Initially we might expect, therefore, that modern Latin American armies would play an even more pronounced role (or in Colombia a pronounced role), to the almost complete exclusion of civilians and constitutional processes. But such has not been the case. In spite of the tremendous balance of force which armies now possess, military organizations do not overwhelm the political sphere in most of the countries of Latin America. It seems, therefore, that the political intrusions of the military must be limited or inhibited by forces other than the direct threat of civilian armed resistance.

The measurement of the degree of military intrusion in politics which I shall use is the frequency of coups. A "coup" is *the removal of the existing chief executive by the armed forces*. Although some ambiguities can arise with this definition of a coup, it is for the most part quite easy to apply. In our discussion "military intervention" is synonomous with "coup."

In itself the coup stands as an important focal point since it is a dramatic and significant event involving, at a minimum, a change in the chief executive. Moreover, a coup threat represents the most important military resource in bargaining with or influencing the executive. If the army can make a credible coup threat, there is a high probability that it may get what it wants, assuming, of course, that it has a clear position. If for some reason the military is incapable of effecting a coup, then its ability to coerce the government will be greatly curtailed. Naturally the military may have other resources, friendships or expertise, for example, but these are decidedly secondary to the ability to eject a chief executive from office.

It is important to keep in mind this resource which determines military power. Frequently writers make statements about behind-the-scenes military influence as if this influence were exercised inevitably and automatically. We should insist that any allegations of military power rest, at a minimum, upon the resources the army holds. I would suggest that their primary resource is the ability to effect a coup. Therefore in situations where the military does not have a credible coup threat one must be cautious about attributing "power" to the military.

What, then, are the causes of military intervention? Viewing the military coup from the perspective of those who must effect it, there are several obstacles which must be overcome. Basic is the fact that deposing the commander-in-chief of the armed forces negates the principle of hierarchy and military obedience. Consequently on the subject of military intervention the chain of command is, de facto, shattered, at least some distance into the ranks. The idea that one or a handful of generals can automatically claim the obedience of the rest of the military if they effect a coup overlooks a crucial point: *these generals would be guilty of gross insubordination.* The hundreds of lesser officers might perfectly well refuse to obey the necessary coup orders and, instead, obey their supreme commander, the president, and throw the instigators of the coup in jail.

The military coup, then, opens a Pandora's box for the armed forces. When the chain of command tears apart, hundreds or, depending on the specific coup situation, thousands of men must make their own private decisions about whom to obey. This rupture of hierarchy and discipline exposes two powerful barriers to coup-making. First, a military organization is based on the notion of obedience. Military men are keenly aware that discipline is the sine qua non of a successful and respectable military organization. This awareness, moreover, is not merely theoretical but drawn from many experiences in which the lack of discipline brought disgrace and defeat to armed forces.

In an account of the Peruvian war against Bolivia in 1841 the Peruvian high command concluded in its examination of the military campaign:

> The most vital interests of the nation may be compromised if political influences undermine the correct posture of chiefs and officials. In the case of the hostility toward General Castilla, a fact manifested on the eve of battle, aside from the fact that it was not justified, it produced the disintegration of the Peruvian command by introducing the corrosive factor of disobedience and the lack of cooperation.[2]

Writing of the successive military interventions in Chile in the period 1924–32, General Carlos Saez Morales makes it his primary aim to show the disgrace that comes to a military organization which becomes involved in politics: "I intend to demonstrate that the armed

2. Estado Mayor General del Ejército, Quinta Sección, *Campaña de Goyeneche en el Alto Perú, 1811; Guerra con Bolivia, 1841*, p. 101.

forces have been only the plaything of the top politicians and, in any case, have been the victims of the environment in which they have had to act." [3] And in discussing the permanent army of Colombia during the civil war of 1899–1902, military historian Jorge Martínez argues that the permanent army could have put down the Liberal uprisings, but that the nomination of officers on the basis of political affiliations and not qualifications undermined the effectiveness of the army. The squabbling among these political chiefs "annulled" the permanent army.[4]

An Ecuadorian general lamented the corrosive impact of politics on military discipline:

> Politics, which for several reasons corrodes, divides and denatures the highest purposes of authority . . . unfortunately penetrated the sacred enclosures of the barracks and . . . shook the disciplinary bonds, turning our army, on several occasions, into a weak and fragile organism.
>
> . . . .
>
> In armies discipline is necessary at every point. . . . Without it there are no barracks, no militia, no patriotism, no instruction, no soldiers, no valor, no flag.[5]

In perhaps the finest treatise on military intervention ever written, retired Paraguayan colonel Arturo Bray described a chain reaction of indiscipline which follows the first act of insubordination in deposing the commander-in-chief:

> If the generals are granted the right to raise themselves up as judges over their hierarchical superior—monarch or president —no reason of obedience will deny this same right to the colonels, so that they in turn criticize the generals, and the commanders, the colonels, and the captains, the commanders; and so on in descending and demolishing fashion until reaching the troops and authorizing the rebellion of the sergeants.
>
> . . . .

3. Carlos Saez Morales, *Recuerdos de un Soldado* (3 vols. Santiago, Biblioteca Ercilla, 1933, 1934), *1*, 8.

4. Martínez, *Historia Militar de Colombia, 1,* 263–64.

5. General A. I. Chiriboga N., *Fuerzas Morales en el Ejército* (Quito, Imprenta Nacional, 1932), pp. 41, 44.

The clear and complete suppression of the concept of hierarchy is synonomous with anarchy in any association run on the
principle of authority; in the armed forces it inevitably produces
a state of dissolution.[6]

There is, then, an aversion within Latin American military organizations toward displacing the commander-in-chief, since a military
coup may severely erode the principle of obedience, a principle that
underlies the function and purpose of the armed forces. The second
barrier to a coup also follows from the disruption of the chain of
command: risk. Those who wish to plan and lead a coup are faced
with a simple but acute problem: will others go along? Will the many
independent actors that the coup context generates side with the coup
effort? Plotters have many reasons to fear that they might not. In
addition to a reluctance to undermine the concept of obedience,
there may be officers who sympathize with the incumbent chief
executive.

In order to determine the degree of support for a coup and to
shape reality in their favor, planners must expend considerable effort
in sounding out and convincing a wide range of military personnel.
In many cases the processes of determining opinion within the military are quite open. In Brazil the *Club Militar* serves as a species of
convention by means of which officers may gauge the sentiment of
the armed forces toward the incumbent government. Prior to the
1962 coup in Peru, a Peruvian army officer reports that an anonymous poll, consisting of questions designed to determine the respondents' attitudes toward a coup possibility, was distributed to officers
by the top command.[7]

Many times, however, the business of sounding out opinion and
setting up a conspiracy is dangerous. The plotters may be discovered
or informed upon at any moment and their careers thus jeopardized.
Even if plotting goes along smoothly and an overt coup attempt is
made, there is still great uncertainty and risk. The number of abortive
coup attempts, it is important to realize, greatly exceeds the number
of successful coups.[8] Almost every case of failure represents some

6. Arturo Bray, *Militares y Civiles* (Buenos Aires, 1958), pp. 139–40.
7. Victor Villaneuva, *El Militarismo en el Perú* (Lima, 1962), p. 210.
8. See the useful compilation of failures by William S. Stokes, *Latin American
Politics* (New York, Thomas Y. Crowell, 1959), pp. 317–19.

form of punishment for the plotters: demotion, removal from active duty, or imprisonment. Military coups, then, are usually risky. This fact might be expected to deter many individuals from attempting to depose the chief executive.

Disruption of discipline and risk would seem to make a coup an unlikely and ill-advised undertaking. Where, then, does the energizing force for a coup come from? In his analysis of the attitudes of the professional military officer, Samuel Huntington provides an insight into this problem. Huntington argues, as I have, that obedience is a basic norm for the officer. But he expands his observations to include some limits to the norm of obedience. On questions of legality (assuming that no acceptable institution exists to decide these issues) and of morality, Huntington argues, the professional soldier's attitude is that the military officer is not bound to obey the civilian commander-in-chief. "So far as ability to judge and apply ethical standards are concerned, the statesman and the soldier are equal." [9]

Latin American military men are frequently forced into situations that require legal or moral decisions. When opposition to the incumbent rulers reaches serious proportions, so that the morality and/or legality of the existing government are called into question, military men find themselves, merely by continuing to recognize the chief executive as their commander-in-chief, making a moral or legal decision. The underlying thrust for military intervention, then, is found in the extremity of conflict which takes place in the civilian sphere and thereby makes the question of supporting or deposing the chief executive a moral one. By "moral" I mean "pertaining to beliefs that appear intensely and widely held in society."

It is important to recognize that the military must be societally oriented to be subject to the moral implications of political opposition. Without this orientation, officers could blindly follow their chief executive, regardless of the consequences to the society. The moral aspect of their behavior becomes apparent only as they see themselves from the societal perspective. In Colombia military personnel are exposed to the same sources of political information and opinion as the rest of the population: families, friends, newspapers, speeches, and books. They are not locked up in the barracks and subject to a

9. Samuel P. Huntington, *The Soldier and the State* (Cambridge, Harvard University Press, 1957), pp. 73 ff., 78.

homogeneous propaganda barrage for an exclusive social, ideological, or partisan political position. Taken together, the armed forces provide a fair reflection of civilian opinion. "The armed forces are, in the origins of their personnel, in the organic composition of their units, in constitution and in mission . . . the society (*el pueblo*)." [10]

Realizing that the military is in and of society, we may reasonably expect it to be sensitive to the prevailing opinion in society. For their information about the state of this opinion, members of the armed forces are likely to look at gross indices such as newspaper comment, congressional opposition, speeches, demonstrations and other forms of public protest. Furthermore, it is the dramatic, immediate aspect of opposition which most forcefully projects a moral choice upon the military. An opinion poll showing a low percentage of "approve" responses has but feeble moral implications. But a vitriolic speech by a prominent leader, a demonstration in which two students are killed, or an arrest of a congressman are events which, placed in a general context of severe opposition, have immediate moral implications.

Stated in its simplest form, therefore, the military is likely to depose a highly unpopular president. If by defending an unpopular president, as in containing violent demonstrations, the armed forces earn a reputation of being "tools of oppression" or "servants of the oligarchy" we may expect the military to do considerable hard thinking. When the president is manifestly unpopular and the military finds itself implicitly or explicitly sustaining him, it is inevitable that members of the armed forces will ask themselves whether they can honorably stand by and ignore the popular clamor.

Under conditions of severe opposition it becomes almost inevitable that both the legality and morality of the government will be called into question. The legislature may prove so intractable that it will approve nothing the president recommends so that the chief executive must bypass it through means of questionable legality. The extremity of the opposition may require that constitutional guarantees be suspended. Even though the constitution provides for such a suspension, the government which places the constitution to one side cannot avoid the taint of illegality and arbitrariness. Political arrests

10. Gonzalo Canal Ramírez, *Del 13 de Junio al 10 de Mayo en las Fuerzas Armadas* (Bogotá, Ediciones Documentos Colombianos, 1957), p. 147.

of questionable legality may be made; certain types of censorship may be practiced.

Even if the legalities of the situation are clear, the moral underpinnings of the regime may be doubtful. It may be legal for the police to kill an unarmed demonstrator in a riot, but is it moral? It may be legal to arrest the vice-president during a state of siege, but is it moral? It may be legal to dissolve political party organizations, rule without a cabinet, close the university, or postpone elections. But the incessant clamor of citizens in the streets creates the impression that these legalities are technical and hollow, that norms of justice and morality have been violated. In such a context military men ask themselves: should we gain the reputation of "enemies of society" to stand by a chief executive whose moral and perhaps legal position is in serious doubt? It ought not to surprise us to find them saying "no."

Frequently the army, and not the police, must face demonstrators and thereby suffer the direct responsibility for casualties inflicted upon civilians. As we might expect, military men detest this role since it burdens them with the acute moral problem inherent in the forcible repression of unarmed civilians. This attitude is illustrated in the comment of a second lieutenant in the Colombian Fifth Brigade (Bogotá, March 23, 1965):

> It is a terrible thing taking care of crowds in demonstrations and riots. They scream at you and call you "beast," "dog," "pig," "assassin," "traitor," and they spit at you, right in the face. And some of your men are saying "shoot, lieutenant, shoot; give the order." But you can't fire. You think of the tremendous political reaction, the headlines: "THREE DEAD ASSASSINATED BY THE ARMY." It's a hundred times better to go after guerrillas or outlaws in the hills. That I don't mind. But maintaining public order is terrible, terrible.

Naturally, a wise chief executive does well to allow the police to handle matters of public order as much as possible. In this way he may hope to dampen the impact of the opposition upon military attitudes. However, since the military does stand behind the police and since it does have the undoubted ability to depose the chief executive, it cannot be sheltered from the moral implications of the situation. The root cause of military intervention in Latin America, then, is the extremity to which political opposition is carried and the moral decision this opposition thrusts upon the military.

Of course it is by no means inevitable that a chief executive face civilian opposition in the most extreme form. The incumbent may have political support. If some groups are supporting the president while others oppose him, a clear moral judgment about him is more difficult to make. If the apparent unanimity of opposition is broken by pro-presidential voices, conflicts become "political" and not moral. Consequently the driving force for military intervention is removed.

When the president has significant civilian support, the military sensitivity to society will operate to inhibit a coup. Why should military officers gain reputations of being "anti-democratic" or "militaristic"? The soldier no more desires to be the villain than the next man. Why should he violate the basic military norm of obedience, risk career, life, and limb to depose "just another" chief executive, a man with opponents and supporters as well? When civilians are divided into support and opposition groups, the military coup loses its thrust as an ethical necessity and takes on overtones of greed and insubordination.

It might be argued, of course, that military men seek the private benefits, particularly prestige, which may be theirs if they effect a coup. There probably is some truth to this view, but it overlooks a critical point: only one man can become the chief executive. Victor Villanueva, a Peruvian army officer, offers an interesting comment on this situation:

> In addition to this reasoning of an ethical or institutional nature [about defending the constitution, protecting the fatherland, etc.] there is added the quite legitimate desire to be the one . . . the national hero destined to pass into history as the savior of the fatherland. But it happens that these fervent desires dwell at the same time in the hearts of many military men, so many that their very abundance comes to neutralize them in a reciprocal fashion.[11]

11. Villanueva, p. 146.

The desire for prestige, although it may explain why one officer is willing to lead a coup, would not be a motivation for the hundreds or even thousands of other military personnel who must cooperate in a coup effort. Cooperation is likely to be achieved, I argue, only when the moral position of the chief executive becomes doubtful. *The coup is, ultimately, a product of the political activity in the civilian sphere.* It is the civilians who generate a coup by withdrawing support from the chief executive and by engaging in vigorous opposition. It is also the civilians who may inhibit a coup by providing the chief executive with significant support while he is buffeted by the opposition. The military role is not autonomous or self-contained; it is reactive, dependent upon the movements of civilian political forces.[12]

I would formulate these observations in the following form:

> *H18. A military coup will take place when (a) vigorous civilian opposition to the chief executive is extremely (unusually) high and (b) when civilian support for the chief executive is extremely (unusually) low.*

I believe that this hypothesis expresses the fundamental conditions which produce a military coup in the Latin American context. I do not mean to deny that a wide range of other conditions, from the weather to chance meetings may not influence the precise moment of a coup. But weather, friendships, and telephone calls will never be sufficient *causes* for a coup. And such variables can have only the slightest preventive effect if the basic conditions for a coup, high opposition and low support, are present.

Unfortunately it is difficult to apply this hypothesis in cross-national comparisons because I have not established numerical levels of opposition and support that produce a coup. In a very broad sense, however, it does seem consistent with the contrast between the Anglo-American and Latin American experiences. If incentives for

12. "The army . . . only reflects the manners and characteristic styles of the prevailing atmosphere." Américo González Merzario, *Política y Ejército* (Buenos Aires, Editorial Yegros, 1955), p. 112. A similar conclusion about a "reactive" role for Latin American military organizations is found in Theodore Wyckoff, "The Role of the Military in Latin American Politics," *Western Political Quarterly, 13* (1960), 745–63. The idea of a reactive role is advanced by Morris Janowitz, *The Military in the Political Development of New Nations* (Chicago, University of Chicago Press, 1964), p. 16. The discussion here has several similarities to that offered by S. E. Finer, *The Man on Horseback* (London, Pall Mall Press, 1962).

political participation are of only moderate strength, as I suggest is the case in the United States and Great Britain, then the intense opposition necessary to provoke a military coup will simply not exist. The United States does not have a sufficient number of leaders and active followers intensely desirous of winning office to develop a vigorous, Latin American style opposition. Without such an opposition, the American military is never required to question the moral or legal position of the chief executive.

The hypothesis may also be applied to the same Latin American country through time. If it is correct, we should find that a coup took place when the executive was faced with unusually severe opposition and retained unusually little support. Testing the hypothesis would require that the investigator establish indices of support and opposition and compute their value for every week or month in the period under study. The index for opposition would contain such items as the size and frequency of anti-government demonstrations, the number of political deaths, injuries, and arrests, the number of anti-government newspapers, and the proportion of congressional time devoted to anti-government speeches. For the index of support one would include the number of pro-government newspapers, the number of top political leaders who participate in the government, the proportion of congressmen who acquiesce to government proposals, and the size and number of political groups and factions which go along with the government.

It is important to note that these measurements of opposition and support employ the obvious, dramatic manifestations. It is possible for a president to censure newspapers, capture interest groups, and exile potential troublemakers and thus have little opposition as I measure it: no street demonstrations, few strikes, a friendly press, and a docile Congress. Foreign observers and exiles may condemn such a regime and allege that the "dictator" is privately hated by the vast majority of the citizens. However, the cues the military finds relevant for interpreting opposition and support do not come from foreign newspapers or opinion polls. Instead the army is sensitive to the clearly visible, dramatic manifestations of opposition which I suggest above for the indices.

With the values for opposition and support thus computed, one may construct a historical graph showing the fluctuations in these

indices through time, as suggested by the hypothetical case diagrammed in Figure 5. If hypothesis H18 is correct, the coups should
have occurred at points of minimum support and maximum opposition as indicated by points A and B in the figure. Such a quantitative
test of the hypothesis for the Latin American countries is beyond the

FIGURE 5

ILLUSTRATION OF TEST FOR HYPOTHESIS H18

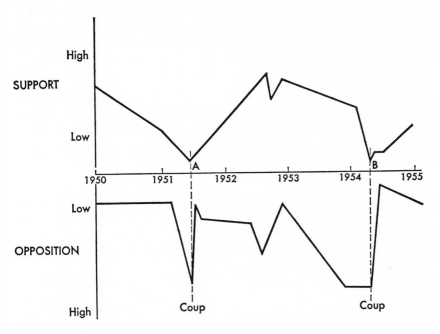

scope of this study. However, it is my impression that the analysis of
military behavior presented here accurately describes the perspectives of Latin American military men and that the hypothesis is consistent, at least in a preliminary fashion, with many coup situations
in Latin America.[13]

13. The best general discussion of military intervention in Latin America is
Arturo Bray, *Militares y Civiles* (Buenos Aires, 1958). Discussions of military-
political problems and specific coups are listed below by country.

Argentina: Alfredo Colmo, *La Revolución en la América Latina* (Buenos Aires,
M. Gleizer, 1932)—an excellent analysis of the coup of September 6, 1930; S. Viale
Ledesma, *6 de Septiembre: El Pueblo, El Ejército y la Revolución* (Buenos Aires,
Ediciones Mercurio, [1930]); Coronel J. Beresford Crawkes, *533 Días de Historia*

THE IMPACT OF PARTY IDENTIFICATION

The hypothesis just advanced leaves unexplained the conditions under which a chief executive will lose support and face an intense opposition. If we assume that in most Latin American countries the incentives for political participation are strong, then all should have

---

Argentina (Buenos Aires, Imprenta Mercatali, 1932); Bonifacio del Carril, *Crónica Interna de la Revolución Libertadora* (Buenos Aires, 1959); Raúl Lamas, *Así Cayó Perón* (Buenos Aires, Editorial Lamas, 1955).

Chile: General Carlos Saez Morales, *Recuerdos de un Soldado* (3 vols. Santiago, Biblioteca Ercilla, 1943)—an excellent inside account of the army during the turbulent 1924–32 period; General E. Monreal, *Historia Completa y Documentada del Periodo Revolucionario 1924–25* (Santiago, Imprenta Nacional, [1929]); Raúl Marín Balmaceda, *La Caída de un Régimen* (Santiago, Imprenta Universitaria, 1933); Raúl Marín Balmaceda, *El 4 de Junio de 1932* (Santiago, Imprenta Universitaria, 1933); General Juan Bennett, *La Revolución del 5 de Septiembre de 1924* (Santiago, Bacells y Cía, n.d.); C. H. Haring, "The Chilean Revolution of 1931," *Hispanic American Historical Review, 13* (1933), 197–203.

Dominican Republic: John Bartlow Martin, *Overtaken by Events* (Garden City, Doubleday, 1966), pp. 343–590.

Ecuador: General A. I. Chiriboga N., *Fuerzas Morales en el Ejército* (Quito, Imprenta Nacional, 1932); Coronel Luis Cabrera, "Informe" in *Informe que el Ministro de Guerra y Marina Presenta al la Nación* (Quito, 1913), pp. 27–70; Martin C. Needler, *Anatomy of a Coup d'Etat: Ecuador 1963* (Washington, Institute for the Comparative Study of Political Systems, 1964).

Peru: Victor Villanueva, *El Militarismo en el Perú* (Lima, 1962); José Luis Bustamante y Rivero, *Tres Años de Lucha por la Democracia en el Perú* (Buenos Aires, 1949); Richard W. Patch, "The Peruvian Elections of 1962 and Their Annulment," American Universities Field Staff, West Coast South America Series, *9* (1962).

Colombia: Gonzalo Canal Ramírez, *Del 13 de Junio al 10 de Mayo en las Fuerzas Armadas* (Bogotá, Ediciones Documentos Colombianos, 1957); Joaquín Paredes Cruz, *Causas y Efectos de una Dictadura* (Cali, 1957); Luis Martínez Delgado, *Historia de un Cambio de Gobierno* (Bogotá, Editorial Santafe, 1958); Tomás Rueda Vargas, *El Ejército Nacional* (Bogotá, Editorial "Antena," 1944).

Paraguay: Américo González Merzario, *Política y Ejército* (Buenos Aires, Editorial Yegros, 1955).

Brazil: Estevão Leitão de Carvalho, *Dever Militar e Política Partidaria* (São Paulo, Companhia Editora Nacional, 1959).

Guatemala: Partido Social Democrático, *La Caída de Jorge Ubico* (2d ed., Guatemala, C.A., 1958).

Venezuela: Ana Mercedes Pérez, *La Verdad Inédita: Historia de la Revolución de Octubre 1945* (2d ed., Buenos Aires, Editorial Colombo, 1953)—an excellent collection of interviews with the officers active in the coup of 1945; Francisco Betancourt Sosa, *Pueblo y Rebeldía: Relato Histórico de la Sublevación Militar de 7 de Abril de 1928* (Caracas, Ediciones Garrido, 1959); *Así se Fraguó la Insurrección* (Caracas, Ediciones de la Revista *Cruz del Sur,* 1958).

similar patterns of intense opposition. Since such energetic opposition often provokes a coup, we might first expect the frequency of military coups to be substantially the same in all these countries. Variations in the frequency between countries as well as within a given country through time would have to be attributed to the more or less chance configurations of political forces, events, and personalities.

It seems possible, however, to attack this problem of coup frequency by isolating structural variables which affect patterns of support (or opposition) and thereby influence the probability of a coup. Although we cannot hope to eliminate circumstantial variables in such an analysis, we may at least advance hypotheses which shape expectations about the likelihood of coups. Perhaps the most important structural condition affecting the likelihood of a coup is the degree of party identification of the electorate because it affects the extent of presidential support.

Political leaders seeking private rewards such as status are quite sensitive to their own immediate political opportunities. Faced with the choice between a strategy of supporting or opposing a chief executive, these participants will select the position that best enhances their personal opportunities. The support strategy has several advantages. One may participate in the government as a minister or agency head and thus gain the reward of status. In addition one may get public credit for accomplishments and obtain employment for active followers, thus establishing a political base for future advances up the ladder of political success. If it appears that the incumbent president has a sufficiently strong hold on the situation that he may determine his successor, it pays to be on his side.

But the support strategy has a critical drawback if the incumbent chief executive is unpopular: collaborators become unpopular. This unpopularity can, if party identification is low, severely damage the supporter's political prospects. The leader must face potential active followers and the electorate solely on the grounds of who he is. He has no established party label on which to campaign, on which to attract votes. If president X is unpopular, and if party labels cannot be relied upon to attract votes, becoming known as an "Xista" is a serious political liability. Consequently, if the popularity of the incumbent president begins to wane (or appears to wane), leaders will seek to disassociate themselves from the government and join the opposition. The desertion of a few leaders reinforces the perception of presidential unpopularity so that the movement into the opposition takes place at an ever faster rate. As a consequence the president may be stripped of significant political support and he must face the likelihood of a coup.

An illustration of this kind of desertion is the experience of Ecuador's President José María Velasco Ibarra, elected in 1960 for a fourth (nonconsecutive) term. Against all other party groupings including the Conservative, Liberal, Socialist, and *Frente Democrático Nacional,* Velasco ran as an independent. He received 52 per cent of the vote, more than the other two candidates put together. In the senate Velasquistas obtained more than a majority of the 35 seats.[14] Nevertheless, a year later Velasco was deposed in a coup after facing intense opposition and was deprived of virtually all political support. Somehow the leaders and active followers who had ridden his coattails had slipped away.

The presence of an electorate with a high degree of party identification counteracts this pattern of eroding presidential support. Leaders may support an unpopular chief executive because they have a label to call attention to. The presence of substantial numbers of party identifiers gives the leaders who support the president a firm margin of security. They can collaborate with the president and in the next election get their votes on the party label. Since the party-identified electorate recognizes and remembers leaders primarily by the labels they bear, leaders may support an unpopular chief executive and still do well in subsequent elections.

The importance of this phenomenon for the military coup is easily seen. Party identification greatly reduces the risks of supporting an unpopular chief executive and therefore increases the likelihood that any president will have significant political support. Earlier I noted that low civilian support for the president was a critical condition in bringing about a military coup (H18). It follows, then, that in those countries where presidents are more likely to have civilian political support owing to the high degree of party identification, coups will be less frequent (assuming other variables to be the same):

14. *Hispanic American Report, 12* (June 1960), 399–400.

H19. In Latin American countries where party identification of the electorate is high, military coups will be infrequent.

H20. In Latin American countries where party identification is low, military coups will be frequent.

These hypotheses suggest that the frequency of military coups in different Latin American countries is not indeterminate but related to the degree of party identification. When applied to the three countries already discussed in detail—Colombia, Ecuador, and Peru—the hypotheses do seem consistent with the data.

Colombia has had three coups in the twentieth century: 1900, 1953, and 1957. The first, that of July 31, 1900, only barely qualifies as a coup. The deposed president, aging Conservative Manuel Antonio Sanclemente, refused, for reasons of health, to come to Bogotá. The government was apparently being run by the ministers who had a rubber stamp of Sanclemente's signature. After prolonged plotting and agitation by both Conservatives and Liberals, the vice-president, Conservative José Manuel Marroquín, assumed the presidency. There was military complicity, however, and Sanclemente was deposed against his will, so the change does qualify as a coup.[15] Three coups in 66 years is, by Latin American standards, a relatively low frequency of military intervention. As already observed, party identification in Colombia has been extremely high, about 80 per cent of the electorate (see also Chapter 9).

In Peru, although some party identification has obtained during this century, it has never reached high levels. During the early years of the century the *Civil* label apparently attracted a significant number of voters since it did remain on the scene for several decades. Since the 1930s the APRA label has made substantial electoral showings, indicating that perhaps about one quarter of the electorate has been identified with it. In recent elections two new parties, the *Acción Popular* of Fernando Belaunde and the *Unión Nacional Odriista* of Manuel Odría have done quite well. But in view of their recent appearance (AP—1955, UNO—1961) it is probable that voters were attracted to the prominent leaders and not to the labels as such. Not more than about 30 or 40 per cent of the Peruvian electorate, then,

15. See Luis Martínez Delgado, *Historia de un Cambio de Gobierno*.

has been identified with a party label. Peru has had six coups in the twentieth century: 1914, 1919, 1930, 1931, 1948, 1962.

Party identification in Ecuador also is relatively low. Although the Liberal, Conservative, and Socialist labels apparently have some faithful followers, examination of the erratic electoral results suggests that the total number of party identifiers is probably not more than about 30 or 40 per cent of the electorate. Ecuador has had eleven coups since 1900: 1906, 1911, 1925, 1931, 1935, 1937, 1944, 1947, 1951, 1963, 1966.

Preliminary data suggest that the hypotheses are consistent with the experience in other Latin American countries. In Guatemala and El Salvador, for example, party identification seems quite low, as inferred from the absence of enduring major party labels. These are also countries where a considerable number of military coups have taken place. On the other hand, Uruguay, judging from the almost total domination of the electorate by the *Blanco* and *Colorado* labels, has a system where party identification is quite high. And Uruguay has not had coups in this century.[16]

The validation of hypothesis H19 is not as clear for Colombia as perhaps we might expect. The coups of 1953 and 1957 seem to represent rather important deviations from the hypothesis. A closer inspection of these two coups reveals, however, that they are consistent with the basic hypothesis (H18) relating support and opposition to the military coup. In 1953 the country had been experiencing a period of increasing political violence growing out of the Liberal opposition to the Conservative government. Bloody clashes between Liberals and Conservatives were taking place all over the country, particularly in smaller towns. Bands of Liberals uprooted by the violence roamed the countryside, presenting a serious threat to public order, a threat which the army constantly struggled to contain. In 1948 there had been a tremendous riot in Bogotá, initially against the Conservative government but degenerating into vandalism which only the army succeeded in containing.

The president in 1953, Laureano Gómez, faced the opposition not

16. The events of March 31, 1933, and February 21, 1942, were not coups by our definition since the chief executives were not removed. See Taylor, *Government and Politics of Uruguay,* pp. 23–30.

only of the Liberals but of a faction of his own Conservative party. A split in the Conservative party was made complete in 1951 with the establishment of a competing Conservative directorate led by ex-president Mariano Ospina. When the coup of General Gustavo Rojas Pinilla occurred on June 13, 1953, Gómez was presiding over a nation racked by incessant violence which had claimed perhaps 100,000 lives. He faced the opposition of the Liberals and the Ospinista Conservatives and retained only the support of his own faction. What is surprising about the coup of 1953 is not that it happened but that it happened so late. In Peru or Ecuador a similar amount of civilian political violence would certainly have provoked a coup long before, at least by 1948 or 1949. The almost criminal reluctance of the Colombian military to put an end to the appalling political violence demonstrates, it seems to me, the importance of even reduced amounts of presidential support—of the Laureanista Conservatives in this case—in inhibiting a coup.

The coup against Gustavo Rojas Pinilla in 1957 also seems consistent with the basic hypothesis. Initially Rojas was supported by both the Liberals and the Ospinista Conservatives in his coup against Gómez in 1953. The Laureanista Conservatives, understandably, opposed him. Rojas, however, decided to form and head a "third force" in Colombian politics. This attempt to create a third party gave rise to serious problems because it meant that Liberals and Conservatives would be deprived of positions and jobs to make way for the Rojistas. By 1957 when Rojas attempted to succeed himself through election by a pocket constitutional convention, the acclaimed leader of the 1953 coup had become a national villain. All the prominent leaders, including Alberto Lleras, Darío Echandía, Alfonso López, Carlos Lleras, Mariano Ospina, Laureano Gómez, Guillermo León Valencia, and Roberto Urdaneta, had turned against him. Without meaningful political support Rojas faced a general strike on May 5, 1957, and was obliged by the army to resign on May 10.[17]

These two coups in recent Colombian history, then, seem consistent with our basic hypothesis (H18). They occurred at moments when political support for the chief executive was at a minimum and opposition was unusually widespread and intense. They indicate that

17. See Martz, *Colombia,* pp. 173–228.

while a high degree of party identification may reduce the frequency of coups over a long period of time, certain chance configurations of political forces and personalities can nullify the effect of this variable in a given instance.

The basic hypothesis (H18) developed to explain military intervention expresses the fundamental conditions for a military coup. While one may advance other conditions to account for a coup, none of these circumstances provides an adequate explanation for the phenomenon. Moreover, if these additional conditions are absent a coup will take place regardless, providing that the conditions stipulated in the hypothesis—extremely low support and extremely high opposition—are present.

Ascribing a fundamental status to any hypothesis about social life is a risky business. But I am willing to take that risk in order to reach a more concise understanding of the reality under study. A forcefully stated hypothesis, even if it may be consistent with only a portion of the data, is far more useful than a meticulous list of many possible factors. An hypothesis, assuming that the meaning of its terms is clear, may be proven or disproven and thus be accepted, qualified, or rejected. Furthermore, a clearly stated hypothesis gives one something on which to build so that other relationships may be uncovered. The relationship I have proposed between party identification and the frequency of coups, for example, was derived from the basic hypothesis which identified presidential support as a critical variable.

To further establish the utility of the basic hypothesis developed in this chapter, it is useful to consider some alternative explanations frequently given to explain military coups. In the following paragraphs I shall examine two of the more popular alternative explanations. A detailed evaluation of these arguments is not practicable, but it is possible to cast some light on their probable validity or utility. The first is the "organizational benefits" explanation for a military coup which might be cast in the following form:

> Hx. Military coups take place when the military organization desires organizational benefits (higher salaries, weapons) which the government refuses to provide.

In the first place, this hypothesis cannot account for the differences in the coup frequency in different political systems. Presumably the members of any military organization in Latin America (or elsewhere) desire a larger budget which would provide newer weapons and higher salaries. Why is it, then, that Colombian, Mexican, or Uruguayan armies do not carry out coups as frequently as the armies of their neighbors? It seems awkward and unconvincing to argue that the soldiers in these countries are strangely selfless, content with

TABLE 7.1

Military Expenditures of Latin American Governments, 1964

Military Expenditures

	as a per cent of GNP	as a per cent of total government expenses
Brazil	3.4	16.1
Peru	3.4	13.1
Paraguay	3.1	30.4
Dominican Republic	n.a.	17.8
Argentina	2.3	15.0
Venezuela	2.2	9.9
Ecuador	2.0	10.0
Nicaragua	1.8	16.5
Chile	1.8	8.8
Colombia	1.3	12.2
Honduras	1.3	10.1
El Salvador	1.2	8.8
Uruguay	1.2	6.2
Bolivia	1.1	6.8
Guatemala	.9	10.5
Mexico	.7	8.2
Costa Rica	.4	2.0
Panama	.1	0.5
for comparison:		
United States	9.0	
Canada	4.5	
United Kingdom	6.9	
Italy	4.1	
Turkey	5.7	

Sources: United States Department of Defense figures presented in: United States Senate, Committee on Foreign Relations, *Hearings on Foreign Assistance, 1966,* 89th Cong., 2d sess. (Washington, GPO, 1966), p. 538; United States Senate, Preparedness Investigating Subcommittee, Committee on Armed Services, *Hearings on Worldwide Military Commitments,* part I, 89th Cong., 2d sess. (Washington, GPO, 1966), pp. 58–59.

rusty tanks and their present salaries—not only awkward, but false.[18] The desire for greater benefits would not account for differences in coup frequency of different Latin American countries.

Furthermore, if this desire is not constant, then it seems reasonable to suppose that those military organizations with relatively poor conditions should be the most anxious for improvement, and hence their countries should, according to the hypothesis above, be characterized by a relatively higher frequency of coups. The figures given in Table 7.1 lend no support to this view. If any association can be discerned it is that countries in which the military budgets are relatively small are *less* prone to coups than the others. Uruguay, Mexico, and Chile, for example, have had no coups for over 30 years.

This hypothesis places the cart before the horse. It says that the military threatens and effects a coup to obtain higher benefits whereas what really seems to happen is that when the military is in a position to effect a coup, owing to the configuration of civilian opposition and support, the chief executive will make attempts to "buy off" the military. But if the military really were seeking private benefits so that it could be bought off, it is difficult to see why (1) there should be any coups in Latin America since, except in the rarest case, the president should be willing to increase military salaries if his survival truly depended on it, (2) as noted above, the worse-off military establishments do not effect coups more frequently. I suspect that it would be found that many chief executives who have been removed by a coup had indeed raised military benefits during their tenure, but obviously to little advantage.[19]

18. See the complaint of one member of the Colombian military over the declining military share of the budget: Brigadier General Alberto Rueda Terán, "El Problema Militar en América," *Revista de las Fuerzas Armadas, 3* (April 1961), 13–18.

19. Two unsuccessful attempts to buy off the military are those of Perón (Robert A. Potash, "The Changing Role of the Military in Argentina," *Journal of Inter-American Studies, 4,* 1961, 574) and Manuel Prado who reportedly signed an officers' pay increase shortly before he was deposed in 1962 (Villanueva, *El Militarismo en el Perú,* p. 293). An excellent study by Charles Wolf, Jr., on the relationship between the fiscal position of Latin American armies and gross political characteristics lends support to the argument advanced here. He found that: 1) greater U.S. military aid to a Latin American country was *not* associated with either its "level of democracy" or a tendency for "democracy" to "erode"; and 2) greater defense expenditures by a Latin American country were *not* associated with either a lower "level of democracy" or with a greater tendency for "democ-

A second explanation frequently offered for military coups identifies alleged ideological conflicts as the cause. The army, it is suggested, has a particular position on matters of social and economic reform and will initiate a coup against the president who greatly departs from this position. Typically the army is alleged to have a "conservative" position so that it would depose "reformist" presidents in "rightist coups." But occasionally a "reform-minded" army is alleged to have ejected a "conservative" president in a "leftist coup." In this way, it is argued, the army determines (usually to the detriment of the lower strata) the social reform policies of successive governments. The hypothesis might be expressed thus:

Hx. The military intervenes when the president is too far left or too far right of its own position.

Much of the literature on politics and political events in Latin America suffers from what I would call the "echoing assumption." In describing the reality before him, the writer makes assumptions which he does not consciously recognize. He then proceeds to describe events within the framework of these assumptions so that his "reality" reaffirms his first principles. In this way the assumptions are further implanted in the literature, not as points which have been doubted and tested, but as echoes bounced off the data.

Nowhere is the echoing assumption more in evidence than on the matter of ideological differences in Latin America, of "lefts" and "rights." There is a firmly held conviction that any country must have a meaningful left-right division in its politics. It seems clear that if one begins with this belief, he will most certainly "find" lefts and rights, even if he has to pin them about on the basis of established journalistic tradition, party labels, or scraps of historical information. The penchant of scholars for left-right labeling probably reflects the unsophisticated state of research on Latin America. Social scientists must order reality in some fashion and the dimension of ideology provides a convenient and familiar manner in which to organize distant and ambiguous data.

---

racy" to "erode." The statistical measure of democracy and democratic erosion was based on a reputational technique developed by Russell H. Fitzgibbon; a high frequency of military coups was probably one characteristic that led respondents to give a country a "low democracy" score. "The Political Effects of Military Programs: Some Indications from Latin America," *Orbis, 8* (1965), 871–93.

But, as I have already suggested, there exists the real possibility that ideology is not a meaningful dimension in most Latin American countries. This is the case in Colombia where the participant incentives of status and employment make matters of program policy incidental to politics. Once one entertains a doubt about the existence of right and left, a reading of various descriptions of Latin American politics reveals that these studies do not provide satisfactory evidence to show that meaningful ideological differences do obtain. Indeed, reading between the lines one can perceive an essentially nonideological politics behind the arbitrary labeling.

Consequently, although writers are in the habit of calling military coups "rightist" or, less frequently, "leftist," these labels are quite untrustworthy. They represent only the writers' implicit assumption —that there *must* be lefts and rights. This point is illustrated in Martin Needler's otherwise excellent study of the 1963 coup against Carlos Julio Arosemena in Ecuador. Were there a right and left in Ecuador? Needler says so, but his observations are contradictory:

> Feeling that an acute need for structural reform existed had been developing for some time. Always popular on the Left, it had achieved new salience with the proposal of the Alliance for Progress. Even the Right took up the theme of reform.[20]

But isn't the Right the enemy of reform? If the Right favors reform, then why not call it Left? What makes the Right right? Significant is the writer's assumption that before he arrived on the scene to discover the Right was left, the Right was right. Trapped by the assumption that there must be a Right, Needler could not use his data to expose the inadequacy of the ideological dimension itself.

When one cuts away the imaginary lefts and rights, Needler's description of the coup is consistent with our basic hypothesis. Arosemena faced widespread opposition and had virtually no support. But Needler's conclusion that this event was a "Right-wing coup" seems extremely unsound.[21] If the reader disregards the unsubstanti-

20. *Anatomy of a Coup d'Etat: Ecuador 1963*, p. 18.
21. One would suppose that if the coup were "right-wing," the deposed president, Arosemena, would be alleged to be a "leftist." But Needler does not take this path. Instead he suggests (p. 48) that the coup was really against former president Velasco Ibarra. Velasco was then in exile in Argentina but might have come back in the following year and won the presidential elections of 1964. Since the coup

ated labeling, his account becomes a description of a system of non-ideological opportunism.

The hypothesis relating coups to ideological divisions, therefore, contains an unwarranted assumption: that meaningful left–right divisions exist in Latin American societies. As stated, the hypothesis prompts the investigator to ask: was the coup right- or left-wing? With the problem posed in this manner, one is inclined to accept the most ephemeral evidence to show "lefts" and "rights." But the fragmentary evidence and scholarly hearsay which "prove" a coup to be left or right are plainly inadequate to demonstrate the existence of a meaningful left–right division in the first place. Once it is doubted that such a division exists, the allegations of "leftist" and "rightist" coups might appear as little more than hasty attempts to make data fit into inappropriate categories.

Of course in the specific context of a coup there will be issues around which, overtly, opposition builds. More familiar illustrations of such issues include new taxes, transportation fare increases, communism in government, inflation, and corruption. But it would be a mistake to assume that it was because the army had an intensely held

---

forestalled these elections, it may have disadvantaged Velasco. Even granting these assertions, we still cannot classify the coup as "right-wing" unless Velasco, against whom the coup was allegedly effected, is a "leftist." Needler realized this in writing his conclusion and therefore alleged that Velasco was "likely to undermine the *status quo*" (p. 48). For this conclusion, Needler has no evidence. Velasco had been president of Ecuador four times before (1934–35, 1943–46, 1952–56, 1960–61) and had left no memories of socioeconomic upheaval. Needler observes earlier in the study that Velasco was erratic in policy matters, that over his career he had been supported by all the different parties, and that "his political philosophy defies description in terms of the normal categories of political discourse" (p. 12). The allegation about Velasco undermining the status quo, then, is gratuitous, appended only to make the left-right labeling work out correctly. The argument is that the 1963 Ecuadorean coup was "right-wing" because (?) it allegedly disadvantaged an exiled leader whose "political philosophy defies description."

In a recent article Needler carries the liberal-conservative, reformist-nonreformist labeling even further. He makes numerical computations of the proportion of "reformist" coups all over Latin America for the last three decades. Nowhere does he say how he classified the coups, nor what characteristics would make them "reformist" rather than conservative. And, out of over 50 coups, he apparently finds not a single ambiguous case! I am hard-pressed to find a single coup which clearly or meaningfully can be classified as either reformist or nonreformist. And the closer I look at each case, the more artificial and inappropriate such labels become. See Martin C. Needler, "Political Development and Military Intervention in Latin America," *American Political Science Review, 60* (1966), 616–26.

position on one or the other of such issues that it effected a coup. Instead, I argue, it is the *opposition* which generates a coup. The *issue* is incidental. If a president has significant political support he can increase bus fares, or be accused of communist infiltration without suffering a coup.

This chapter is an attempt to explain the relatively low frequency of military coups in Colombia. By casting the explanation in general form I have developed two hypotheses that may be applied to other Latin American countries. These hypotheses describe, in effect, two contrasting patterns. In one there is a relatively high degree of party identification and a relatively low frequency of military intervention. In the other, party identification is relatively low and military coups are more frequent.

Aside from proving useful as a rough tool for predicting the likelihood of coups in a Latin American country, the hypotheses about party identification and military intervention provide a practical insight for policy-makers who seek to prevent military coups. The analysis suggests that one road to prevention is increasing party identification.

Certain constitutional changes, for example, might cause party identification to increase. A shorter period between elections might accelerate the growth of party identification, since each election would perhaps serve to revitalize party organizations and the use of party labels. Off-year congressional elections, when there are no presidential candidates on whose coattails leaders may run, might stimulate the use of labels before the electorate. Deprived of the name of a vote-getting chief, the congressional candidates would necessarily use labels more prominently. Perhaps use of off-year elections in Colombia in 1832–60 (and today as well) might be associated with the high party identification there.

However, before too much thought is expended on ways to increase party identification and thereby reduce the possibility of a military coup, one ought to decide whether the coup is an undesirable institution. As I shall endeavor to show in the next chapter, there are circumstances under which a military coup may well be the lesser of two evils.

CHAPTER 8

THE DEFENSIVE FEUD AND
THE FRENTE NACIONAL

We believe that in Santander another method of defense should be adopted. Our brothers of that department work against their own interest if they continue respecting the lives of those who do not respect theirs.

> Nuestra Bandera *(Liberal weekly of Popayán, Cauca), March 1859, cited in Gustavo Arboleda,* Historia Contemporanea de Colombia *(6 vols. Cali, 1935), 5, 575.*

From 1946 to 1953 Colombia experienced a period of political violence surpassing in duration and intensity anything recently experienced in this hemisphere. Whereas in other Latin American countries the annual number of political deaths seldom exceeds a few dozen, the tally for this Colombian episode runs into tens of thousands. If one also includes the criminal violence such as banditry and simple homicides, which were probably indirectly caused by the initial political violence, then the number of deaths may exceed the hundred thousand mark as suggested in one calculation.[1]

Up to this point I have accepted a simple relationship between the strength of incentives and the intensity of political conflict (H4). I have reasoned that the more keenly people want a certain object, the more energetic or costly will be their actions to attain the object. In the political realm these higher costs are what I mean by "more intense conflict." As it stands, this hypothesis (H4) is useful in a broad sense for it provides an avenue of explanation for lasting cross-nation differences in the level of political conflict. With it one may proceed to identify the specific conditions which affect incentives and thus construct a hypothesis relating these conditions to the level of

1. Guzmán et al., *La Violencia en Colombia, 1,* 292.

political conflict. I have attempted to do this in elaborating hypothesis H4a.

Nevertheless, the relationship between the strength of incentives and conflict intensity will apply only approximately because differences in political structures may cause the *same* incentives to find expression through different, and more or less violent, channels. This point is important for understanding variations in political conflict between different Latin American nations, for in many of these countries, it appears, incentives are similar in nature and strength to those in Colombia. This proposition could be defended in several ways; here I shall assume that the original hypotheses (H1 and H3) advanced to explain incentives are valid and do apply to many other Latin American countries. If incentives are roughly similar in these other countries, then why did Colombia achieve such preeminence in political violence? The answer, I believe, lies in structural conditions.

The usual approach to political "unrest" in Latin America is grounded on the assumption that socioeconomic "privation of the masses" is the cause of political violence. This belief is another illustration of an echoing assumption. It orders the data for the writer rather than being tested by the data. In interpreting the events in Colombia one writer argues, "What occurred in Colombia between April 9, 1948, and Rojas' rise was due to no accident; it resulted from the meshing of the forces behind an authentic social revolution." [2] But the events do not support this interpretation. The major dimensions of violence in 1946–53 [3] were not socioeconomic. The conflict took place not between rich and poor, peasant and landowner, employee and employer but between two socially heterogeneous political parties. Socioeconomic issues were not raised with particular urgency; instead it was political claims and political fears of one party against the other which characterized the demand context. The issue was, essentially, which party would gain permanent occupancy of the government. Nor was the solution to the conflict socioeconomic; it was political. Initially it consisted in the removal of the Conservative president, Laureano Gómez, by the army. Ulti-

2. Vernon Lee Fluharty, *Dance of the Millions* (Pittsburgh, University of Pittsburgh Press, 1957), p. 150.

3. It is inaccurate to date the period of violence from 1948 as Fluharty does. The assassination of Gaitán and the Bogotazo marked a point, albeit dramatic, in a pattern already established.

mately a more lasting solution was found in the 16-year political arrangement whereby the Liberals and Conservatives share public offices, including the presidency. Finally, for what it may be worth, Colombia was a relatively well-off Latin American country. And during the period 1945–50 Colombia enjoyed a period of relative prosperity.[4]

THE DEFENSIVE FEUD

The basis of my analysis is the idea of a *defensive feud*. By employing the modifier "defensive" I am attempting to capture a specific meaning of "feud" which is customarily lost in everyday usage. This meaning refers not to any fight or quarrel but to a particular kind of conflict. A defensive feud is a struggle between two groups in which each side recognizes the existence of a mutually acceptable solution less costly than fighting, but that solution cannot be reached. That is, each side finds a common solution preferable to fighting, yet each side continues to fight. Clearly a defensive feud is an uncommon type of conflict. It is not our usual expectation that conflicting groups will avoid making a truce which both find preferable to continued struggle. Such a pattern may obtain, however, if there are conditions which make it impossible to reach and maintain this desired truce.

4. Naturally it is difficult to gather conclusive evidence on this point. However, some figures are suggestive. Employment in Bogotá (blue-collar) rose about 13% from 1945–49. *Real* wages of blue-collar workers (i.e. corrected for inflation) in Bogotá rose 20%. These figures strongly suggest that the 1948 riots known as the Bogotazo cannot be attributed to "increasing deprivation of the masses." In 1951 and 1952 a certain deterioration in these and other economic indicators can be observed in comparison with the 1949–50 figures. But none of the indices (blue-collar real wages in Bogotá, blue-collar employment in Bogotá, blue-collar employment in the departments of Cundinamarca, Boyacá, Norte de Santander, and Santander) in 1952 fell to the 1945 levels. Inspection of the wages of different categories of farm laborers in different regions indicates that money wages rose considerably from 1945 to 1951, about doubling in most cases. From 1951–52 a slight decline in the money wages of agricultural workers was registered (the cost-of-living indices for blue-collar workers and white-collar workers also declined slightly in 1952). I cannot calculate the real wages of farm workers in this period because there is no cost-of-living index computed for them. But judging from the change in the Bogotá *obrero* cost-of-living index (which increased about 70% in the period 1945–51), it seems probable that farm workers (whose money wages about doubled from 1945 to 1952) were somewhat better off in 1952 than they were in 1945. See *Anuario General de Estadística 1947*, pp. 351, 482–83, 494–501; *Anuario General de Estadística 1951–1952*, pp. 334, 368, 371, 376–79.

To illustrate the defensive feud we might construct a hypothetical example. Two men are in joint possession of a hundred dollars and a court of law will decide how it is to be divided between them. The judge, however, may be bribed and will award the full hundred dollars to the man making the highest bribe offer. Only the highest bribe offer will be accepted by the judge; if no bribes are made the judge will divide the sum evenly, 50 dollars to each man. Both men are avaricious, unscrupulous, and (rightfully) mistrustful of each other.

The eventual outcome, given these conditions, seems obvious. Each man will proceed to make bribe offers to the judge. The man who makes the first five-dollar offer acts in the belief that he will be awarded the full hundred dollars which, subtracting the cost of the bribe, gives him 95 dollars, or 45 more than he would have had without making the bribe. But the other man reasons similarly: that a ten-dollar offer will still bring him 90 dollars or 40 more than under a "fair" decision, and 90 more than if he took no action.

Up until the amount of each man's bribe offer has reached 50 dollars, the conflict is a simple struggle. There does not exist a mutually acceptable solution which both find preferable to struggling (making higher offers). Each man stands to gain more by winning with a bribe than by accepting the unbribed decision. But beyond the 50-dollar mark a defensive feud obtains. Each man knows he will gain more by withdrawing his bribe offer *if the other does so as well* than he would get by continuing to make higher offers. But if the other man cannot be relied upon to stop, then it is productive to continue to raise the offer. At higher levels of bribe offers each man will receive less than if a no-bribing agreement could have been kept, but he still gets more than if he allows his opponent to make the highest offer. The end point in this situation would be the bribe of $99.99; the "winner" gets one cent net profit, the loser, nothing. But, it must be emphasized, each man is acting rationally given his mistrust of the other.

The idealized Tennessee mountain feud provides a practical illustration of the defensive feud. Each side is fighting for its physical survival which it sees threatened by the other. But neither clan, taken as a whole, desires to fight in preference to a true. Each would give as its reason for fighting "if we don't get them, they'll get us," or "they started it, we must defend ourselves." Each side would prefer to stop fighting if it could obtain guarantees that the other would also stop. By inquiring into the hill feud more closely we might arrive at the general conditions which make the defensive feud possible.

First, each group must perceive that attacks upon one of its members are attacks upon all. If John is shot in the leg by a member of the opposing clan the rest of his side must consider John as one of them. Without this condition of identification the bipolar group conflict cannot obtain and violence would be nothing more than individual conflict.

The inability to reach a binding agreement would be created by two conditions: decentralization and partisan channels of communication. Decentralization, or the inability of either leaders or majorities to control all members of the group, enables only a few "hotheaded" members to initiate hostilities and thus cause the other side to mistrust their entire clan. And if communication takes place only within each clan, then each side will bias its perceptions of the other and reinforce its conviction that opponents are basically evil and cannot be trusted. From a perfectly fair fight between the "hotheads" of each side, for example, two drastically conflicting reports are brought home. Each report finds the other side guilty of unprovoked aggression, with the home side fighting heroically against unjust odds. Control of these actors by the elders of the clans in the first place, would have prevented the clash altogether. Objective communication of the events could have prevented the other members of the clan from arriving at a distorted view of the intentions of the entire other side.

Finally, a feud may be stopped at any point by the intervention of a third force with the ability and will to prevent the fighting. A police force or national guard could physically separate the sides or make it prohibitively expensive for any members of either side to take hostile action against the other. These reflections may be summarized in a preliminary hypothesis:

Hp. A defensive feud is likely when each of two highly self-identified groups perceives that no guarantees exist to prevent the other from depriving it of important values and no third force exists to terminate the conflict.

This general hypothesis may be recast to make it directly applicable to political conflict within a nation. Instead of clans, the likely units are political parties: large groups of leaders, active followers, and voters bound together in their common identification with a party label and their common interest in the fate of that label. The important value being disputed will probably be control of the government; each party will fear that the other intends to monopolize public office indefinitely.

Fair elections would be, of course, insurance against such a monopoly since different parties would each get some positions and each would have a long-term hope of winning a majority. But fair elections will be undermined if incentives are so strong that participants are greatly concerned about the outcome. They will be inclined to tamper with electoral processes to assure a favorable result, employing campaign sabotage, police harassment of opponents, favoritism to supporters, manipulation of public jobs, and actual frauds. Furthermore, participants who have strong incentives will be extremely apprehensive about what happens in elections, ready to scream "fraud" if in danger of losing. Hence they will fear a fraud even when none is taking place. Participants with weaker incentives are not greatly interested in arranging frauds, nor intensely concerned about the possibility of fraud against them. Therefore strong incentives, by undermining the guarantees against political monopoly which elections would provide, cause the *fear* of indefinite exclusion from office. This fear is a necessary condition for a defensive feud.

Decentralization of the parties is a necessary condition for a defensive feud because it prevents leaders from contracting a binding truce between the parties. Beyond the control of top leaders, a few participants may engage in electoral fraud, and thus convince the other party that their entire party cannot be trusted.

A system of only two parties also seems a necessary requisite for a defensive feud. If there are important third or fourth parties, they may play a balancing role, preventing either of the two major parties from establishing an indefinite monopoly of the government and removing the fear of such monopoly.

Partisan channels of communication assist the development of the reciprocal belief in the evil intentions of the other party, which undermines the possibility of interparty truce. Upon reflection it would seem that such partisan channels are themselves a product of strong incentives. If these incentives are of a private nature (status, employment) the channels will not carry biased program policy communications, as I suggested in Chapter 4. But on matters of a strategic nature—intimidation of voters, discharge of public employees —those holding strong incentives will, in response to their keen interest in such matters, establish strongly partisan channels of communication.

Finally, in a national political system the only third force capable of terminating a defensive feud is the armed forces. Assuming the other necessary conditions to establish a defensive feud, only the armed forces could, by taking control of the government themselves, end the conflict. Hence, for a defensive feud to persist, the military must be prevented from intervening.

The hypothesis can now be stated:

> *H21. A defensive feud is likely in a system where (1) incentives for political participation are strong, (2) only two parties exist, (3) party identification with those parties is high, (4) the parties are decentralized, (5) partisan channels of communication (at least on strategic matters) exist, and (6) the military is prevented from intervening.*[5]

It is useful to note, parenthetically, that wars between nations rarely, if ever, are defensive feuds. Two of the conditions necessary for a defensive feud are missing in most cases of international strife. First, nations are, as far as their military behavior is concerned, highly centralized. Secondly, warring nations can almost always reach and maintain solutions to their conflict, which they both find preferable to fighting, if such solutions exist. The spatially defined basis of international conflicts—boundaries, enclaves, straits—provide mutually perceptible thresholds or "sticking points" at which the war may be terminated or not started at all. The Korean war, for example, was not a defensive feud with each side drifting unwillingly and uncontrollably into war. A conscious decision was made by one

5. This hypothesis contains a certain repetition. I have already (H19) advanced a connection between high party identification and military intervention so perhaps (6) is unnecessary. I also suggested that partisan channels of communication will arise when incentives are strong so perhaps (5) is also redundant. But it is useful, I believe, to present the hypothesis in its complete form. It may be of assistance to refer to Figure 6 where the hypothesis is diagrammed to show the suspected relationships.

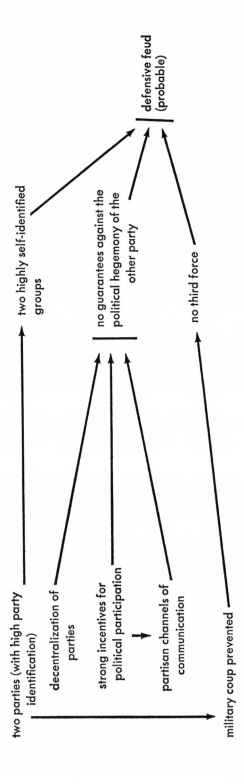

FIGURE 6

ANALYSIS OF THE DEFENSIVE FEUD

side to risk war in crossing a border. The war ended as soon as both sides found stopping on the truce line preferable to the actual and future costs of fighting.

The centralization of hostile states and the mutually perceptible quality of the status quo lines that define the violence-provoking acts give, in effect, these hostile states "guarantees" against the uncontrolled and inadvertent encroachment of one by the other. Even in the event that the status quo is ambiguous, many tenable solutions can be negotiated or arbitrated and then held to by both sides. Boundaries can be affixed, territories exchanged or divided. If war is produced or continues, it is only because the sides feel that they have too much at stake (reputation, economic interests, ideological principles) to accept possible compromises.

In one sense the Frente Nacional arrangements (discussed below) have transformed the Liberal-Conservative rivalry into a confrontation more resembling international conflict—and they have thereby prevented a defensive feud. The arrangements for exactly sharing legislative seats and alternating the presidency between the parties are, in effect, status quo lines. They constitute mutually perceptible thresholds the crossing of which would represent a deliberate and unequivocal provocation. Whereas before, during the defensive feud, tens of thousands of independent party activists took the marginal actions that, cumulatively, menaced the existence of the opposite party, now only the highest leaders have the power to provoke civil war and that through a dramatic, unequivocal deed (e.g. an incumbent president refusing to relinquish his office to a successor from the other party).

THE COLOMBIAN EXPERIENCE, 1946–1953

Did a defensive feud take place in Colombia during 1946–53? In 1946 the Liberals, who had held the presidency since 1930, divided in the presidential elections, enabling the minority Conservative candidate to win:

Conservative: Mariano Ospina Pérez	565,849 votes
Liberal: Gabriel Turbay	441,199 "
Liberal: Jorge Eliécer Gaitán	358,957 " [6]

6. *Anales de Economía y Estadística*, supplement to Nos. 17 & 18 (May-June 1946), "Estadística Electoral," p. 3.

Given this distribution of forces each party had good reason to fear that the other would attempt to exclude it from the government. The fear was quite real since a tendency toward exclusion had appeared again and again in Colombian history. The party controlling the presidency possessed the necessary weapons to erode the electoral strength of the other party. Moreover, given the manifestly intense interest in officeholding, it was virtually inevitable that at least some members of the presidential party would employ these weapons to secure their political objectives.

The instruments for establishing political hegemony include intimidating voters by violence at the local level, harrassing the out-of-office party candidates in their campaigns, using biased electoral boards and commissions, particularly at the local level, buying off active followers by the in-office party with offers of employment, and undermining opposition party machinery by the discharge of appointees so that the party could not practice favoritism to counteract the favoritism practiced by the ruling party. Table 8.1 shows the electoral dimensions of the establishment of hegemony following the Liberal takeover in 1930. This pattern is characterized by a lowering of the opposition party vote until it refuses to participate. As competition declines the voter turnout in the ruling party declines.

TABLE 8.1

The Establishment of Liberal Hegemony, 1930–1938

Election	Liberal vote	Conservative vote*
1930, president	369,934 (45%) victory by plurality	240,360 213,493 ——————— 453,853 (55%)
1931, representatives	401,993 (51%)	384,948 (49%)
1933, representatives	604,372 (63%)	361,571 (37%)
1934, president	938,934 (100%)	no participation
1935, representatives	420,547 (100%)	no participation
1935, city councils	435,721 (65%)	234,435 (35%)
1938, president	511,947 (100%)	no participation

*I have disregarded the tiny number of blank, void, and third-party votes.

Sources: *Anuario General de Estadística 1935* (Bogotá, 1936), p. 428; Instituto Colombiano de Opinion Pública, *Factores Colombianos* (Bogotá, 1964), p. 73.

In the period following 1946 each party feared the establishment of hegemony by the other. The Conservatives recognized that the majority Liberal electorate (established by fraud, they claimed) represented a threat to their continued possession of the presidency. If the Liberals gained the presidency again the Conservatives could expect to be excluded indefinitely. The Liberals feared that the Conservatives would annul their electoral majority by the intimidation and manipulation of the electorate and thus establish an indefinite period of Liberal exclusion from the highest offices. It seems reasonable to suppose that each party was desirous of establishing hegemony and was willing to sustain certain costs (violence) to do so. But after 1946 leaders and majorities of each party concluded that the indefinite exclusion of the other was far too costly, that it was preferable to reach some kind of sharing agreement.

Some of the first instances of violence occurred late in 1946, shortly after Ospina took office. In the department of Nariño there were clashes between Liberals and Conservatives in Ancuya, Funes, Túquerres, and Sandoná. In Sandoná, where Conservatives were celebrating a religious festival, Liberals were observing (or planning to agitate), a fight ensued, the army was brought out on the side of the Conservatives, as ordered by the Conservative mayor, and three Liberals were killed.[7] Each party read this and scores of similar events in quite different ways. The Conservatives considered that the Liberals were using violence to intimidate Conservative voters; the Liberals concluded that Conservatives and Conservative government officials were attempting to impair Liberal officeholding opportunities. Early in 1947 Liberal leader Gaitán presented the government with a list of 57 clashes in various towns which the Liberals considered to be government-instigated.[8]

7. *Semana*, November 11, 1946, pp. 6–7. It is on this source, the weekly newsmagazine *Semana*, that I largely base my account of this period. During the period under study this magazine, founded in 1946, was a highly successful attempt to bring impartial, detailed, and depth reporting to Colombian journalism. For a readable account of this period see: John D. Martz, *Colombia* (Chapel Hill, University of North Carolina Press, 1962), pp. 42–169. In general Martz reports the conflict as a strictly political one, although he occasionally inserts fragments of a deprivation-of-the-masses theory: "peasants and workers were increasingly unwilling or unable to carry on under existing conditions. So the first smoldering outbreaks of violence began in isolated rural areas" (p. 50).

8. *Semana*, April 19, 1947, p. 6.

The intensity and frequency of such incidents suggest that they were not "normal" or inevitable products of political friction. The particular political context was one which gave each party ample reason to fear that the other would attempt to eliminate it. At the local level the fears were about a street-cleaning job, about the police chief, about the mayor. Each event had significance well beyond the locality since it confirmed fears about what was happening to the electorate and to officeholding opportunities. Each party had it within its grasp to exclude the other; each party was on the verge of being excluded by the other.

It is difficult to determine exactly when the conflict became a defensive feud, but I would suggest that this point was reached by the end of 1947. Throughout that year there were increasing signs that leaders could identify an acceptable truce situation, that they found it preferable to continued violence, but that they could not implement it. When he came to office, President Mariano Ospina was among the first to attempt to establish a truce. He had appointed a cabinet of six Liberals and six Conservatives in an effort to give guarantees to both sides. But each side felt that this coalition was a smokescreen behind which the other party tampered with the electorate at the local level while its hands were tied by its commitment at the national level. And clashes did indeed occur at the local levels. "President [Ospina] does not understand how a program of peace and conciliation, and of mathematical distribution of offices goes on reaping cadavers in its implementation in Nariño." [9]

Toward the end of 1947, in September, the rising clamor for some end to the violence led party leaders to subscribe to a formal pact of *Unión Nacional*. Reached between Liberal leader Gaitán and Conservative leaders Laureano Gómez and Roberto Urdaneta, the pact stipulated an end to all political intimidation and retaliation, and proposed a system for investigating each conflict to determine the real culprits.[10] In essence the leaders were seeking to provide guarantees for each side. Each adopted a position of "we'll stop if you'll stop." But the leaders did not have it in their power to stop the many thousands who would be involved in clashes. And the provisions for impartial determination of culpability failed because no one in the country was considered impartial. The violence continued.

9. Ibid., November 11, 1946, p. 7.
10. Ibid., September 6, 1947, pp. 3–6.

One month later Laureano Gómez accused the Liberals of having used 1,800,000 fraudulent voting cards in the city council elections just held, in clear violation of the pact. Gaitán in turn insisted the Conservatives were not holding up their end of the pact.[11]

Another attempt at union followed the April 9, 1948, riots. On that day Liberal leader Gaitán was assassinated in Bogotá. Neither then nor since has it been shown that any group was responsible for that deed. But in the inflamed state of partisan opinion, many Liberals interpreted the assassination as the work of the Conservatives. A riot ensued, directed initially against the government and government buildings and the Conservatives, but finally degenerating into sheer vandalism. In attempting to contain the mobs and restore order the army fired upon the rioters on many occasions. In several other cities the riots were repeated.[12]

In an effort to somehow contain the corrosive and increasing violence, the Liberals consented to reenter the cabinet of President Ospina. (They had left on March 10, 1948, claiming that the government was abusing their good will in undermining the Liberal position behind their backs.) This attempt at coalition lasted about one year until the Liberals withdrew once again arguing, as before, that their presence in the cabinet had only given Conservatives greater freedom to erode the Liberal position. Conservative ministers had resigned two weeks before alleging that the Liberals were using their position in the government to assist and defend Liberal lawlessness.[13] *Semana* summarized the basic problem leading to the Liberal refusal to participate in the government:

> The origins of this crisis are not . . . an indecipherable mystery. They are . . . in the obscure and threatening political atmosphere which the country has been breathing as a consequence of the *lack of effective and workable guarantees* on the part of lower-echelon authorities.[14]

In the presidential elections of 1949 the Liberals, who had nominated Darío Echandía, refused to go to the polls, declaring that they were prevented from exercising their rights by Conservative-govern-

11. Ibid., October 18, 1947, pp. 4–5.
12. See Martz, pp. 55–68.
13. *Semana*, May 1, 1948, pp. 5–6; June 12, 1948, p. 5; March 12, 1949, pp. 5–6; May 14, 1949, p. 5; May 28, 1949, pp. 5–7.
14. May 28, 1949, p. 5 (italics mine).

ment intimidation. Conservative Laureano Gómez won uncontested. By this time the violence had begun to take on a second, more deadly aspect, that of vicious personal crimes, banditry, and guerrilla activity. In many of the villages the pattern of aggression and reprisal, with civil authorities heavily implicated in partisan violence, became a situation of kill or be killed. The disruption caused by deaths, burnings of homes, and theft of livestock generated armed bands of partisans who committed shocking atrocities.[15]

It seems reasonable to suppose that if a similar situation had been reached in the last century, events would have taken a different turn. Some of the national Liberal leaders would have gone out into the countryside, recruited sizable armies, and made an attempt to destroy the Conservatives by force. The regular army and Conservative recruits would oppose them. But in 1949 the open civil war solution was not possible. The regular army would have held overwhelming firepower against any civilian army. As a consequence the battle remained in clandestine form. In the long run the dispersed guerrilla resistance was perhaps more costly because there was no way a truce could be signed. The war of 1899-1902, costly as it was, at least found a relatively definitive termination in the truce signed aboard the U.S. battleship *Wisconsin*. But in 1949–53 there was no way a truce could be made with the combatants because they were not unified under any central command.

In the face of truly awesome violence leaders tried again, late in 1951, to reach a binding truce. Liberals Alfonso López and Carlos Lleras and Conservatives Gilberto Alzate, Luis Navarro, and José María Villarreal, at the behest of temporary President Urdaneta, signed a pact which provided for an end to press censorship, an end to newspaper invective, establishment of political freedoms and free elections, and an end of guerrilla activity with no reprisals to be made against those who laid down arms.[16] Momentarily the pact had some

15. Guzmán et al., *La Violencia en Colombia*. While the authors of this volume perform a useful task of documenting the nature and extent of the violence, they seem confused when it comes to establishing an intelligible explanation. After toying with jargon (the recent import "dysfunction" included) they finally surrender with a six-page list of nearly 100 "causes" which covers every imaginable social condition, historical event, tautology, truism, and cliché (*2*, 410–15).

16. *Semana*, September 8, 1951, p. 5; September 22, 1951, pp. 9–10; October 13, 1951, pp. 9–10.

effect. There were new outbreaks of violence the next week but the party newspapers voluntarily refrained from fanning the fires. "Liberals and Conservatives have continued to have faith in the agreement. They know that total peace must arrive inevitably. They do not want to take these events as pretexts . . . to resume the war of the linotypes." [17] But shortly thereafter, when the government arrested four Liberals for "plotting against the public order," the pact lapsed.[18] The Liberal leaders could not approve of the arrest of their men; the Conservatives could not let them go.

La violencia continued to run its course until June 13, 1953, when an army coup removed Conservative President Laureano Gómez and placed General Gustavo Rojas Pinilla as chief executive. With the exception of the Laureanistas, political leaders acclaimed Rojas. The acute tensions between Liberals and Conservatives were relaxed by the presence of a nonpartisan figure in the presidency, and there was apparently a lull in guerrilla activity. Although Colombia suffered from an unusually high homicide rate and banditry for at least a decade after 1953, most instances of rural violence after that date were criminal and not political in the sense that they were apparently not connected with either gaining political office or influencing government policy. By 1965 rural violence and banditry had greatly diminished and all but a very few outlaw chiefs had been imprisoned or killed.

A review of this period demonstrates, I believe, that a defensive feud took place and that socioeconomic conditions played little role in the conflict. The three major attempts at a truce (1947, 1948, 1951) centered entirely on the problem of *political* guarantees. These pacts and the various sharing arrangements devised during this period demonstrate that the leaders could identify a truce which they found preferable to continued fighting. But they could not carry out the basic idea of coalition with long-range guarantees for both sides. An examination of the circumstances shows that all of the conditions hypothesized as necessary for a defensive feud were present.

There were only two political parties, and party identification with these labels was high. Each time an individual or group was involved

17. Ibid., October 20, 1951, p. 11.
18. Ibid., October 27, 1951, p. 9.

in a conflict the Liberal and Conservative labels borne by these actors gave the clash national significance. Between these two parties, the fear of political exclusion took on real and desperate meaning owing to the strength of participant incentives. Each party had good reason to believe that the other sought hegemony. Members of each side understood and had witnessed the corrosive effects of office-seeking upon the electoral process. Elections could not, in themselves, provide a guarantee for each party, because too many participants were too interested in the outcome to resist tampering with them.

A critical link in the pattern of defensive feuding was the inability of leaders to control all the members of their parties. It was this decentralization of party structure that undermined all attempts at agreement. While leaders desired all violence to cease, they could not control the local police captain or guerrilla, the town councilman or agitator. It took only a small number of irresponsible party members at the local level to convince all members of the other party that the first party held hostile intentions.

Partisan channels of communication greatly assisted the development of partisan mistrust of the other side. Each event occurred not in a neutral, apathetic climate, but in a pre-established atmosphere of hostility. Instances of violence then conformed to expectations. The assassination of Gaitán, for example, led to serious repercussions because Liberals already expected that such a deed could only be the work of Conservatives.

Newspapers were, for the most part, highly partisan. It is inaccurate, however, to lay the responsibility entirely upon the publishers, because if newspaper readers had desired more objective publications, economic competition probably would have caused such papers to emerge. As it was, newspapers merely provided the partisan material which readers already sought. Even presumably objective material was interpreted in conflicting ways by the papers of each side. A pastoral letter of the archbishop, issued in July 1951 urging peace and an end to violence, was interpreted differently by the Conservative *El Siglo* and the Liberal *El Tiempo*. Each paper accused the other of "falsification." [19]

There are various indications that Liberals and Conservatives lived

19. Ibid., July 21, 1951, p. 5.

in separate compartments. Many leaders noted in 1965 that in those times (1946–53) Liberals and Conservatives would not even greet each other. Given such exclusive patterns of communication it is easy to see how each side was able to sustain and reinforce the conviction that the other desired hegemony at any cost. The problem of finding a neutral, objective view is described by *Semana*:

> To establish the truth, the humble truth in each case [of violence] is converted into a prodigiously difficult task. The journalistic organs of the Conservatives and the leaders of that collectivity systematically attribute the origin of bloody events ... to the leaders and members of the Liberals. The Liberal press and the leaders of that collectivity insist, in turn, on pointing out as the cause of the bloody episodes the government and the local leaders of the Conservatives in each town. But neither the government nor the political parties find themselves able to prevent them.[20]

Finally the third force capable of preventing the defensive feud, the armed forces, did not intervene until events ran their bloody course. Ultimately, in 1953, a coup did occur. By removing the Conservative president from office and placing a neutral figure (Lieutenant General Rojas) in the presidency, the military did succeed in breaking the defensive feud. But military intervention came surprisingly late, long after extremes of political violence had been reached. As noted in the previous chapter, one explanation for the tardy intervention of the Colombian military is the high degree of party identification, which enabled the chief executives—Mariano Ospina and Laureano Gómez—to retain sufficient support to prevent a military coup.

These findings about the defensive feud and the role of the military necessitate readjustment in the usual evaluations of certain Latin American political institutions. In much of the scholarly literature there is a strong inclination to judge Latin American phenomena in terms of the United States. By American standards a fragmented, personalist party system is "bad" and so is military intervention. But this judgment overlooks a fundamental difference between most

20. Ibid., March 27, 1948, pp. 5–6.

Latin American systems and the United States: the great strength of incentives for political participation in the former region.

In the United States, where incentives are much weaker, there does not exist a real and pressing fear that one party will attempt to exclude the other. Participants realize, quite correctly, that their opponents are not sufficiently anxious to gain office to employ violence or fraud on any significant scale. Their guarantee against political exclusion lies in their recognition that not enough people care enough to attempt it. The reverse side of the experience is that in those occasional cases when electoral manipulation is practiced or alleged, Americans have not appeared to become particularly upset about the matter. In many places in the United States, including some southern states and some urban centers, citizens were, for long periods of time, quite convinced that local electoral practices were corrupt. Although there certainly were protests and reform movements, the reaction was seldom energetic or violent.

If one attempts to explain fair elections in the United States as reflecting an intense commitment to democratic institutions ("legitimacy"?), then surely this commitment should have produced explosive violence wherever fraud was practiced or alleged. Fraud in the United States has not been an explosive issue because most participants—leaders and active followers—have not been sufficiently keen about winning office. I am not saying that Americans do not approve of fair elections. They do. So do Colombians. It is because Colombian participants have so much more at stake in elections that their free and fair operation is constantly threatened.

The lower strength of incentives in the United States also prevents defensive feuding by undermining possible partisan channels of communication. Political leaders in the United States are not so keenly interested in political outcomes that they establish highly partisan communications for themselves and give highly partisan accounts to the electorate. The assassination of John F. Kennedy in 1963 illustrates the different character of American political communication. Certainly the possible complicity, the rumors, the ambiguity which surrounded that event contained as much explosive potential as the assassination of Gaitán. But Americans, participants and citizens, leaped to the conclusion that no important political group could possibly have done such a thing. In the atmosphere of neutral communications political leaders quickly allayed potential doubts and fears.

The strength of incentives of political participants in Latin America, however, drastically alters the requirements for guarantees against political monopoly. Elections may not be guarantees because there *are* many persons willing to tamper with them. The occasional fraud cannot be passed off or overlooked, because outcomes are considered too important. Partisan channels of communication are established so that competing parties gain a distorted view of each other. These implications of strong incentives, added to an established two-party system, make the defensive feud a real possibility.

THE FRENTE NACIONAL

The defensive feud of 1946–53 was broken, as I noted, by the military coup of Rojas. Both parties having been displaced from the presidency, it was possible for the leaders to work out, during 1957, an arrangement for bipartisan government. Following the coup against Rojas in 1957 these agreements were made amendments to the constitution by a plebiscite on December 1, 1957, approved by 95 per cent of the voters.[21] The provisions for bipartisan government until 1974 are known as the *Frente Nacional*.

In working out the Frente Nacional party leaders, headed by Liberal Alberto Lleras and Conservative Laureano Gómez, made every effort to provide ample guarantees to each party that its equal status could not be challenged by the other.[22] Some measures included had been attempted in the 1946–53 period. Ministries are shared equally between the parties, with the Minister of Interior (political appointments) being of the opposite party to the president. Governorships are divided equally between Liberals and Conservatives, and governors and mayors must, in turn, divide their cabinets equally between the parties. An earlier attempt to assure bipartisan

21. Martz, p. 264.
22. There is little divergence between the analysis given here and the manner in which party leaders assessed the mechanics of the Frente Nacional; see: Alberto Lleras Camargo, *Sus Mejores Páginas* (Segundo Festival del Libro Colombiano, n.d.), pp. 178–98, especially p. 190; Carlos Lleras Restrepo, *Hacia la Restauración Democrática y el Cambio Social* (2 vols. Bogotá, 1963), *1*, 153–79.

representation in the legislature was expanded: both houses of Congress, all departmental assemblies and municipal councils must have an equal number of individuals registered under the Liberal and Conservative labels. Furthermore, a two-thirds majority is required in these bodies for approval. Thus one party cannot, by winning over just one member of the other party, enact a measure injurious to that party.

The keystone of this arch of bipartisan coalition is the alternation of the presidency. After each four-year term the presidency must pass to a member of the opposite party. In 1958–62 the president was Liberal Alberto Lleras; in 1962–66, Conservative Guillermo León Valencia; in 1966–70, Liberal Carlos Lleras Restrepo, and in 1970–74 it will be a Conservative. The alternation of the presidency solves the basic question which was not solved in the period of political violence: Who will eventually emerge the winner, Liberals or Conservatives? During the earlier period the Liberals feared, certainly not without reason, that in their cooperation with Conservative presidents they were merely witnessing the transition to Conservative hegemony. The provision for presidential alternation provides each party with a basic guarantee that in the long run the other cannot emerge victorious.

The arrangements of the Frente Nacional now make the Liberal–Conservative division of the vote *completely irrelevant*. By getting more or less of the vote neither party changes its share of legislative representation, nor its quota of governorships and mayors, nor its chances at the presidency. Even if one party label gets only one vote, it gets half of all positions. Since the division of the vote no longer affects officeholding opportunities between Liberal and Conservative participants, it no longer makes sense for either party to fear the other.

The experience in the period 1958–66 clearly demonstrates that the Frente Nacional has succeeded in its primary objective. It has provided satisfactory guarantees for each party against the possibility of being excluded by the other. In fact, it has tended to provide guarantees to all factions of both parties as well as to the small third party (ANAPO) of Rojas Pinilla. The arrangements for dividing the executive and legislative positions have made it impossible for any group or faction to monopolize electoral resources or carry out fraud on any significant scale. Consequently, elections have been fair and peaceable.

Although the direct struggle between bearers of the Liberal and Conservative labels has been prevented, the system has not lost in competitiveness. Running under each party label, at the local and national level are many competing factions. These factions provide an outlet for any real or imagined preferences of the electorate. If any significant difference in program policy positions did exist between the various candidates and factions, the Frente Nacional itself provides no obstacle to the selection among these policies by the electorate.

Of course, Colombia does not have what one could reasonably call a tranquil political system. Participants are still keenly interested in winning office; the Frente Nacional has not altered incentives in any way. There are diatribes heavily laden with invective, quasi-violent demonstrations, campaign sabotage, partisan newspapers, parliamentary riots, and student clashes with the police. But the conflict takes place along factional lines and not between Liberals and Conservatives. The multiplicity of factional groups, the shifting nature of their alliances, and the dispersion of electoral resources makes a defensive feud generated along factional lines improbable.

The Frente Nacional has worked magnificently. Its success is both a tribute to its creators and an excellent illustration of how a change in political structures may greatly reduce political violence. During 1958–66 Colombia has had five consecutive congressional elections which have been highly competitive, quite fair, and relatively free of violence. This sequence marks an undisputed first in Colombian history. The three presidential elections, while not closely contested, were free of repression and characterized by little violence. After about five years of press censorship (1952–57) there is now an almost appalling freedom of the press. Rojas Pinilla agitates publicly for a military coup; the communists, openly implicated in waning guerrilla activity, cover newsstands with fierce anti-government literature. Finally, there exists no condition of defensive feuding, and it seems unlikely that such a conflict could come about under the Frente Nacional.

The hypothesis (H21) given to explain the phenomenon of defensive feuding points only to the variables that make this pattern probable. It does not contain enough information to predict the precise limits of the process, nor the timing. It is rather like saying that a man walking on a steep, slippery roof is likely to fall. This statement points to two critical variables, steepness and slipperiness, which greatly affect the likelihood of a certain outcome. But it does not specify all the variables, so we cannot predict when he will slip or how far he will fall.

Similarly the hypothesis about the defensive feud, when applied to Colombia, will not yield a precise explanation of the extent and timing of any particular episode. But since the basic conditions have been present in Colombia at other times, it is reasonable to suppose that defensive feuding has taken place frequently in Colombian history. There is suggestive evidence for this possibility.

In the period following the Liberal capture of the presidency in 1930 there was considerable violence. In the following elections the problem of exclusion and guarantees arose in dramatically similar form to the period after 1946. One source reports, perhaps exaggerating, over 6,000 deaths during 1930–34.[23] This period bears, in fact, an almost perfect correspondence to the 1946–50 experience. The Conservatives had an electoral majority which they annulled by division. The Liberal president, Enrique Olaya Herrera, was responsive to the Conservative congressional majorities and formed a coalition ministry. Political violence exploded at the local levels. Leaders were unable to prevent violence, although they apparently sought to do so. Conservative Roberto Urdaneta Arbeláez wrote of Liberal President Olaya:

The Government and Olaya Herrera personally made every imaginable effort to stop the bloodshed and the Liberal directorates cooperated with the executive toward the same end; but the matter continued. . . . Once the first bloody attack of Liberals against Conservatives or vice-versa was produced, the process would develop automatically.[24]

23. Guillermo Salamanca, *La República Liberal* (2 vols. Bogotá, Editorial Centro, 1937), *1*, 339, 349.
24. From *El Materialismo contra la Dignidad del Hombre* cited in Guzmán et al., *1*, 25.

It seems probable, then, that the period following the Liberal victory in 1930 was also an example of defensive feuding. The violent electoral campaign of 1922, while it probably cannot be classified as a defensive feud, illustrates the strong tendency toward such conflict in the Colombian system. In this instance the Liberals attempted to contest Conservative control of the presidency but found their way blocked by the partisan and violent activity of public officials.[25] A close inspection of the various civil wars of the nineteenth century might show that they were largely products of the variables discussed above: that they constitute cases of defensive feuding.

The experience of Uruguay reinforces the finding that a two-party system is a dangerous alternative for Latin American countries—dangerous, that is, unless special sharing arrangements can be made between the parties. Uruguay is the only other Latin American country which has been characterized by the dominance of only two parties since the nineteenth century. In the nineteenth century there were several wars between the Colorados and Blancos over, judging from the nature of the truces, the question of party hegemony in the government. But the Uruguayans were fortunate in being able to establish a durable sharing arrangement. Initially, probably owing to the highly regional distribution of party strength, it was possible to divide up departments. Following the civil war of 1872 the minority Blancos obtained control of four departments; an agreement in 1897 expanded this control to six departments.[26]

The development of a plural executive in which the minority party is represented falls in the pattern of providing each party a guaranteed position in the government. We might strongly suspect, then, that the Uruguayan system does contain the necessary conditions for a defensive feud, but that various sharing arrangements are instrumental in counteracting the tendency toward such conflict.

The conclusions that might be drawn from this analysis of the defensive feud include: (1) military intervention in a Latin American country can be, under certain circumstances, a highly desirable phenomenon; (2) of all the possibilities for party systems, an established (high party identification) two-party system contains particu-

25. Samper Bernal, *Breve Historia Constitucional y Política*, pp. 173–91.
26. Taylor, *Government and Politics of Uruguay*, p. 18.

lar dangers for a country where incentives for political participation are strong; (3) the dangers of a two-party system can be offset by guaranteed sharing arrangements; (4) if such arrangements cannot be made, then a personalist (low party identification) party system or multiparty system is probably preferable to an established two-party system.

PART THREE

THE COLOMBIAN SYSTEM
IN OPERATION

CHAPTER 9

THE PARTY SYSTEM:
I

That which was lacking and continued to be lacking from beginning to end was Conservative unity, which the National Directorate sought and hoped for. But it was faced by a de facto situation impossible to change. Personalist cliques, old factions, antagonism, envy and the desire for pre-eminence and wealth had seized the majority of political leaders.

Impossible seemed the unity of people who, while professing the same political sentiments, were profoundly separated by personal interests and ambitions, absolutely opposed, with antagonisms between clique and clique and between person and person, in the nature of a war without quarter.

> Aquilino Gaitán P. *(member of the Conservative National Directorate, 1928–30),* Por Qué Cayó el Partido Conservador *(Why the Conservative Party Fell) (Bogotá, Talleres Mundo al Día, 1935), pp. 10, 14.*

Most Americans believe their political parties exhibit little cohesion. They see them as fractured, fragmented agglomerations of disparate elements, remarkable for their disunity. But such a conclusion can only be relative to the variations found in other countries. Measured against their British counterparts, the American parties are, in certain respects, less united. Measured against Colombian parties, however, the American groupings are by no means examples of disunited parties. Alongside the competitions and divisions which occur within Colombian parties, the American Republicans and Democrats are models of unity. Indeed, the most outstanding characteristic of Colombian political parties is a degree of factionalism which astonishes the American observer.

The definition of political party employed in this study is focused upon the label. Collections of people acting under the same root label are a political party. The number of parties in a nation is, by definition, the number of root labels receiving a significant number of votes. The validity of this label-oriented definition of party rests upon the importance of labels in binding voters and, often, groups of leaders together. Other formal definitions of parties, which typically include some degree of organization as a defining characteristic, are extremely difficult to apply in practice. Is, for example, the U. S. Democratic party fifty state organizations or one national? An argument on such a question could continue indefinitely, involving further definitions of "hierarchy," "cohesion," or "common interest." In fact, when we say "the Democratic party" or "the Labor party" or "the Liberal party" we usually mean, perhaps without recognizing it, the collection of participants identified by such labels.

"Factionalism" means here the presence of candidates bearing the same party label but competing with each other in *general* elections. This definition is particularly useful for two reasons. First, competition in general elections represents the ultimate in party division. All political parties exhibit internal divisions at some level: cell meetings, party elections, or conventions. But as long as a party presents one candidate in the final elections, party leaders indicate that more unites them than divides them. The presence of competing candidates in general elections represents a qualitative difference in the level of party conflict; party leaders have indicated that the conflict within the party is as great as conflict between parties. Secondly, this definition of factionalism is easy to apply in a quantitative manner. One need only note the number of competing lists (candidates) with the same label which appear in general elections.

In Colombia factionalism takes place at both the national and local levels. Nationally there were five factions in 1965, three Liberal and two Conservative, as well as a small third party, ANAPO (see Table 9.1). The national factions are semipermanent groups of political leaders that compete with each other and establish separate organizations with separate headquarters, party committees, and congressional groups. At the local level, national faction lines tend to be reflected in separate groups of local leaders in most departments. But even within these local branches of national factions there are divisions, expressed in competing lists for Senate, House, and city council positions—factions of factions. The Officialist Liberals, for example, ran five competing lists in Atlántico in the 1964 election for representatives; in the same election the Movimiento Revolucionario Liberal ran three competing lists in Boyacá. In addition to factions of factions at the local level one will find "independent" Liberals and Conservatives adding their lists to the mélange.

TABLE 9.1

Colombian Parties and National Factions, 1965

	Leader	Votes in 1964 election	
LIBERALS:			
Liberal Oficialista*	Carlos Lleras Restrepo	752,527	(33.3%)
Movimiento Revolucionario Liberal, Linea Blanda	Alfonso López Michelsen	284,952	(12.6%)
Movimiento Revolucionario Liberal, Linea Dura	Alvaro Uribe Rueda	96,895	(4.3%)
Movimiento Independiente Liberal**	Fernando Mazuera Villegas	7,129	(.3%)
CONSERVATIVES:			
Conservador Doctrinario (Lauro-alzatistas)	Alvaro Gómez Hurtado		
Conservador Unionista (Ospinista)	Mariano Ospina Pérez	802,282	(35.5%)***
THIRD PARTY:			
Alianza Nacional Popular	Gustavo Rojas Pinilla		
from lists registered as Conservative	293,183		
from lists registered as Liberal	16,495		
Total ANAPO		309,678	(13.7%)
	Blank and void votes	7,727	(.3%)
	Total vote	2,261,190	(100.0%)

*Includes 14,090 votes for independent Liberal candidates.

**Registered in the 1964 elections as Movimiento de Izquierda Liberal; existed only in Cundinamarca.

***Includes 8,282 votes for independent Conservative candidates.

What causes factionalism? In the United States, Great Britain, and many other nations this phenomenon seldom occurs. In Colombia it has been a way of life. To explain the contrast we need to consider both incentives and structural variables.

First, the analysis assumes that party identification is high. If party identification of the electorate is low, then whatever the conditions that prompt intraparty division they will not lead to factionalism. Since the party label has little electoral value where party identification is low, dissident politicians will not be inclined to use it. Instead they will adopt new labels. Only if the party labels attract substantial numbers of votes will competing leaders continue to use them. Factionalism as I have defined it, therefore, will not occur where party identification is low.

To party leaders factionalism promises certain rewards and entails certain costs. Among the costs of founding a faction is a substantial injury to the party collectivity in the following senses: (1) the presence of a competing party list is likely to diminish the party's success at elections by dividing its vote; (2) in diminishing electoral success the factionalist is reducing the probability that the party's programs or policy preferences will be reflected in government policy; (3) the presence of open competition at elections between party factions is likely to confuse voters, disenchant them, and detract from the party image, thus impairing the long-run future of the party as a whole; (4) the presence of open electoral competition is injurious to party idealism and purposefulness, feelings which may be important for leaders and active followers. The potential factionalist, therefore, might find the damage to the party collectivity an important cost of becoming a competing party candidate.

Probably the most important benefit that factionalism can bring a leader is getting into office. By launching his candidacy in opposition to other party candidates, the politician may stand a better chance of winning the desired office. He may have been left out completely as an official party nominee, or very poorly placed on a list; consequently his chances of winning are better if he runs independently under the party label.

These two dimensions, then, seem fundamental in determining the calculations made by the potential factionalist: (1) the value of the party collectivity to him and (2) the value of gaining office for himself. What incentive will lead participants to value the party collectivity highly and the office little so that factionalism seldom occurs? What incentive causes participants to care little for the party collectivity and highly value the office itself so that factionalism will be rampant?

In a system where the incentive is program, leaders do not seek office for private rewards. They want to get things done, to realize programs in accord with their preferences. It would follow that leaders with a program incentive will find the value of the party collectivity salient in their perspectives. Their image of a political party is not an organization designed to deliver personal benefits of office but an efficient way for like-minded people to get things done in politics. Loyalty to party, faith in the party's role, unity for the realization of common aspirations: these are facets of the program-motivated leader's perspectives. He values the party collectivity, and the idea of getting into office at the expense of that collectivity is distasteful.

The leader with a status incentive has a reversed view. For him the party collectivity means little; the status of the office itself is his object. Loyalty, unity, program or doctrine, party image: these dimensions will not be important for the patricipant who seeks status. Getting himself into office *is* the basic reason why he is in politics. Consequently, leaders with a status incentive are favorably disposed to become factionalists if it is to their private advantage.[1]

PUNISHMENT FOR FACTIONALISTS

The nature of incentives is also likely to affect the pattern of punishments dealt out to factionalists. These punishments will, in turn, affect the risks (costs) of opposing the official party nominee and therefore affect factionalism. Essentially, the idea of punishment for factionalists rests upon the view that the party collectivity has value and therefore injuries to that collectivity are "crimes."

If the leadership incentive is status, the party collectivity has little

---

1. To avoid making the discussion too complicated, I shall not include an explicit analysis of the role of active followers. The basic outlines of such an analysis are perhaps self-evident: active followers with a program incentive will resist factionalists; active followers with an employment incentive will support factionalists if they can satisfy their need for employment.

value and leaders will not be inclined to establish punishments for factionalism. Punishing a factionalist, it should be noted, always entails a cost for those who must punish: they incur the antipathy of the victim. Leaders with a program incentive are willing to accept this onus to protect the party over the long run. But leaders with a status incentive, seeking their own immediate advancement, do not want to reject any potential support.

Experience in Colombia illustrates this hypothesis. The factionalist, although he might receive admonitions and pleas from national faction leadership before the election, is accepted back into the faction whether he wins or not. He is taken back because the leaders of the faction want to have his electoral strength and his vote (if he won). To refuse him, while it might be salutory for the long-run interest of the party or national faction, has the immediate effect of driving the factionalist into the camp of political opponents. Since leaders are interested in their own personal advancement, they are not disposed to make the sacrifice of refusing the support of an ex-factionalist in order to strengthen the party or national faction in the long run.

This analysis may be expanded to explain the general development of norms and techniques which prevent factionalism. A law, for example, which prohibits people from using the party label unless officially approved by the party should not be seen as the basic explanation for low factionalism in a system. Instead it is probably the result of leadership interest in protecting the party collectivity. Similarly, such things as centralized finances or a hierarchical party structure are basically the outgrowth of a desire of participants to protect the unity of the party in those cases where division damages the party collectivity. To call such norms the reasons for party unity is misleading because it does not explain why the leaders who adopt and support these practices want unity in the first place.

It is easy to see why mechanisms to prevent factionalism have not been adopted in Colombia: leaders do not want them. If an attempt were made to give one group legal control of the party label, a tremendous storm of protest would arise and politicians would endlessly bicker over who should control the label. One does not have to guess what would happen if party primary elections were used; they are already used unsuccessfully by the Liberals. Leaders who do poorly call them a fraud and a farce, then run their own lists in general elections and often win.

FACTIONALISM OF PROGRAM-MOTIVATED LEADERS

There exists, of course, the possibility of factionalism where leaders have a program incentive. In the United States, for example, groups of leaders within each party have sharp differences over civil rights policy. Such differences with the rest of the party on a policy issue might result in the presentation of competing candidacies in general elections. However, although this possibility seems credible, there is reason to doubt the existence of extensive factionalism among program-motivated leaders. For them the new policies espoused would be important, and it would be embarrassing to use the old party label. Ideological dissenters would be anxious to demonstrate their purity; they would want to appear distinct from the old party which, in their view, stands for something different and reprehensible. As a consequence, when an open division is produced by leaders with a program incentive, we would expect them to form a new party (use a new label) and not become factionalists. Policy conflicts have given rise to many new labels in the United States, including Populist, Non-Partisan League, Socialist, Progressive, Farmer-Labor, Liberal, and Prohibitionist.

If the policy conflict within the party is not severe when placed in the total context of the party program, then it seems likely that the factionalists will quickly rejoin the party. They might run in one election against the old party with the old label, but then a decision will be made. Either the new policies are different enough to merit the formation of a new party or, in the total context, they are not. As a consequence factionalism, if it occurs at all in a system where the incentive is program, will be minimal and brief. The idea of using, for years and years, the same party label to identify a basically different program would be repulsive to leaders with a program incentive.

These reflections suggest, therefore, that the semipermanent national factions (Laureanistas, Ospinistas, Oficialistas) which are characteristic of Colombian parties are not founded on policy differences.

The foregoing discussion may be summarized in several hypotheses:

H22. Factionalism will not occur where party identification is low.

H23. Where party identification of the electorate is high and the incentive for leaders is program, factionalism will not be prevalent.

H24. Where party identification of the electorate is high and the incentive for leaders is status, factionalism will be prevalent.

Before discussing the extent of factionalism in Colombia, we should examine the evidence for the conclusion that party identification is high. Ideally, party identification is determined by a public opinion poll in which respondents are asked if they consider themselves Republicans, Democrats, Independents, or something else. Since I have not conducted a poll, indirect evidence must be employed to determine the approximate degree of party identification. One indication of high party identification is the stability of the party vote from election to election. If voters are identified with the labels, the vote given to those labels will be relatively constant over a period of time in a given town or region. If voters are not identified, then the vote of each party in a region may fluctuate wildly, being affected by issues, candidates, and the pattern of campaigning.

In spite of the changes in party regime, partial frauds, intimidation, violence, migration, social and economic change, and simply the passage of time, a number of departments have retained party majorities election after election. Antioquia, at least since 1867–80, has been Conservative. Atlántico, Cauca, Valle, Cundinamarca, and Tolima have produced substantial Liberal majorities in all the clearly competitive elections since 1930 (1930, 1946, 1947, 1958, 1960, 1962, 1964). Huila has maintained a moderate Conservative majority during the same period.

A more detailed demonstration of the stability of the party vote comes from comparing the proportion of the vote given to one party in different towns in two successive elections. I have made such a comparison for 20 randomly selected towns (electorates from 600 to 3,500) in the department of Cundinamarca for the elections of 1962 and 1964. By plotting the Liberal percentage of the total vote in

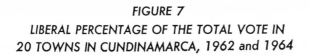

FIGURE 7

LIBERAL PERCENTAGE OF THE TOTAL VOTE IN
20 TOWNS IN CUNDINAMARCA, 1962 and 1964

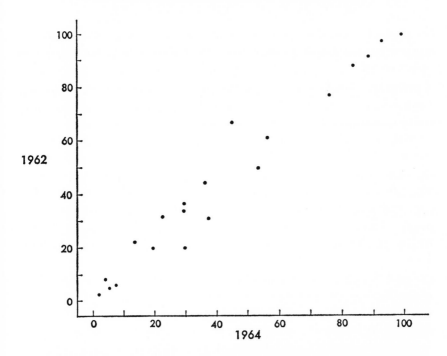

Source: Compiled from data given in *Organización y Estadísticas Electorales* for 1962 and
1964. The results for the elections to the House of Representatives were used in both cases.
The 20 towns were selected alphabetically, Agua de Dios through Chocontá.

1962 against the Liberal percentage in 1964, a scatter diagram can
be constructed as shown in Figure 7. If the proportion of Liberal vote
from election to election varied widely and randomly, then the dots,
each representing a town, would be randomly distributed. If the
proportion of the Liberal vote was constant in each town from
election to election, then the dots should fall on a perfectly straight
line. The association produced in Figure 7, while not perfect, is quite
close, particularly when one realizes that turnout in the 1964 election
declined by about 35 per cent in these towns. Such a change in turnout introduces fluctuations since members of each party may not stop
voting in exactly equal proportions in each town.

Another piece of indirect evidence for high party identification comes from a survey of 400 students at the National University in Bogotá. Asked to identify the political party of their parents, 59.2 per cent said Liberal and 28.7 per cent said Conservative.[2] Although students at the National University are not representative of the electorate, their parents, most of whom have not attended university, do represent an approximate sample of the medium urban strata. Since it seems generally true that identification is somewhat over-stated when assessed by others, the party identification of the parents is probably slightly less than the 88 per cent reported by the students. On the basis of this and electoral evidence we may conclude that the party identification of the Colombian electorate is quite high.[3]

Ever since the political parties emerged over a hundred years ago, factionalism has been their typical state. During the second half of the nineteenth century, competing factions emerged in both parties. The Liberals had their *Gólgotas, Draconianos, Radicales,* and *Nuñistas.* The Conservatives frequently divided in presidential elections during the period 1869–80 and finally, upon gaining the presidency in the 1890s, split into two factions known as *Nacionalistas* and *Históricos.* In recent times the Conservative split between Laureanistas and Ospinistas (*Doctrinarios* and *Unionistas,* as they are sometimes called) dates from about 1951; the Liberal split between Oficialistas and Movimiento Revolucionario Liberal dates from about 1959.

In the twentieth century one party or the other has divided, in presidential elections, in 1903, 1918, 1930, 1942, 1946, 1958, 1962, and 1966. But the other presidential elections were not bi-

2. "La Universidad de Espaldas al Sistema" in *Acción Liberal,* August 1965, p. 79. The survey was made by Fadul, Peñalosa, and Associates and was presented by Mario Latorre Rueda. The students *themselves* expressed their sympathies thus:

None	22.0%	Christian Democrat	13.5%
Liberal (all types)	24.7	Communist	7.7
Conservative	3.7	Nationalist	4.5
Socialist	15.7	Others, no answer	8.0

3. Local observers have generally noted the high party identification in Colombia: "Each Colombian adds to his own characteristics as a distinctive essential of his personality the belonging, from the cradle, to one of the two traditional parties into which public opinion is divided." Rafael Azula Barrera, *De La Revolución al Orden Nuevo* (Bogotá, Editorial Kelly, 1956), p. 11. See also Guillermo Hernández Rodríguez, *La Alternación Ante el Pueblo* (Bogotá, Editorial América Libre, 1962), p. 168; Sánchez, *Sociología Política Colombiana,* pp. 5–6.

polar. There were no general presidential elections in 1910 or 1954; in the elections of 1914, 1926, 1934, 1938 and 1949 there was only one candidate. In spite of the manifest existence of only two parties, Colombia has had only one presidential election in this century which was fought along party lines, with two candidates, one Conservative and one Liberal, that of 1922.

It is difficult to obtain data on factionalism in local elections prior to 1949. Sources indicate that there were competing lists in some departmental elections in the Conservative party during the 1920s and in the 1929 elections.[4] In the 1947 and 1949 congressional elections the Liberals, while locked in a desperate battle with the Conservatives, presented two or even three competing lists in most departments.[5] Since the Frente Nacional was established in 1958 factionalism at the departmental level has, for reasons I shall examine, increased substantially. It is not unusual to find as many as ten to twelve competing lists of candidates for the House of Representatives all using the same label. Although the third party, ANAPO, is both small and focused on a living man, Gustavo Rojas Pinilla, it has not been immune to factionalism. In the 1964 elections for representatives, a dissident ANAPO list appeared in Cundinamarca (it got only 825 votes), and in Caldas (it got 374 votes).[6]

It might be argued that factionalism at the department level is not the result of the status incentive, but rather could be a conscious strategy adopted by program-motivated leaders seeking to obtain more seats for their national faction. This argument would rest on the observation that, given the electoral system in use in Colombia, a party or national faction could increase its seats by dividing its votes between two or more lists. That factionalism is a conscious strategy to increase representation is, however, not true.

For one thing, the complexities of the electoral system and the elections make it practically impossible to use a multiple-list strategy

4. Guillermo Salamanca, *La República Liberal, 1,* 41; Aquilino Gaitán P., *Por Qué Cayó el Partido Conservador* (Bogotá, Talleres "Mundo al Día," 1935), pp. 27–30, 36–43.
5. *Semana,* March 29, 1947, pp. 5–6; records of the Registraduría Nacional del Estado Civil.
6. Registraduría Nacional del Estado Civil, *Organización y Estadísticas Electorales, 1964* (Bogotá, 1965), pp. 14, 22. Unless otherwise noted, 1964 electoral data given below are compiled from this source.

to advantage. With the list system of proportional representation employed in Colombia, it can be seen in retrospect that a national faction might have gained a seat through factionalism.[7] Instead of giving all its votes to one list, it could give a second list enough votes to gain a seat on the second, smaller, quotient. But in order to use a multiple-list strategy to advantage, one must know the following facts before the election: (1) the total vote (on your side of the Liberal-Conservative barrier); (2) the total number of lists other factions will present; (3) the total votes these other lists will receive; (4) the total vote you will receive. In addition one must control (5) the number of lists your national faction presents, and (6) the number of votes each of your lists receives. Since national faction leaders seldom know these things or control the number of their lists and votes, a multiple-list strategy cannot be used to advantage.

In fact, leaders generally believe, rightly, that factionalism hurts the party or national faction. They know that if a list does not get beyond a certain number of votes (between 3,000 and 10,000 in the 1964 elections for representatives) then it can only be injurious since it will not win and will draw away votes from the other list(s) of the national faction. At election time feeble attempts are made by leaders of national factions to discourage factionalism, but the national directorates are hesitant to make energetic condemnations of specific factionalists since they would have little effect except to alienate the leaders involved.

In investigating the 1964 elections I encountered only four cases of explicit condemnation of factionalists by the Officialist Liberal national directorate: Jorge Mojica Márquez (who won) and Gustavo Humberto Rodríguez (who lost) in Boyacá;[8] and Rafael Isidro Rodríguez (who lost) and Nestor Urbano Tenorio (who lost) in Valle.[9] None of the candidacies was withdrawn following the denunciation. That three out of four lost indicates little about the effectiveness of denunciation since the national directorate attacked only those factionalists who already appeared weak. In a number of instances the national directorate formally approves of factionalism,

7. The electoral system can be described as a list system of PR with a simple quota and largest remainders. The mechanics are described in C. G. Hoag and H. H. Hallett, *Proportional Representation* (New York, Macmillan, 1926), p. 414.

8. *El Tiempo,* March 14, 1964, p. 21.

9. *El Espectador,* March 14, 1964, p. 14.

in spite of the bad image it gives the national faction. In the 1964 elections for representatives, the Officialist Liberal national directorate publicly approved competing lists in the departments of Chocó, Atlántico, and Nariño.[10] The general leadership attitude is that factionalism is undesirable but that it really cannot be fought effectively.

Leaders are correct in judging factionalism to be destructive to their respective national factions. In the 1964 elections to the House of Representatives, the Officialist Liberals lost to their opponents (MRL and ANAPO running lists on the Liberal side of the Liberal–Conservative barrier) several seats through division at the local level: one seat in Norte de Santander, one seat in Santander, and one seat in Valle. In no department did the factionalism of Officialist Liberals gain them more seats than they would have had by running only one list.

On the Conservative side, the Frente Nacional Conservatives (Ospinistas, Laureanistas, and Alzatistas) who united momentarily on the national level lost to ANAPO through factionalism: one seat in Antioquia, one seat in Nariño, and two (both) seats in Meta. Although in the department of Valle one seat was gained by factionalism this division was clearly not a conscious strategy. The victorious list was that of the *Movimiento de Restauración Conservadora* of César Tulio Delgado who, as the "restoration" title indicates, campaigned against the supposed decadence of the regular party.

The case of Meta noted above illustrates the extreme lack of interest most leaders have in the fate of their party. In the department of Meta only two representatives are elected on each side of the Liberal–Conservative barrier. A plurality system is used here so that the list with the most votes gets both seats. The Conservatives, with almost twice as many votes as ANAPO divided three ways, and ANAPO won both seats: [11]

Conservatives			ANAPO
List 1	List 2	List 3	List 1
3,118	2,904	2,175	4,154

10. *El Tiempo*, March 15, 1964, p. 20; *El Espectador*, March 14, 1964, p. 12.
11. *Organización y Estadísticas Electorales, 1964*, p. 31.

The Conservatives were undoubtedly aware of the possibility that ANAPO could win, but each faction was willing to risk a party defeat in the hope that it would gain the plurality and win both seats. Local factionalism, then, is not a conscious strategy adopted by leaders to gain more seats. It is destructive to the party (or, under the Frente Nacional, to the national faction) and leaders know it.

Most observers, Colombians and foreigners, have not made the obvious deduction about the Colombian system from the patent fact of endemic factionalism. What does it mean when a leader who claims to have a radically new program for the salvation of the country continues to run on the old party label? What does it mean when leaders of a national faction, who say they have a new and vitally important program, subdivide in local elections, thus giving the movement an image of "squabbling opportunists" and endangering the faction's chances to win seats?

The answer seems quite clear. Leaders are disregarding party, national faction, and alleged programs for their own private benefit. Such behavior is inconsistent with the proposition that either parties or national factions have "profound ideological differences." In analyzing American politics we frequently assume that politicians are maximizing only their officeholding opportunities. But as I hope to make clear in this study, the behavior of politicians who *really* seek office for private benefit contrasts markedly with how American leaders behave.

In the analysis of American national party conventions, for example, we occasionally accept the assumption that participants (delegates) are motivated by a pure sort of selfishness. We suppose they want to nominate a winner to receive patronage from him. But we have overlooked the explanation for the very existence of the convention as a viable, decision-making body. As the experience in Colombia dramatically illustrates, party conventions will be institutions for settling intraparty disputes only if party leaders find the value of the party collectivity greater than the value of private, personal rewards.

In Colombia the national party convention has been a recent and imperfect development. The Conservatives, prior to the late 1940s, attempted to nominate presidential candidates by the congressional party. The Liberals used small conventions (10 to 20 delegates) of top party leaders in the last century; by the 1940s these had grown much larger (over 100 delegates) and included leaders from all departments.[12] But party conventions have not been successful in preventing the emergence of competing candidacies. In 1946 Liberal Jorge Eliécer Gaitán and his group simply refused to accept the decision of the Liberal convention to nominate Gabriel Turbay. In 1962 Conservative Jorge Leyva refused to accept the Conservative convention's nomination of Guillermo Valencia. In practice, party conventions, both national and departmental, have not served to heal divisions. If a division exists, then the convention is attended only by members of one faction and the other faction stays away. For example, Mariano Ospina and his group refused to attend the Conservative convention on November 20, 1964, because it was dominated by Lauro-alzatistas.[13] Thus the practice is for each national faction to hold its own convention, and conventions reaffirm rather than heal party divisions.

In concluding this discussion of factionalism I should note that the hypothesis (H24) predicting factionalism where the incentive is status and party identification is high also appears to apply to Uruguay. Party identification is high in Uruguay and the dominant incentive for leaders is status; and Uruguayan parties are characterized by rampant factionalism.[14]

THE DISTRIBUTION OF ADVANTAGE

Up to this point I have mentioned only one structural variable affecting factionalism, the degree of party identification. By directing attention to incentives, I have attempted to provide a basic explanation for a broad, enduring contrast in the amount of factionalism in Colombia compared to the United States or Great Britain. The

12. *Semana*, March 1, 1947, pp. 6–7, and May 7, 1949; Eduardo Rodríguez Piñeres, *Diez Años de Política Liberal, 1892–1902* (Bogotá, Librería Colombiana, 1945), pp. 7, 41; Aquilino Gaitán, pp. 66–67.

13. *El Tiempo*, November 16, 1964, p. 1.

14. Taylor, *Government and Politics in Uruguay*, pp. 59 ff. We might also suspect that the hypothesis is consistent with the persistent factionalism which has taken place under the label *"Radical"* in Argentina since the 1890s; see Peter G. Snow, *Argentine Radicalism: The History and Doctrine of the Radical Civic Union* (Iowa City, University of Iowa Press, 1965).

analysis may be refined, however, by inspecting certain structural variables which encourage or discourage factionalism.

Many structural arrangements, of a legal, social, or political nature, affect the distribution of advantages for the potential factionalists. These arrangements make it more or less difficult to win as a factionalist and thereby increase or decrease the amount of factionalism. If a new electoral law makes it easier for a factionalist to win than before, for example, we would predict that more participants would take their chances as factionalists. This observation can be applied to other party phenomena as well, such as the formation of new parties. If structural changes cause the distribution of advantage to shift in favor of the leaders of the new parties, then more new parties will appear.

These reflections are subject to an important qualification: they assume that participants are seeking to advance their personal careers; they assume that the leader is calculating only the risks and gains to his own career so that as soon as being a factionalist becomes less risky and more profitable he will respond accordingly. But if the participants are not primarily interested in their own personal advancement, they will be much less responsive to changes in the distribution of advantage. If participants already find the value of the party collectivity greater than the value of office per se, they will tend to ignore structural changes which make it easier for the factionalist to win office. These two different perspectives are a direct consequence of the nature of incentives, so we may formulate the hypotheses:

> *H25. Where the incentive for leaders is status, leaders will be relatively sensitive to (changes in) the distribution of advantage for factionalists or new party leaders.*
>
> *H26. Where the incentive for leaders is program, leaders will be relatively insensitive to (changes in) the distribution of advantage for factionalists or new party leaders.*

With these two fundamental hypotheses a wide range of specific phenomena may be analyzed.

One general condition is the concentration or dispersion of administrative resources (appointments, jobs, favors, electoral machinery, etc.). If these resources are concentrated in the hands of one clique of party leaders, factionalists are discouraged because they cannot easily gain the resources to win in elections. Moreover, if they stay with the leading clique, their chances for advancement are greater since that clique monopolizes the advantages. Consequently we may advance the hypothesis:

> *H25a. In a system where status is the incentive for leaders, factionalism will increase as administrative resources are more dispersed among competing groups.*

This hypothesis has a direct application to the effect of the Frente Nacional on factionalism. In essence, what the Frente Nacional has done is to make the construction of national or departmental monopolies of political resources almost impossible. By the requirements of parity between the parties at every level (ministers, governors, departmental secretaries, mayors, municipal secretaries) it has become difficult to construct a cohesive clique of public officials which would dominate a region.

A governor must appoint his departmental secretaries from both parties, as must mayors. Furthermore, since these executives are sensitive to the distribution of seats among the various factions in departmental assemblies and city councils, the major national factions all tend to get a share of administrative resources, including both high appointive positions and jobs for active followers. Finally, the balanced distribution of forces provides freedom from official harassment and reasonably fair elections for even the most insignificant factionalist. This is not to say that administrative resources are removed from the electoral context or distributed evenly to all possible factionalists. But compared to pre-Frente Nacional days, considerable dispersion of these resources has taken place.

Consequently, predicting by hypothesis H25a, factionalism should have increased under the Frente Nacional. In Table 9.2 I have computed the average number of lists presented for elections for representatives in the departments. Consistent with the hypothesis, the number of lists has increased substantially in the Frente Nacional elections (1958, 1960, 1962, 1964), compared to the number of lists in the pre-Frente Nacional election of 1949.

Two other applications of the distribution-of-advantage hypothesis (H25) can be noted in Table 9.2. First, it appears that the party with a president coming to office or in office exhibits a depressed level of factionalism. In 1949, when a Conservative president was in office and another Conservative appeared to be coming to office, the Conservatives had almost no factionalism. In 1958 the Liberals, who had a president coming to office, exhibited a lower level of factionalism than the Conservatives. The presidential effect on factionalism is still noticeable in later elections although other conditions obscure the magnitude of the changes. The Conservatives exhibited a depressed level of factionalism in 1962 and 1964 with Conservative President Valencia respectively coming to office and in office.

TABLE 9.2

Factionalism at the Departmental Level:
Elections for Representatives, 1949–1964

| Year | Average number of lists per department | | Total |
	Liberals	Conservatives	
Pre-Frente Nacional			
1949*	2.2	1.1	3.3
Frente Nacional			
1958	1.6	3.1	4.7
1960	3.8	2.9	6.7
1962**	5.0	2.7	7.7
1964**	6.3	3.5	9.8
1966 prediction	6.0	5.0	11.0

*Only the 15 departments in existence in 1949 are included. Regions which have been made departments after that time are left out of the computation.

**None of the ANAPO lists in 1962 and 1964 is included in the tabulation. ANAPO lists registered both as Conservative and as Liberal, as well as dissident ANAPO lists, are considered third party lists and therefore are neither Liberal nor Conservative. Hence, if no factionalism had taken place in either party, the average number of lists should be 1.0, and the average number of total lists should be 2.0 per department.

Source: Figures compiled from records of the Registraduría Nacional del Estado Civil; figures for 1962 and 1964 were compiled from the bound publications of the Registraduría, *Organización y Estadísticas Electorales* for 1962 and 1964.

The president-to-be has the ability to discourage factionalists through his control of appointments. Staying with the party is more profitable and opposing it more costly when that party has a president coming to office or in office (but not leaving office). In effect, he alters the distribution of opportunity against the factionalist in his party. The dispersion of administrative resources caused by the

Frente Nacional has, of course, reduced the president's ability to deter factionalists.

Another condition affecting the distribution of opportunity can be discerned from the figures in Table 9.2: the impact of priests. In many areas priests influence the voting of their parishioners and thus act to congeal the electorate into a limited number of blocs. This makes it more difficult for the upstart factionalist to gain voters in an energetic street campaign. Of course, priests frequently support different factions and their effect is, in any case, not conclusive. But nevertheless they reduce the number of "free-floating" voters and thus make factionalism somewhat more difficult. Since most priests are Conservatives, we would expect the stabilizing impact of clerical intervention to be felt most in the Conservative party. As a consequence, Conservatives should have a lower, long-run level of factionalism.

Examination of Table 9.2 bears out this expectation. In 1960 the presidential effect favored lower factionalism of the Liberals. But actually the Liberals had a slightly higher amount of factionalism than the Conservatives since the clerical effect depressed factionalism in the Conservative party. In the 1962 and 1964 elections when both the presidential effect and the clerical effect operated to depress Conservative factionalism, that party had markedly lower factionalism than the Liberals. In 1966 the presidential and clerical effects were out of phase again and we should find, when the data are compiled, approximately equal amounts of factionalism in both parties (see 1966 prediction in Table 9.2).

AUSTRIA: A COMPARISON

The increasing factionalism in Colombia under the Frente Nacional contrasts sharply with the experience of the Austrian parties under a similar arrangement. After the end of World War II the Austrians adopted an arrangement under which the two major parties, the Socialist party and the People's party, governed in coalition, sharing political offices. The arrangement provided that both parties had to concur if government action were to take place.[15]

Under the coalition system the Austrian parties appeared to re-

15. The coalition was broken in April 1966 by the decision of the People's party to run the government independently.

main as immune to factionalism as before. Each party was united and well-disciplined, despite the discomforts of acceding to compromise solutions. The lines of conflict remained as before. The Socialists opposed the People's party, conflict taking place over differing proposals for government policy. To settle differences, a system known as "Junktim" was adopted, which identified the compromise position on the basis of the electoral returns in the most recent election. If, for example, the Socialist vote had declined in the last election, the compromise solution would move more toward the position of the People's party.[16]

The investigator might expect to find in Colombia similar mechanisms for settling disputes between the parties on policy matters. But in fact, the Colombian coalition bears almost no resemblance to the Austrian one. The parties are divided and conflict takes place along factional lines within these parties. Policy conflicts are hardly discernible; they certainly do not occur between the parties. The explanation for this contrast lies, I believe, in the nature of incentives in the two systems. In Austria the apparent dominant incentive for leaders is program. The satisfactions of leaders come primarily from shaping or attempting to shape society in accordance with their ideals.[17] As a consequence the adoption of a coalition system did not produce factionalism or alter lines of party conflict. The program-motivated Austrian leaders valued the party collectivity and, with minor exceptions, continued within their respective parties and remained willing to discipline party rebels.

THE DISTRIBUTION OF ADVANTAGE IN DIFFERENT DEPARTMENTS

What differences are there in factionalism in the different Colombian departments? Our interest in this question stems from the im-

16. See: Frederick C. Engelmann, "Haggling for the Equilibrium: the Renegotiation of the Austrian Coalition, 1959," *American Political Science Review, 56* (1962), 651–62; Herbert P. Secher, "Coalition Government: The Case of the Second Austrian Republic," *American Political Science Review, 52* (1958), 791–808; Charles A. Gulick, "Austria's Socialists in the Trend Toward A Two-Party System: An Interpretation of Postwar Elections," *Western Political Quarterly, 9* (1958), 539–62.

17. See Charles A. Gulick, *Austria from Hapsburg to Hitler* (2 vols. Berkeley, University of California Press, 1948).

portance given Antioquia as a deviant case. I have observed that in Antioquia the dominant incentive, while still status, tends to be closer to the program side of the status–program continuum (see Figure 1, Chapter 1) than in the rest of the country. We should expect then, by hypotheses H23 and H24, that Antioquia will have relatively less factionalism than other departments.

Taking first the number of lists presented in departmental elections as the measurement of factionalism, we encounter a difficult problem. Table 9.3 presents the number of lists registered in the legislative

TABLE 9.3

Local Factionalism in Each Department:
Elections for Representatives, 1949–1964

Number of lists, both parties*

Department	Election year					Total lists, five elections
	1949	1958	1960	1962	1964	
1. Atlántico	5	5	10	17	13	50
2. Nariño	4	4	11	9	16	44
3. Boyacá	3	4	7	13	13	40
4. Cundinamarca	3	7	7	6	15	38
5. Magdalena	6	6	7	8	9	36
6. Bolívar	3	4	8	9	10	34
7. Antioquia	3	4	7	7	12	33
8. Valle	3	5	5	7	10	30
9. Caldas	2	4	5	6	11	28
10. Norte de Santander	2	4	6	7	9	28
11. Santander	4	6	5	6	7	28
12. Tolima	3	4	7	7	6	27
13. Huila	3	4	6	4	6	23
14. Chocó	3	5	4	5	5	22
15. Cauca	2	4	5	4	5	20

*All ANAPO lists have been excluded from the tabulation.

elections in each department. A department in which no factionalism had occurred would have seen, in each election, only two lists, one Conservative and one Liberal (ANAPO lists are excluded from the tabulation). Thus the total number of lists would be ten had there been no factionalism in any of the five elections. As is immediately apparent from the variations present, a number of structural conditions, both circumstantial and long-term, may affect the distribution of opportunity for factionalists in each department. Consequently the effect of a possible difference in incentives between Antioquia and other departments would be obscured by variations in these structural features.

What are these structural variables? We note that the three departments with lowest factionalism are all backward, with small urban centers and little industrialization. But when an attempt is made to correlate factionalism with industrialization, urbanization, or literacy, no significant association is found. Nariño, Boyacá, and Magdalena, for example, are also backward departments but they exhibit high factionalism. One thinks of many other conditions which might affect factionalism: topography, family patterns, municipal administration, patterns of agricultural exploitation, and so on. There are also temporary political conditions: the presence of one popular leader, a particular falling-out of some leaders, a coalescence of other leaders. Finally, there is a general problem: how dispersed (or neutral) are the administrative resources in each department? Unfortunately I do not know which variables affect interdepartmental distributions of opportunity, let alone how to measure them. Consequently there is, for the moment, no way of knowing whether Antioquia has less factionalism, as measured by the number of local lists, when variables affecting the distribution of opportunity are held constant. I do not know how to hold these variables constant.

On another measurement of factionalism, support for "dissident" presidential candidates, results are more encouraging. If it is true that Antioqueños are less prone to factionalism, then their support for dissident presidential candidates should be less. Party leaders will show a somewhat greater interest in the party collectivity and will be more inclined to support the "official" party nominee. Their support, in turn, would produce a greater vote for this nominee and a relatively smaller vote for the "dissident." The "official" party candidate can be identified as the man chosen by the customary nominating process.

The two presidential elections which can be employed for this purpose are those of 1930 and 1946. In 1930 the Conservative congressional party chose Guillermo Valencia as the nominee; Alfredo Vásquez Cobo was the dissident. In 1946 the Liberal party convention chose Gabriel Turbay; Jorge Gaitán was the dissident.

In this demonstration we are able to eliminate many of the circumstantial variables since the elections are sixteen years apart and occur
in different parties. If a department gave relatively little support to
the dissident in *both* elections, we might conclude that the party collectivity has somewhat greater value for leaders in that department.

In Table 9.4 the results of these two elections are compiled. When
each department is given a combined score for both elections
(the sum of the department's rank in 1930 and in 1946) Antioquia
ranks first, as the only department which gave markedly little support
to both dissidents. I should note, incidentally, that a similar result
can be obtained from analysis of the 1962 presidential elections.

TABLE 9.4

*Support for Dissident Presidential Candidates,
1930 and 1946, by Department*

Department	1930 Proportion of Conservative vote to dissident (%)	Rank	1946 Proportion of Liberal vote to dissident (%)	Rank	Total score*
1. Antioquia	15	3	9	1	4
2. Caldas	39	7	24	3	10
3. Santander	55	8	11	2	10
4. Magdalena	6	1	54	10	11
5. Norte de Santander	34	6	39	6	12
6. Cauca	24	5	52	8	13
7. Bolívar	6	2	76	13	15
8. Tolima	57	9	49	7	16
9. Boyacá	77	12	24	5	17
10. Nariño	79	13	24	4	17
11. Atlántico	20	4	83	14	18
12. Valle	59	11	53	9	20
13. Huila	58	10	70	12	22
14. Cundinamarca	83	14	68	11	25

*The total score is simply the sum of the rank in 1930 and the department's
rank in 1946. The lower the rank or total score, the less support given by party
voters to the dissident. Substantially the same final result could have been
achieved by adding the percentage of party vote received by the dissident in
each election.

Source: Compiled from election results given in *Estadística Electoral*, supplement to Nos. 37 to 39 of *Anales de Economía y Estadística*, July 1948, pp.
22–23.

Although some adjustment of the figures are necessary to correct for the bipartisan nature of the Valencia candidacy, it can be demonstrated that dissident Conservative Jorge Leyva got less Conservative support in Antioquia than in almost any other department.

Other evidence about factionalism in Antioquia conforms to our expectation of lower division in that department. For example, when the Lauro-alzatista Conservative directorate was established in November 1964, formalizing a split with the Ospinistas, competing Conservative directorates soon appeared in most of the other departments, including Tolima, Cundinamarca, and Valle. Antioquia, however, managed to exist with a united Conservative party as late as August 1965. When the Lauro-alzatistas came in and held their own convention to establish a separate directorate, *La República,* in its editorial condemning the division, first noted: "The Conservatives of Antioquia have been, throughout history, the most homogeneous and best disciplined in the country." [18] A number of leaders, in Antioquia and outside, confirmed this observation.[19]

We might cautiously conclude, then, that factionalism does tend to be somewhat lower in Antioquia. This observation, however, is tempered by the complexities inherent in accounting for interdepartmental comparisons of factionalism.

INCENTIVES AND PARTY SYSTEM ANALYSIS

The preceding discussion has been confined to the phenomenon of factionalism within political parties. We can extend the analysis to another feature of party systems: the number of parties. My purpose will not be to construct any complete theory of party development, but rather to illustrate the importance that incentives must have in any such theory.

18. *La República,* August 15, 1965, p. 4.
19. It is significant to note that in Antioquia the Conservative leaders were much more inclined to avoid denominations of factions. Of the 11 Antioqueño Conservatives responding to my survey, six refused to choose either "Lauro-alzatista Conservative" or "Ospinista Conservative" to identfy themselves, but instead wrote in "simply Conservative," or "independent Conservative." Out of the 59 Conservatives in the rest of the sample, only three identified themselves as "independent Conservatives" (See Appendix Table 1).

The best-known hypothesis advanced to explain the number of political parties in a country is the electoral system hypothesis. This states that the use of a single-member, single-ballot election system will give rise to only two parties, but the use of a system of proportional representation will result in many parties. The electoral system hypothesis rests upon the assumption that if an electoral system reduces the representation given to a party, then voters will desert that party, causing it to disappear. If, for example, an attempt is made to establish a third party where the single-member district system is used, this attempt will fail, the theory runs, because until the party grows large enough to win a plurality in the district, votes for it are wasted. In order not to waste their votes, voters decline to support the third party and vote for one of the two major parties which have a chance of winning.

If proportional representation is used, however, votes for small parties are not wasted. They are added up over a large circumscription which elects many representatives, and even a small party will get some representation. Consequently, voters are not wasting their votes and they will continue to support (begin to support) small third or fourth parties. Thus a system of proportional representation will produce a multiparty system.[20]

The electoral system hypothesis overlooks, however, the impact of incentives on the behavior of leaders and active followers. Indeed, it ignores participants completely, treating them as a constant in any system. But it does seem clear that they constitute the backbone of any political party. If there are many leaders and active followers willing to fight long and hard, their party probably will gather a significant electorate. Whether such participants are numerous and determined, however, will depend on the nature of their incentives as well as the distribution of opportunity afforded by the electoral system. If leaders and active followers are motivated by a program in-

20. I have made this presentation quite brief since I suppose readers to be familiar with the arguments involved. For full treatments of the electoral system hypothesis see: Maurice Duverger, *Political Parties*, trans. Barbara and Robert North (2d ed. London, Methuen, 1959), pp. 206 ff; John G. Grumm, "Theories of Electoral Systems," *Midwest Journal of Political Science*, 2 (1958), 357–76; Donald V. Smiley, "The Two-Party System and One-Party Dominance," *Canadian Journal of Economics and Political Science*, 24 (1958), 312–22; G. E. Lavau, *Partis Politique et Réalités Sociales* (Paris, 1953).

centive, they are likely to be willing to sustain their party in spite of electoral disadvantages. Such participants are seeking the realization of certain policy preferences and not private rewards of officeholding. They will not give up the fight simply because the electoral system discriminates against them at the moment.

This may be an explanation for the rise of, for example, the British Labor party. According to the electoral system hypothesis, the Labor party should not have grown and survived, since for years (1910–24) it suffered underrepresentation in terms of votes. If the leaders had been interested primarily in getting themselves into office, they would have given up and entered one of the other parties. But, I strongly suspect, their incentive was program; consequently they were not sensitive to the disadvantages laid on them by the electoral system (see hypothesis H26). Indeed, there are a number of exceptions to the electoral system hypothesis in Europe itself where many parties arose under the disadvantages of a plurality system and *then* proportional representation was adopted.[21] I suspect that these cases would be consistent with an hypothesis that made electoral systems irrelevant to the number of parties where the incentive for leaders is program.

When the incentive for leaders is status, however, we should expect the electoral system hypothesis to apply. A system of proportional representation distributes advantage in favor of the founders of new parties. If these founders hold a status incentive, they will respond to the new opportunities, as suggested in hypothesis H25. But this expectation overlooks one more point: *a party label, if many voters are identified with it, is itself an advantage.* If a system has only two parties to begin with and identification with those party labels is high, then it requires leaders with a program incentive to break out and establish a third party, even with proportional representation. In renouncing the use of the old label, the politician is renouncing votes. If he is seeking status, then it is inefficient to struggle to establish a new party label.

The unsuccessful efforts of Jorge Gaitán to found a third party in the 1930s and of ex-minister of war Alberto Ruiz Novoa to establish a new political organization in 1965 illustrate the drawbacks of rejecting old, vote-getting labels. The new leader cannot persuade

---

21. See the excellent research on this matter by Grumm.

enough leaders (and active followers) to fight an uphill battle with him—and indeed he may have little interest in an uphill fight himself. Gaitán deserted his *Unión Nacional Izquierdista Revolucionaria* after two years of difficult going to accept a position on the Liberal list of representatives.[22] Ruiz deserted his *Movimiento Democrático Nacional* to become a Liberal after five months of unpromising effort.[23]

This analysis goes far to explain why Colombia, which has employed a system of proportional representation since 1910,[24] has seen no third parties—a direct contradiction of the electoral system hypothesis. A third party did not arise in Colombia not because leaders were insensitive to the distribution of advantage, but precisely the opposite. Colombian politicians have realized that the established labels confer votes, and these votes are more important to them than alleged policy conflicts with other party leaders.

ANAPO: THE MAGNETISM OF AN EX-PRESIDENT

Recently it has become somewhat inaccurate to say that Colombia has only two parties, for there now exists a third of significant strength, ANAPO (*Alianza Nacional Popular*). The ANAPO was founded by and is built upon the name of Gustavo Rojas Pinilla, ousted from the presidency in the coup of 1957. In 1962 it received 4 per cent of the total vote, in 1964, 14 per cent, and in 1966, 18 per cent.[25] The Frente Nacional arrangements have been of great assistance to this party by providing a relatively free electoral climate; and the proportional representation system has benefited it.

In elections under the Frente Nacional there compete legally only two parties, Liberal and Conservative. No other party can run in the elections. However, it is a simple matter to legally register lists of a

22. J. A. Osorio Lizarazo, *Gaitán* (Buenos Aires, Ediciones López Negri, 1952), pp. 161–75.

23. *El Espectador,* May 10, 1965, p. 1; *El Tiempo,* May 10, 1965, p. 29. Oddly enough, after trying to disband the MDN, Ruiz, at the urgent behest of those he left stranded, apparently continued to play a figurehead role in the waning movement; see *El Tiempo,* August 27, 1965, p. 32.

24. Samper Bernal, *Breve Historia Constitucional y Política de Colombia,* p. 159. From 1910 to 1930 a modified plurality system that assured representation to the runner-up was employed; since 1930 full PR has been used. See Dix, *Colombia: The Political Dimensions of Change,* pp. 130, 250.

25. *Newsweek,* April 4, 1966, p. 55.

third party as Liberal or Conservative so that in practice third parties are not impeded from running and winning. ANAPO first entered lists on the Conservative side, but in 1964 began to enter Liberal lists as well. In this way ANAPO competed for the seats available to Conservatives (one half of the total in each department) and also for the seats available to those calling themselves Liberals. Although legal registration under the old party labels may have assisted ANAPO, the organization does have a new label and therefore is a new party.

ANAPO demonstrates what seems to be the only basis for a third party in a system where party identification with two labels is high: an ex-president. As we know from studies of the American electorate, voters rely on simple cues for their choices. The only such cue with an appeal approaching that of established party labels would be a well-known name. Ex-presidents, because they are men of prestige and prominence, are therefore useful electoral material. Leaders with a status incentive will join them because they offer an opportunity for faster advancement than in an established party faction. Many ex-presidents in Colombia, even formerly unpopular ones, have returned to politics and gathered large political followings. However, most of them have been party figures and have led new factions of the old parties.

Rojas, although formerly a Conservative himself, was not a party figure. Instead of heading a faction, he created a new label. As an ex-president he attracted enough support to become a meaningful political force. That Rojas had been scorned as a corrupt dictator when removed from office and later condemned by the Senate and deprived of his citizenship rights did not deter eager supporters. For status-motivated leaders, *today* and *me* are infinitely more important than yesterday.

After three elections ANAPO has enjoyed only limited success.[26] When Rojas dies, its prospects will be extremely bleak. As soon as ANAPO *looks* as if it has no political future, it *has* no political future because leaders will desert in great haste. Since the votes of the organization are tied to a man and not so much to a party label, when that man leaves the scene many ANAPO leaders will adopt established labels once again.

26. It is, I believe, a realization that ANAPO can never carry him to the presidency which leads Rojas to agitate for a military coup.

Rojas has demonstrated, however, that an ex-president (and only an ex-president, I believe) can provide a sufficient basis for a third party in Colombia. Only the vote-getting power of an ex-president is strong enough to induce sizable numbers of leaders to relinquish the electoral appeal of established labels.

The examination of the electoral system hypothesis presented in the preceding pages illustrates the utility of incentive theory in the analysis of party systems. The changes and qualifications to this hypothesis developed here may be summarized thus:

> *H27. Where the incentive for leaders is program, the electoral system (SMSB, PR) does not affect the number of parties.*
>
> *H28. Where the incentive for leaders is status, a single-member, single ballot electoral system will lead to the formation of two parties in each district (and probably to a two-party system).*
>
> *H29. Where the incentive for leaders is status a proportional representation electoral system will produce a multiparty system if party identification is low when PR is adopted.*
>
> *H30. Where the incentive for leaders is status a proportional representation system will not produce a multiparty system if party identification with only two labels is high when PR is adopted, unless a third party be based upon an ex-president.*

It is interesting to note in passing that H30 apparently also applies to Uruguay. As I have suggested, the dominant incentive in Uruguay seems to be status, and party identification is high with only two labels. Although PR is employed in that country, the system continues to be characterized by two major parties.[27]

This analysis will, of course, require further qualification as new cases and considerations come to light. Although this particular use of incentive theory to develop hypotheses about political parties and electoral systems may be inadequate, it is difficult to see how a theory of party systems can be constructed without including incentives.

27. Taylor, pp. 19, 47, 49.

CHAPTER 10

THE PARTY SYSTEM:

II

Q. *What if there are people who want to be candidates and are not on the directorate's list?*
A. *They can launch their own candidacies as dissidents. There are a lot of these. And if the person has votes, if he has a force of his own, then he wins.*

> Interview with the president of a Conservative municipal directorate for Bogotá, (Bogotá, March 17, 1965).

The basic units of the Colombian party system are not the parties (people bearing the same label) but are, instead, the national party factions, composed of participants seeking to obtain the status of political office. This chapter advances a general hypothesis which predicts the characteristics of such factions in a system where the incentive for leaders is status, where party identification is high, and where a free political environment obtains. By "free political environment" I mean a general observance of the freedoms of speech, press, and organization and a competitive electoral climate.

DECISION-MAKING IN THE NATIONAL FACTIONS

A national faction generally has three elements: a chief who is the coordinator and spokesman of the faction and its potential presidential nominee; a national directorate composed of from three to a dozen top leaders; and a congressional group including all faction members who hold House or Senate seats. At the departmental level the leaders generally divide themselves into separate groups following national faction lines. Consequently one will find departmental directorates and legislative groups (in the state assembly) which are branches of the national factions. Even at the municipal level the national faction lines may persist, giving rise to competing cliques of leaders, each of which identifies itself as "belonging to" or "following" a distinct national party faction.

The penetration of national factions into departmental and even municipal levels is a consequence of the partial centralization of the national political structure. The president appoints governors, who in turn appoint mayors. Consequently if local leaders seek the removal of a mayor they need to influence the governor; or to remove a governor, they must influence the president. Local leaders need political support at the higher levels to make changes in their executives.

The means whereby an executive may be coerced are quite simple. Each level of government—national, departmental, and municipal—has a locally elected legislature. Each town has its locally elected town council; each department has its departmental assembly. The approval of these bodies is necessary to run the administration (budgets and taxes) and to enact laws and ordinances. Consequently legislative bodies may be used to bring the administration to a standstill. If enough assemblymen or municipal councilors vigorously oppose all measures before them, the executive is greatly handicapped, and indeed becomes practically incapable of governing.

Suppose, for example, that in a certain department the Ospinista Conservatives decide that the governor has not been responsive to their demands. Their departmental directorate then "breaks relations" with the governor. This break involves three actions: (1) the Ospinista departmental cabinet secretaries will resign; (2) the Ospinista group in the assembly will engage in bitter opposition; and (3) the Ospinista leaders on the national scene will prevail upon the president to remove the governor in question. Since the president is faced with the threat of losing the support of the Ospinistas in Congress, he will be inclined to replace the governor. Since he is faced with the threat of losing Lauro-alzatista Conservative support if he favors the Ospinistas, he will probably delay considerably before he appoints a replacement. In response to a similar conflict on the municipal level, the governor will, through similar mechanisms, be prompted to replace the mayor.

It can be seen, then, that the various directorates (or informal cliques of top leaders where a directorate is not established) play a critical decision-making role. It is they who decide if and when to break relations with an executive. In addition, the directorates usually decide which leaders shall be approved by their faction for appointment to administrative positions (ministries, departmental secretaryships, etc.). Obviously, the executives (president, governors, mayors), in order to please the factions, are responsive to their wishes about who should receive the faction's share of appointments. Finally the directorates appoint or influence the selection of subordinate directorates of the faction (national of departmental, departmental of municipal), and compose or influence the "official" faction list of candidates in elections.

Clearly, then, the directorates (or less formal groups of top leaders) are important decision-makers in party matters. Our interest in party phenomena, however, lies not so much in determining exactly who makes the decisions or the processes of decision-making as in identifying the basic forces that produce these decisions. In this way we may note the persistent, underlying characteristics of party decision-making. A first proposition is:

> *1. An individual's position in the national faction is commensurate with the electoral resources he commands.*

By "position" I mean such posts as member of a municipal, departmental directorate and candidate for various elective and appointive positions. These candidacies range from last on the list of candidates for the local city council (unlikely to win) to faction-approved candidate for appointment as minister of the national government. The above proposition suggests that getting ahead in Colombian politics depends not so much on who you are, on who your friends are, or on what you stand for, but rather upon the votes you can get.

Of course there are many ways to get votes: hard work in the local neighborhood, energetic oratory, owning or writing for a newspaper, writing a book, or simply by being a good coordinator of cliques of leaders and active followers. High status in the community—being a doctor, ex-mayor, etc.—is an electoral asset because in the status-conscious Colombian environment lower status individuals will get pleasure simply from being associated with, being known as "friends of" a higher status individual.

The basic determinant of a leader's position in the national faction is his electoral resources because ultimately the strength of the faction depends on votes. Although there are and have been many different methods of naming persons to directorates and composing lists of candidates, the result will tend to be the same under any system: positions go to those with electoral resources. There are, for example, at least five distinct methods whereby directorates may be chosen, all of which are used or have been used: (1) election by the congressional party (for national directorates); (2) primary elections within the party; (3) election by conventions; (4) appointment by the superior directorate (national of departmental, departmental of municipal); (5) appointment by the faction leader. Each of these systems has tended to produce the same results: popular leaders find themselves on the directorates.

In the event that a given system of decision-making does not produce directorates with a maximum of electoral support, the system will be changed, either formally or in practice. For example, the Liberals (later, Officialist Liberals) have had, at least since the 1940s, a system of private party primaries and successive conventions to select directorates at each level. The members of the municipal directorates are elected by a primary in which all Liberal voters were supposed to participate; the municipal directorates send a number (calculated on the size of the Liberal vote in the town) of delegates to a departmental convention where a departmental directorate is elected; each departmental directorate sends delegates to a national convention where the national directorate is elected.

But like so many paper schemes which provide for mass participation in selecting organizational leadership, the primary-convention system does not work satisfactorily. In order to vote in the party primary one has to obtain a party membership card, pay dues, and attend the election. These barriers—not to mention deliberate favoritism practiced by some party secretaries (e.g., "I'm terribly sorry we have no more membership cards; the national directorate was supposed to send us 5,000 last week")—produce primaries in which only a small fraction of the party voters participate. As a consequence those men with a good stock of membership cards and friends in local neighborhoods do well in the primaries, while intellectuals, wealthy people, and even prominent politicians, do poorly. Although there is always a need for the "local operator" on directorates, there is also a need for persons of prominence, wealth, and intellect. If the faction does not capture their resources, someone else will.

Therefore the national directorate of the Officialist Liberals was, in the 1964 party convention, formally given powers it had already exercised: authority to remake (amplify) the departmental directorates. The purpose behind this measure was to enable the national directorate to include persons with useful electoral resources who had been left off the departmental directorates owing to the vagaries of the primary election process. In this way divisions (factionalism) could be somewhat curtailed. In 1965 the national directorate remade many directorates, including those of Bogotá, Cundinamarca, Antioquia, and Boyacá.[1]

Contrary to the theory, it appears that the Liberal municipal directorates are only infrequently chosen by the primary system. A report on the 1947 elections observed that the municipal primaries, if they were held at all, were not important.[2] In 1965 it appeared that the departmental directorate of Cundinamarca, in consultation with the leaders of each town, was naming the municipal directorates. By the end of August at least 43 had been named.[3] Apparently the same thing had happened in 1963.[4]

But it would be a mistake to suppose that the members of the departmental directorates appoint municipal directorates in accordance with their personal predilections. Their object in naming directorates is to conciliate and unite local cliques as much as possible and see that the men most likely to be supported by the active followers and voters are named to the directorate. Time and again, in interviews, departmental leaders pointed out that the most important requisite for being named to municipal directorates was the ability to command votes, to "have force" in the locality.

A Colombian party or national faction is interested in survival, and ultimately survival depends on votes. Whatever the formal arrangements for selecting party leaders at the different levels, the

1. *El Tiempo,* June 4, 1965, p. 1.
2. *Semana,* March 1, 1947, pp. 6–7.
3. *El Espectador,* August 7, 1965, p. 1; August 24, 1965, p. 7; and August 28, 1965, p. 3. *El Tiempo,* August 14, 1965, p. 7.
4. *El Espectador,* September 10, 1963, p. 8.

practical result must be substantially the same: men with the greatest possible electoral support are picked.

The above observations can be restated in proposition form:

> 2. *The margin of discretion which leaders at any level have to appoint or nominate lesser leaders to positions in the faction is quite limited.*

It contradicts the notion (prevalent in the U.S. and Colombia) that in Colombia the directorates or top leaders exercise autocratic control of lesser leaders. In most cases, top leaders cannot afford to exercise their personal preferences in naming directorates or composing lists. They face not only the competition of other national factions but also the quite real, indeed inevitable, problem of factionalism within their own national faction. Interviewees repeatedly pointed out that in the selection of individuals to fill a list of candidates or to be named to a directorate one cannot name "just anybody." A "just anybody" list of candidates would be faced in an election by the real, vote-getting leaders running as dissidents. The party label belongs to no one by right; it belongs simply to those who get votes under it.

For this reason party leaders spend considerable time sounding out opinion, cajoling, convincing, and choosing optimal combinations of leaders for directorates, lists, and appointments. The constant threat of factionalism makes this process mandatory. Of course, frequently no amount of cajoling and juggling with positions will enable higher leaders to heal a local schism. In such a situation no system of nomination and selection will work. If a primary election gives victory to one faction, the other will call the election fradulent; if the higher directorate names one faction for the directorate, the other will cry "favoritism" or "oligarchy." If the higher directorate names men from both factions to the local directorate, it will simply break apart into the two factions.

A member of the Conservative departmental directorate of Cauca explained the constraints on the directorate in the process whereby the municipal directorates were selected:

> You can't just name a municipal directorate from Popayán; it won't be accepted. You have to go to the municipality and hold

meetings and consultations and find out who's popular, and who hates who, and try to persuade.

At the national level there are similar constraints. The major national factions elect leaders at their conventions. The chief of the faction consults about the relative standing of the leaders, meets with the most influential ones, and together they arrive at the slate which will have the greatest support and be least likely to cause division. Can this slate be very different from the one the convention would elect anyway? If it were, serious problems could arise as the November 20, 1964, Lauro-alzatista convention illustrates.

Alvaro Gómez, the chief of the Laureanista Conservatives had drawn up a list of candidates for the national directorate. He had taken into account the prestige and popularity of the various leaders as well as the demands of the Alzatista Conservatives regarding the size and composition of their representation. Attempting to exercise his discretion, Gómez had omitted from the proposed list Jorge Leyva, a popular but dangerously ambitious leader. When the time for elections in the convention came, however, many delegates began a chant of "LEY-VA, LEY-VA." Gómez was in a difficult position. If he went ahead with his pre-selected list, ignoring the demand for Leyva, he ran the risk of launching Leyva as the chief of another faction. To prevent this, Gómez expanded the size of the proposed directorate by one and included Leyva.

Even in the ANAPO of Gustavo Rojas Pinilla there must be a basic sensitivity to the electoral resources of leaders. Although factionalism is much reduced, it stands as a threat as indicated in the cases of Cundinamarca and Caldas, noted in Chapter 9. Furthermore, Rojas is interested in securing the greatest number of votes. He believes that exercise of his personal judgment is the most satisfactory method to achieve an ideal directorate, as indicated in this interview:

Q. How is the new national directorate of Rojismo going to be named?

ROJAS. I, as chief, will name it.

Q. But General, doesn't this contradict the popular and democratic orientation of your movement?

ROJAS. But you understand that in a convention [the directorate] would be very difficult to designate; the same thing would happen to us that happened to the Officialist [Liberals].[5]

What Rojas meant about the convention system being a "difficult" method was not that some kind of directorate could not be named, but that it was an awkward instrument for naming the best directorate in terms of electoral strength.

Of course, most leaders have a marginal degree of discretion as to appointments and nominations. They cannot name an unknown bootblack to a list; neither can they avoid naming the most popular local politicians. But there are many individuals with apparently equal electoral resources, each of whom would have some utility on the team. A directorate may decide, for example, that it would like to balance its list with a university student or a woman. Although the choice is restricted to half a dozen active, popular individuals, a choice must still be made. Certainly personal friendships, family connections, or trustworthiness will influence this choice. And, of course, we may expect to find considerable jousting and horse-trading going on among the members of directorates as each attempts to augment the strength of his personal clique.

But such sparring and favoritism, it must be remembered, take place within the basic constraints imposed by electoral necessity. Although top leaders (members of directorates) customarily make the important party decisions, their freedom of choice is illusory because the costs of exercising their power freely are, in broad terms, prohibitive. A man may have a gun, for example, and therefore he is powerful in a formal sense. He can kill anyone in sight. But the costs of using this gun are prohibitive since they involve being charged with murder. Consequently the power of the man with the gun is usually illusory since he chooses not to incur the costs of using it.[6]

5. *Sistema,* April 1, 1965, p. 25.

6. I am employing here the "opportunity cost" conception of power advanced by John C. Harsanyi, "Measurement of Social Power, Opportunity Costs and the Theory of Two-Person Bargaining Games," *Behavioral Science,* 7 (1962), 67–80. In practice this approach is not greatly different from the analysis of power in terms of resources, since we consider as "resources" only those actions which participants are willing to take under the circumstances of the conflict situation. The Queen of England, for example, could dissolve Parliament on her own whim. But since she is never willing to take such action (given the high costs) the ability to dissolve Parliament is not considered a resource of hers.

A statement like "the real power of electing belongs to the directorate, and the nominal power belongs to the people" is profoundly mistaken.[7] Also mistaken is the view that a "reactionary" party leadership imposes "reactionary" candidates on the electorate, while men with "progressive" programs are autocratically suppressed by party leaders. In the first place the existence of "reactionary" leaders is mythology (see Chapter 4). But even if such leaders could be found, the above description would not apply. If a man can achieve by any means, including an attractive program, a significant electoral following, then the national faction to which he wants to belong will not spurn his support. In this sense Colombian politicians are anything but personalistic; they are businessmen. If a successful leader has dirty hands, a strange program, or a record of past disloyalty, it does not matter. He has votes. That matters. The idea that personal animosities are the guiding force in Colombian politics is quite incorrect. Such animosities are the fruit of a deeper struggle, the struggle for office. When in this struggle it becomes convenient to unite with a former enemy, animosities disappear or are suppressed immediately.

This explanation of why leaders are constrained by electoral necessities rests upon the assumption that a competitive electoral context obtains. Under the Frente Nacional elections, for legislative bodies in particular, have been highly competitive. But we might wonder whether the electoral climate was sufficiently competitive in pre-Frente Nacional days to make electoral necessities the primary leadership constraint.

My impression is that while the electoral climate has been made more competitive through the Frente Nacional, it had a competitive texture in pre-Frente Nacional days. The three-way presidental elections of 1930 and 1946 were certainly highly competitive. The presidential elections of 1918 and 1942 (between factions) and 1922 (between the parties) were hotly contested although the outcomes were rather one-sided. Even in those cases when one party ran only one presidential nominee unopposed, he was unopposed because he had convinced enough leaders that it would be unprofitable to back

7. José Lorenzo Mariño, "Los Derechos Políticos," *El Espectador Magazine Dominical*, August 15, 1965, p. 15. The same proposition is found in Dix, *Colombia*, p. 207: "Real control of both parties rests with the party directorates."

a second candidate. An unopposed presidential candidacy was the result of much hard work and a position of unsurpassed popularity. Finally, local elections, particularly for city council positions, were usually competitive between factions and/or parties.

Aquilino Gaitán, in his excellent practical account of the Conservative defeat of 1930, provides some insights into the bases on which party leaders made their decisions. Gaitán was a member of the three-man Conservative national directorate in 1928–30. He recounts that, in composing directorates for the departments, the national directorate attempted to heal divisions by giving representation to different factions. At the same time it attempted to give the greatest representation to those leaders who, as could be determined from the national directorate's observations and consultations with other leaders, were strongest in the department. Some individuals, however, were dropped or added at the request of high church officials or influential political leaders.[8] He also notes that in composing the lists of candidates the primary consideration was the electoral strength of each man.[9] This constraint is consistent with his description of a Conservative party racked by divisions and competing factions.

BEHAVIOR OF NATIONAL FACTIONS

3. Except in elections, national factions are cohesive in their behavior on the political scene.

This proposition comes perhaps as a surprise. Judging from the divisiveness of national factions in elections we would hardly have expected any degree of cohesion in their behavior in other contexts. It would seem that a pattern of "every man for himself" would also obtain when action was taken on the political scene. But in fact national factions are quite cohesive in spheres other than elections. When a directorate decides to oppose an executive at a given level, the cabinet appointees of that faction will resign, the legislative group

8. Aquilino Gaitán, *Por Qué Cayó el Partido Conservador,* pp. 13–19.

9. Ibid., pp. 39–40, 44–45. In one case, for example, the incumbent Conservative president, Abadía, objected to one alternate on the directorate's list of candidates for representatives for Cundinamarca. A member of the directorate replied that the presence of this man on the list "would assure the votes of the street-car workers, which were numerous" (p. 40).

will attempt to block passage of anything the executive might want or need, the higher directorate of the faction will express dissatisfaction to the executive on its level, and faction newspapers will oppose the executive in question.

I employ the term "cohesive" to describe this phenomenon rather than "well-disciplined" because national faction unity is largely a voluntary "sticking together" and is not induced by threats of punishment. Indeed, since each person holds his position largely as the result of his own electoral resources, there is little the faction could do to punish a rebel, who always has the alternative of switching to another faction.

What makes national factions cohesive? To answer this question we must first explain their existence. National factions arise because participants have discovered that it is more efficient to act in concert with other leaders than alone. By pooling their resources, leaders can coerce executives to allot them more positions. They can bargain effectively for a presidential nomination. They can defend their active followers in bureaucratic positions and, through the vertical links, they can protect each other from threats from above or below. It follows, therefore, that the faction acts to protect the interests of all the members. On those matters which affect the health of the faction generally, so that each participant stands to gain or lose equally, faction members will agree on the course of action.

Suppose, for example, the issue is withdrawing support from a governor. Participants will weigh the matter in these terms: Has cooperation been beneficial for us? Are we getting enough mayorships? Enough public jobs? Is an opposing faction cutting us out of what belongs to us? Will going into the opposition bring us a sufficient electoral return? If we go into the opposition can we topple the governor anyway? The leaders of the national faction on the departmental directorate weigh these questions and consult widely with other faction participants. When they make their decision it will be based on the balance of opinion within the faction. Many leaders will acquiesce because they agree with the reasoning that the faction will be better off if the action is taken. The rest will support the decision because they do not see the strategic implications very clearly one way or the other but realize that the leaders are acting to protect the opportunities of all faction members.

Cohesion, then, is produced because faction members all have the same strategic perspective vis-à-vis other national factions. When a decision is taken to withdraw support from an executive, the cabinet appointees will resign in every case. They resign not because they are coerced by the faction (indeed, they probably played an important part in making the decision to withdraw support) but because it is strategically convenient for the faction to which they belong and it is the faction that will carry them to higher offices, including the presidency. The legislative group, many of whom would be on the directorate which decided to withdraw support, engage in the necessary harassment of the executive because such activity benefits all of them. Consequently the legislative groups of the national factions are cohesive on most votes, even those which appear to have only faint strategic implications (see Chapter 11).

The cohesion of national factions in nonelectoral behavior is impressively consistent with the proposition that leaders have a status incentive. It seems thoroughly inconsistent with the opposite view, that leaders have a program incentive. Suppose, for example, we assume that cohesion is the product of commonly held programs or ideological views. Then why should not this same cohesion obtain at election time as ideological participants unite to gain the maximum support for their faction? Or one could argue the reverse and suggest that divisions at election time were the product of divisions over program. But then these divisions should carry over into voting patterns, causing the national factions to exhibit disunity.

Members of national factions divide at elections because in this context what is good for one member is not good for another. But they tend to remain united in their behavior toward executives and policies because in this context what is good for one is good for all and vice versa. Both phenomena are consistent with the proposition that Colombian leaders hold a status incentive, that they are increasing their private opportunities to hold higher political offices. The difference in behavior is produced by a different context.

4. The behavior of national factions on the political scene is primarily the product of a struggle over the distribution of public employment, political positions, and the opportunities for political positions.

4a. The behavior of national factions is not greatly influenced by the social composition of their membership, the nature of their electorates, or announced programs or policy positions.

This proposition is perhaps the most fundamental observation that can be made about Colombian national factions. It is overlooked by American writers who paint Colombian politics as struggles of lefts and rights, of reformers and reactionaries. I argue that one can best explain (and predict) the behavior of national factions by attempting to determine the strategic implications of the context for each of them. Conversely one can make very little sense out of Colombian politics by studying the formal pronouncements made by leaders in the past, the social composition of the faction, or the nature of its electorate.

Perhaps the best way to demonstrate this proposition would be to examine a few representative illustrations.

1. Alfonso López Michelsen, founder and leader of the Movimiento Revolucionario Liberal (MRL Linea Blanda) made the elimination of the Frente Nacional a central theme of his opposition campaign. In 1958 he wrote that the two-thirds majority requirement for approval of measures in legislative bodies was undesirable because it would, among other things, make the Frente Nacional difficult to amend. Following his criticism to its logical conclusion he stated: "I sustain that to place the opposition, which might arise tomorrow, in such a blind alley [with the two-thirds requirement to amend the constitution] will always be an ill-advised policy and a serious commitment on the part of those who propose it." [10]

Several years later, in 1965, López continued to carry the banner of opposition and to advocate doing away with the Frente Nacional.[11] But when asked about eliminating the two-thirds rule, as many leaders were then suggesting, he opposed such a change. As leader of a minority political faction he realized that the two-thirds rule gave his MRL much greater leverage to block other factions and coerce the

10. In Alfonso López Michelsen, *Colombia en la Hora Cero* (2 vols. Bogotá, Ediciones Tercer Mundo, 1963), *1,* 224 and passim.

11. Briefly the MRL had collaborated with the government in August-September 1962, after its impressive electoral gains. But it received only one ministry and no governorships and so retired, concluding that it deserved more positions (which, given its electoral strength, it did).

president. He felt, regarding the two-thirds rule, that "One shouldn't play with the constitution." [12] All this looks curiously inconsistent. Does López really want to do away with the Frente Nacional, in which case one must indeed "play with the constitution?" The abolition of the two-thirds rule would be an almost indispensable prerequisite for abolishing the Frente Nacional, since, as it is now, two thirds of Congress would have to approve amendments ending the Frente Nacional before 1974. Did López mean what he said in 1958? Did he mean what he said in 1965?

An examination of the strategic context makes his behavior intelligible. In 1958 it was logical to add to the list of reasons for opposing the Frente Nacional the undemocratic and rigid aspects of the two-thirds rule. López was apparently preparing to be that opposition "which might arise tomorrow," and therefore reasoned that the more complete the attack, the better his position. But in 1965 these attacks became inconvenient—he then was leader of a faction which benefited from the two-thirds rule.

2. In preparing for the Lauro-alzatista Conservative convention on November 20, 1964, the Alzatista Conservatives released a document stating the conditions under which they would agree to participate in the convention. Their conditions dealt exclusively with the selection of leadership. Primarily, they insisted that they get half of the seats on the new national directorate and that they themselves decide who these members should be.[13] There were no demands for platform concessions, program positions, or ideological stances. The absence of such demands reveals the lack of interest leaders have in policies. The divisions or wings that exist in the American or British party systems are centered on program differences, and it would be almost inevitable that any document stating conditions of cooperation (if indeed cooperation were withheld) would express the desire for ideological or policy concessions.

3. In the period July-September 1965 the Ospinista Conservatives began an intense campaign against President Valencia's division of the six cabinet posts available to the Conservatives. By this system, dubbed *"milimetría"* the Ospinista Conservatives received two cabinet posts and the Lauro-alzatistas, four. The Ospinistas insisted that

12. Interview in *El Espectador,* April 12, 1965, p. 1.
13. Printed in *El Tiempo,* November 13, 1964, p. 21.

Valencia break the pattern of milimetría, maintaining that it was "unconstitutional." Obviously they were not interested in constitutionality, because if Valencia broke milimetría by giving the Lauroalzatistas five ministries and the Ospinistas only *one,* the Ospinistas would most certainly withdraw support. In short, the Ospinistas wanted three ministries instead of two for their support.[14] It was never even hinted that they desired a particular policy or policy change from Valencia.

Why did the Ospinistas wait until August 1965 to make their demand? Indeed, in June 1964 it was their opponents, the Laureanistas, with only two ministries, who opposed milimetría.[15] The answer lies in the fact that the Ospinistas, like every other faction, feared being eclipsed by competitors. Given only two ministries to the four of the unified Lauro-alzatistas, it had begun to look as if the Ospinistas were a waning force. With the congressional elections approaching in March 1966, the Ospinistas realized that belligerence would pay dividends either way. If Valencia acceded to their demands for three ministries, they would gain a position of equality with the Lauro-alzatistas and a reputation for toughness and ability to defend their own; if he refused, the Ospinistas would take to the opposition with the theme that Valencia, with the support and guidance of the Lauro-alzatistas had run the country to the ground. On this platform they could hope to increase their electoral strength.

Valencia, after weeks of calculated delay, finally announced, on September 1, a new cabinet which did not break milimetría. To have done so would have immediately thrust the Lauro-alzatistas into the opposition. The Ospinistas divided on how to react. Some wanted to adopt a strict opposition strategy, others thought that such a move would endanger the candidacy of Liberal Carlos Lleras for president in 1966. The Ospinistas had allied with this candidacy, in the hope that when Lleras came to office, almost everything Conservative would be theirs (ministries, governorships). The national directorate of the Ospinistas finally issued a decision that the strategy should be left in the hands of their chief, ex-president Mariano Ospina. Ospina decided on a position of qualified support: accept the ministries (so

14. *La República,* August 1, 1965, p. 1; *El Espectador,* August 3, 1965, p. 1, and August 10, 1965, p. 1.
15. *El Tiempo,* June 14, 1964, p. 21.

the Lauro-alzatistas would not get them and use them to sabotage the campaign of Lleras) but harass the president in Congress, and speak out against the government quite freely.

In miniature, such conflicts are constantly erupting at the departmental and municipal levels. The threat to withdraw support from an executive is constantly made by all factions (except, of course, those already in the opposition). In virtually all of the scores of "crises" provoked by withdrawals, the matter in conflict concerns the distribution of positions. Neither reporters nor participants make an attempt to hide the practical struggle for positions behind allegations of program conflicts. The following are typical of comments which have appeared in daily newspapers:

> The city council [of Pasto, capital of Nariño] has not been able to meet lacking the attendance of Conservative councilmen who . . . in a letter [to the mayor] said that they would not attend any council session as long as the government and the Liberal councilmen maintain the decision to name a Liberal manager of the municipal public works agency. . . . Liberals and Conservatives both insist that the managership belongs to their party.[16]

> [In the department of Meta] the departmental directorate of *Unidad* Conservatives [Ospinistas] postponed until tomorrow the meeting they had arranged with Governor Arango Jaramillo, which has as its purpose the redistribution of departmental cabinet secretaries which belong to the Conservative party in this department. There is concern to learn the final outcome of this impasse since a withdrawal of support by the Unionista departmental directorate [Ospinista] from the government of Meta may be produced.[17]

> The departmental directorate of the [Ospinista] Conservatives of Cundinamarca confirmed today its refusal to continue to cooperate with the administration of Governor Francisco Gaviria Rincón.

And this extract from the declaration of the Ospinista departmental directorate explains why:

16. *El Espectador,* May 8, 1965, p. 4B.
17. *La República,* April 29, 1965, p. 9.

Notwithstanding the firm hopes which [Ospinista] Conservatives of Cundinamarca held with respect to an improvement over the disgraceful period characterized by the administrative partiality in favor of factional ambitions, in reality it has re-emerged again in equal or worse form . . . from the moment . . . the Secretary-ship of Gobierno was given to [a Laureanista].[18]

The Officialist Liberals and Ospinista Conservatives withdrew support on February 24, 1965, from Manuel Orozco Fandino, governor of the department of Magdalena. In an open letter to President Valencia a leader of the Officialist Liberals gave a long account of the reasons for withdrawal:

[The governor] disregarded the rights of the authentic Liberal majorities and named some secretaries who had to be considered challenges to these majorities. . . .

In the Department of Finance the participation of the [Officialist] Liberals scarcely reached 20 per cent, and these in insignificant positions. In the Department of Agriculture, after the massive discharge of 54 workers, the Liberals remained in a ridiculous minority. . . .

Just barely were we saving the Departments of Public Works and Public Health, whose chiefs struggled to block the Laureanista voracity, which was one of the reasons why they were removed.[19]

Sometimes the claims had a comical ring:

Unionismo [the Ospinista Conservatives] had refused the secretaryship of agriculture, occupied by Doctor Jaime Duque Estrada, because this portfolio has no budget and its only function was that of caring for a farm with a herd of 40 pigs.[20]

But comical or not, these claims and counterclaims constitute the warp and woof of Colombian politics. It is difficult for an observer to glance at these daily happenings and still believe that politics is a struggle between reformers and reactionaries.

---

18. Ibid., March 6, 1965, p. 3. The secretary of Gobierno is in charge of lesser appointments and is consequently a key man.

19. *El Tiempo,* February 25, 1965, p. 9.

20. *La República,* May 6, 1965, p. 10. The above was in explanation of the Ospinista withdrawal in Meta, foreshadowed in the earlier citation.

4. In 1965 there was a noticeable difference in the social status of the members of the three major Bogotá municipal directorates. The directorate of the Ospinista Conservatives was composed of men of medium-high status, well-dressed, and mainly in professional occupations. The Bogotá directorates of the Lauro-alzatista Conservatives and the Officialist Liberals were similar; their members were of lower status, many dressed quite poorly, some were even limited in their ability to read. That is, in social composition the Liberal and Lauro-alzatista directorates were more "popular" than the Ospinista directorate.[21]

One might suppose that the Liberals and the Lauro-alzatistas would have followed similar policies, and that these policies would be opposed to those of the Ospinistas. But it did not happen this way. The Officialist Liberals and Ospinista Conservatives remained supporters of the Liberal mayor of Bogotá, Jorge Gaitán Cortez. The Lauro-alzatistas withdrew support on April 22, 1965, and bitterly opposed Gaitán after that date. Why? "Mayor Gaitán Cortés Tolerates And Promotes the Undue Exercise of Political Favoritism," as the Lauro-alzatista *El Siglo* headline went.[22] The Lauro-alzatistas felt (probably not without reason) that their men in the administration were being selectively fired, and the hiring favored the Ospinista and Officialist Liberal groups.

The search for a social composition explanation of the behavior of Colombian factions (when differences exist) runs aground because the incentive for virtually all leaders is status. If they were seeking program satisfactions, looking for policies or social groups to defend, a social-background explanation might be useful. Participants would tend to defend policies favorable to the social group from which they came. But Colombian politicians, seeking the status of political office, do not find their social backgrounds relevant for their behavior.

5. An interesting addition to this observation concerns the geographical location of party strength. It happens that some of the parties and factions do not receive equal electoral support from

21. It was not my impression that this pattern was repeated on a national scale. It seemed in Atlántico, for example, that the Lauro-alzatistas were of higher status than the Ospinistas. Whether there is any general tendency for directorates to have members of different status is an interesting problem. Perhaps more recently founded cliques or factions generally tend to have younger and lower status members. But I have no data that throw light on this speculation.

22. April 22, 1965, p. 6.

cities and from towns and villages. The differences in the vote from these two areas for the various political groups are tabulated in Tables 10.1 and 10.2. This observation is perhaps surprising because it is reasonable to expect that, if the groups do not adopt distinct programs, an urban-rural split in the vote will not occur. A thought-

TABLE 10.1

Urban–Rural Division of the Party Vote, 1947

City and Department*	% Liberal	% Conservative
Medellín	57	43
rest of Antioquia	45	55
Cartagena	77	23
rest of Bolívar	65	35
Tunja	64	36
rest of Boyacá	43	57
Manizales	55	45
rest of Caldas	50	50
Popayán	57	43
rest of Cauca	60	40
Bogotá	73	26
rest of Cundinamarca	56	43
Cúcuta	76	22
rest of Norte de Santander	40	60
Bucaramanga	68	29
rest of Santander	61	38
Ibagué	70	29
rest of Tolima	63	35
Cali	63	35
rest of Valle	61	39

*To simplify the presentation I have considered the rest of the department less the capital city to be "small town-rural." In general this assumption is adequate for our purposes: the single capital city is overwhelmingly *the* city of the department and the rest are small towns and villages. Since some departments, such as Caldas and Valle, do have other cities, my technique slightly understates the urban–rural differential. It should be noted, however, that compared to the differentials produced in other departments, Manizales is surprisingly Conservative, being the only large city in Colombia which, in a competitive election, has produced a Conservative majority, e.g. in 1946.

Figures may not add across to 100 because of the presence of small numbers of third party (Socialist) votes.

Source: Based on the results of the 1947 city council elections given in *Estadística Electoral,* Supplement to Nos. 37 to 39 of *Anales de Economía y Estadística,* July 1948, pp. 8–21.

ful examination of the phenomenon suggests, however, that this split has little to do with program policies of the different groups.

First we observe that the Liberal label, even prior to the Frente Nacional, has done better in the cities than in the small towns; conversely the Conservatives have done relatively better in the towns and countryside. In Table 10.1 these differentials have been computed for ten selected cities and their respective departments. The division of the vote is by no means total and there are a few exceptions to the pattern. Manizales, a city in Caldas, has tended to be almost as Conservative as the rest of the department; the countryside in Cauca has been strongly Liberal so that Popayán, while having a Liberal majority, is less Liberal than the rest of the department. Nevertheless, the division is significant and requires an explanation.

Since this differential vote resembles the Democratic–Republican division of the vote in the United States, we are at first tempted to explain it in the same manner. The large cities in the United States tend to give the Democrats a higher vote than "upstate" because for many years the Democratic party has favored groups located predominantly in the cities: Catholics, unemployed, trade unionists, Negroes, Jews, and immigrants. But an examination of Colombian leadership attitudes does not reveal, as it does in the United States, that party leaders are differently disposed toward urban groups. American Republican leaders, for example, are markedly less in favor of government urban housing programs and labor unions than Democratic leaders.[23] But Colombian Liberal and Conservative leaders show no marked difference in their attitudes toward these matters (Table 4.1). When asked to identify "the most serious problem facing Colombia," leaders of both parties virtually ignore agrarian problems (Table 4.5).

The urban–rural split in Colombia, I believe, is not related to either present programs or past accomplishments of the parties. Instead, it results from the impact of the church on party identification and voting behavior. As I noted in Chapter 4, most priests are identified with the Conservative label. Insofar as they give political advice to their congregations, it will tend to be in favor of the Conservative label. In urban centers, however, there are more channels of com-

23. McClosky et al., "Issue Conflict and Consensus Among Party Leaders and Followers," *American Political Science Review, 54* (1960), 412–13.

munication, literacy is higher, people are drawn into contact with conflicting views and become less dependent on priests for information and advice. It follows that the amount of pro-Conservative label advice which city dwellers notice is less than that received by village inhabitants, and consequently Conservatives do relatively better in the villages than in the big cities. Regardless of the general level of the Conservative vote in the entire department, the Conservatives get more in the villages and countryside than in the cities.[24]

An inspection of Table 10.2 reveals the same general pattern persisting in the 1964 elections for representatives, although the addition of the MRL faction of the Liberals and ANAPO somewhat complicates the picture. We notice that ANAPO strength lies disproportionately in the cities and MRL support comes disproportionately from the villages and countryside. The ANAPO urban strength is easily explained. A new party, without clerical support, would do better among the more independent urban citizens than among the backward, suspicious rural voters. But the rural strength of the MRL, which has captured a large proportion of the rural Liberal vote, seems surprising. Apparently the rural support of the MRL was accidental, a result not anticipated by its founder, Alfonso López. In the 1962 elections one observer reported that his campaign was "deliberately urban-centered." [25] In 1965, when he opposed certain measures backed by the labor unions and the government (a strategic position in consequence of his opposition strategy), he announced that he was defending the peasants.[26] I asked a leader of the MRL, and friend of López, about this matter in 1965:

Q. What social group does the MRL represent?
A. Well López *says* it's the peasants. But that's post facto.
Q. What do you mean?

24. The department of Cauca has been an exception. In Caldas only the city of Manizales is deviant; in Pereira and Armenia, two other cities of Caldas, Liberals do much better than in the department at large. I suspect that the Liberal strength in the countryside of Cauca may be the result of the renegade pro-Liberal church wing which emerged in that department around the war of 1860–61 (see Chapter 4). As a consequence perhaps priests in Cauca tended to be pro-Liberal and the effect described above would work in favor of a higher Liberal vote in the countryside.

25. Kenneth F. Johnson, "Political Radicalism in Colombia: Electoral Dynamics of 1962 and 1964," *Journal of Inter-American Studies*, 7 (1965), 15–16, 20.

26. *El Espectador,* April 12, 1965, p. 1.

A. That first he saw the election results and then he explained them by saying he was for the peasants. Post facto.

But if López decided he favored the countryside *after* he got his support there, why did he get rural support in the first place? And why did his rural vote drop off somewhat in 1964, *after* López allegedly decided to defend the peasants? A clue to this appeared when

TABLE 10.2

Urban–Rural Division of the Vote, 1964

	Percent of the vote for:			
City and Department	Officialist Liberals	MRL, Blanda and Dura	ANAPO*	Conservative
Medellín (732,510)	34	9	17	39
rest of Antioquia	19	20	14	47
Cartagena (191,270)	48	19	0	31
rest of Bolívar	44	20	0	36
Tunja (53,970)	31	5	41	22
rest of Boyacá	28	10	24	39
Manizales (181,420)	31	9	17	42
rest of Caldas	30	18	14	37
Popayán (65,440)	51	9	8	31
rest of Cauca	42	20	1	35
Bogotá (1,406,230)	48**	9	26	16
rest of Cundinamarca	33	15	10	42
Cúcuta (141,540)	35	22	32	11
rest of Norte de Santander	13	13	13	61
Bucaramanga (235,720)	36	18	32	14
rest of Santander	19	21	15	45
Ibagué (154,590)	33	24	19	23
rest of Tolima	29	23	18	30
Cali (750,770)	44	14	20	21
rest of Valle	22	24	24	30

*The votes for ANAPO have been summed from lists entered as Conservative and from lists entered as Liberal.

** The MIL in Cundinamarca was not part of the Officialist Liberals but its small vote has been added in here.

Sources: The figures have been compiled from the results of the 1964 election for representatives, given in *Organización y Estadísticas Electorales* for the 1964 elections. Figures may not add across to 100 because of the presence of null or blank votes and because of rounding. Population of the cities given in parentheses was taken from *Factores Colombianos, 1964.*

some interviewees noted that the MRL seemed to be strong in those areas where the Liberal-Conservative fighting in 1946–53 was most violent.

Adopting a thoroughgoing stance of opposition, López included an attack on the Frente Nacional, against the idea of coalition or cooperation with the Conservatives. In addition to being a more "profound" position of opposition, an attack on the Frente Nacional could be expected to bring in the highly partisan Liberal voters who hated Conservatives. It turned out, however, that the intensely partisan Liberals were not in the cities but in the small villages where the political conflict had been most bloody, giving rise to strong partisan hatreds. López lost some of this rural support from 1962 to 1964 because as the memories of violence grew dimmer and the Frente Nacional was successful in restoring peace, an anti-Conservative position lost appeal.

A preliminary test of this interpretation may be made by inspecting the MRL vote in four towns in Nariño: Ancuya, Funes, Sandoná, and Túquerres. These were the towns, mentioned in Chapter 8, where Liberal-Conservative violence broke out shortly after Ospina took office in 1946. We make the crude assumption that because these incidents occurred at an early point and were prominent enough to be reported, the Liberal-Conservative conflict was more acute in these towns than in the department in general. If our analysis is correct these towns should have given unusually high support to the

TABLE 10.3

The MRL Partisan Backlash in Nariño

Proportion of total Liberal vote for MRL*
Per cent

	1962	1964
Ancuya	70	63
Funes	64	42
Sandoná	66	47
Túquerres	24	37
Entire department of Nariño	21	20

*Both the Linea Blanda and Linea Dura are included. Notice that the proportions are of only the *Liberal* vote, not the total vote. Data compiled from the elections for representatives.

Source: *Organización y Estadísticas Electorales* for 1962 and 1964.

MRL in 1962 and somewhat less in the 1964 elections. The figures in Table 10.3 indicate that three out of the four towns do fit this expectation. It is likely, then, that the MRL vote in 1962 and 1964 was predominantly a partisan backlash and unrelated to programs López might have propounded.

In the preceding pages I have described some basic characteristics of Colombian political parties. They were explained (and presumably could have been predicted) by the proposition that the dominant incentive for Colombian leaders is status. It is possible, therefore, to present these characteristics as dependent variables in an omnibus hypothesis, thus:

> *H31. In a country where the incentive for leaders is status, where party identification with two or three parties is high and where political freedoms are observed, there will be national party factions with these characteristics:* [27]
>
> *1. Leadership positions will be allocated largely on the basis of each individual's electoral resources.*
> *2. Higher leaders will have a relatively narrow margin of discretion in selecting lower leaders.*
> *3. The factions will be relatively cohesive in their behavior on the national political scene, except in elections.*
> *4. The behavior of the national factions will be primarily the product of a struggle over the distribution of political positions and the opportunities for political positions; their behavior will not be greatly influenced by the social composition of their membership, the nature of their electorates, or announced program policy positions.*

27. It seems necessary to stipulate a reduced number of party labels since at some point as the number of party labels increases it becomes inefficient to subdivide a party into national factions. The small size of such factions would make them inconsequential units on the political scene. I would guess that a national faction would not be a viable unit unless it had at least about 10% of the vote.

CHAPTER 11

THE COLOMBIAN
CONGRESS

Q. *Why is attendance in Congress for votes, even apparently important votes, low?*
A. *Well our congressmen just haven't gotten the idea that a vote is important. If I am writing a letter or reading an interesting magazine and they say, "there's a vote; come and vote," I prefer to finish the letter or the magazine. I just can't be bothered. We think Congress is for speeches, not votes.*

> *Interview with a member of the Colombian House of Representatives (Bogotá, September 2, 1965).*

An American observer is easily deceived by the Colombian legislature. At first glance it seems to resemble the American Congress. There are two chambers: a Senate (96 members) and a House of Representatives (184 members). The concurrence of both houses is required for the passage of legislation. Senators are elected every four years and must be over 30 years old; Representatives are elected every two years and must be over 25. Each house elects its own officers and has standing committees to which its members are assigned and to which legislation passes before final disposition is made on the floor.[1]

Aside from these superficial similarities, however, the Colombian Congress stands a world apart from the American body. In virtually all its processes, practices, and underlying characteristics, the Colombian legislature is what the American Congress is not. As it turns out,

1. There are a few contrasts in formal arrangement with the American body. Colombian Senate seats are apportioned to the departments on the basis of population, instead of a fixed number to each state (two) as in the United States. Also, Colombian representatives are elected from department-wide circumscriptions under a system of proportional representation. In the United States representatives come from single-member districts within each state.

the many contrasts are consistent with the incentive analysis followed in this study.

One of the many contrasts with the American Congress is the astonishingly high rate of turnover. In Table 11.1 the continuity

TABLE 11.1

Continuity in the Membership of the Colombian Congress

Base year	Total members	Number returning for second consecutive term	Number returning for three consecutive terms
House of Representatives			
1925	112 (100%)	14 (12.5%)	6 (5.4%)
1935	119 (100%)	24 (20.2%)	7 (5.9%)
1960	152 (100%)	34 (22.4%)	12 (7.9%)
Senate			
1923	48 (100%)	8 (16.7%)	3 (6.3%)
1935	56 (100%)	10 (17.9%)	
1958	82 (100%)	24 (29.3%)	

Source: Anales del Congreso; Anales del Senado; Anales de la Cámera (beginning in 1923 these documents contained lists of congressmen elected for each session from which continuity could be calculated).

rates for the Senate and the House have been calculated for three different periods: Conservative rule (1920s); Liberal rule (1930s); and the Frente Nacional (since 1958). In all three cases, turnover is remarkably high, with only about one fifth of the representatives or senators returning for a consecutive term. Only a very small number of legislators, less than 10 per cent, will experience three successive terms. In Table 11.2, continuity for the United States House of

TABLE 11.2

Continuity in the U.S. House of Representatives

Base year	Total members	Number returning for second consecutive term	Number returning for three consecutive terms
1959	437 (100%)	373 (85.4%)	294 (67.3%)

Source: Compiled from the *Congressional Record.*

Representatives is calculated for the period 1959–63. Of the representatives elected in 1959, 85 per cent returned for a second term; 67 per cent returned for three successive terms.

In Colombia between 5 and 10 per cent of the representatives in a given year will miss one term and return two years later (Table 11.3). Returnees from further back in the past will, in quite small numbers, augment the number of experienced representatives present in any given year. But even including all these sources of continuity it seems safe to say that over half of the representatives at any moment have never been in the House before.

Initially we might seek an explanation for high turnover in the intensity of electoral competition. This explanation, however, is at variance with some important facts. First, if it were electoral competition that caused turnover, more legislators would reenter Congress after one term of absence. Being relieved of the supposed distractions of officeholding, the ex-congressman would be free to reactivate his old contacts and devote his full time to getting reelected. There is little evidence, however, that this in-out-in pattern obtains (see Table 11.3).

TABLE 11.3

Alternate Membership in the Colombian
House of Representatives (in-out-in)

Base year	Total members	Number of representatives skipping one term and then returning
1925	112 (100%)	9 (8%)
1960	152 (100%)	12 (8%)

Source: Compiled from *Anales del Congreso; Anales de la Cámera.*

Secondly, if a congressman really wants to stay in office, he has many resources which his aspiring opponents lack. He has considerable prestige, governmental connections, a position of greater prominence and publicity. The resources open to other candidates, such as street campaigns and face-to-face politicing are also available to the incumbent *if he is willing to expend the necessary effort.* If it is true that the legislator's desire to stay in is as strong as his desire to get in, then he has a clear advantage over his opponents.

By examining the attitudes of the legislators themselves we discern that electoral competition does not account for turnover, for these men lack the will to return before elections even arrive. Many will frankly voice a desire not to return. Others I interviewed were noncommittal or indifferent: "perhaps," "I haven't thought about it," "if they want me," "we'll see what happens." Being so weakly motivated to return, these men are likely to lose out in the struggle to regain their seats. Getting reelected is generally an exhausting task and demands considerable motivation.[2]

Studies of American state legislatures support the view that motivation and not electoral competition mainly account for turnover. Hyneman observed that turnover was highest in the least party-competitive states (Indiana, Iowa, and Maine) and lowest in the more competitive areas (New Jersey, New York, and California). Simply by noting that less than one third of the legislators not returning ran in primary or general elections he could conclude that electoral competition was not the primary cause of turnover.[3]

Turnover in the Colombian Congress is not the result of electoral competition but, instead, of the status incentive of leaders. Colombian leaders are seeking the prestige inherent in the position of representative or senator. And that prestige adheres to an ex-representative as well as an incumbent. In this sense the office is like a medal or award which, once achieved, is always possessed and requires only proper display and occasional polishing to serve as a status indicator. If it is only prestige one seeks from Congress, then a career in the legislature becomes an unnecessary cross to bear.

The Colombian congressman will, with few exceptions, follow one of two paths after his first term. Either he will retire, having gained the title he sought, or, depending upon his ambitions and expectations, he will seek to win a higher title and move into the pre-presidential ring of senators, ministers, and governors. A relatively high

2. See, for example, California Representative Clem Miller's efforts to stay in touch with his constituency, which involved a grueling 18-hour day: Clem Miller, *Member of the House* (New York, Charles Scribner's Sons, 1962), especially pp. 74–79.

3. Charles S. Hyneman, "Tenure and Turnover of Legislative Personnel," *The Annals of the American Academy of Political and Social Science, 195* (January 1938), 21–31. His computations for turnover in ten states combined showed that only 35.4% of his sample of 10,152 legislators were first-termers. This figure is not strictly comparable with ours, but would not be far from showing a 65% continuity rate, compared to the 20% rate for Colombia. Eulau et al. discovered greater electoral competition is associated with a greater willingness to return: "Career Perspectives of American State Legislators," in Marvick, ed., *Political Decision-makers*, pp. 218–63.

proportion of representatives move up to the Senate in the next election (between 10 and 20 per cent, see Table 11.4). In Colombia there are basically two patterns of political motion: in and out, or in and up. The career-type pattern of staying in at the same level for long periods of time is extremely rare.

TABLE 11.4

Movement of Representatives to the Senate in Colombia

Base year	Total representatives	Number of representatives who became senators at the next elections
1925	112 (100%)	9 (8%)
1960	152 (100%)	31 (20%)

Source: Compiled from *Anales del Congreso, Anales de la Cámera, Anales del Senado.*

In the United States, by and large, a congressional position is taken seriously as a career. An American congressman gets a continuing satisfaction from defending constituencies and working out policies, and hence wishes to retain his seat. Getting reelected and doing the business of a legislator is indeed taxing, but most American congressmen consider the satisfactions worth the costs. They are just as anxious (if not more so) to be reelected as they were to gain the seat for the first time. We may, therefore, make the obvious hypotheses explicit:

> *H32. In a system where status is the incentive for leaders, legislative turnover will be high.*

> *H33. In a system where program is the incentive for leaders, legislative turnover will be low.*

We can test these hypotheses within Colombia. As I have already suggested, the incentive for leaders in Antioquia tends more toward the program side of the status-program continuum than the leadership incentive in the rest of the country (see Figure 1, Chapter 1). Consequently we should expect a lower turnover of representatives from that department than from the rest of the country. By measuring turnover over the period 1925 to 1945, in the three departments of Antioquia, Cundinamarca, and Boyacá, we may gain some evidence to support this expectation. During this period Antioquia and

Cundinamarca were similar in size of population, industrialization, urbanization, and size of congressional delegation. Boyacá had the next largest congressional delegation and serves as a check on the amount of accidental or spurious variation possible in such a comparison. As is evident in Table 11.5, Antioquia had a significantly higher continuity rate: 25.5 per cent of all the representatives elected from Antioquia during this period returned for a second consecutive term; the corresponding figure for Cundinamarca was 15.3 per cent, and for Boyacá, 17.5 per cent.

A second remarkable contrast between the Colombian legislature

TABLE 11.5

Continuity of House Members from the Departments of Antioquia, Cundinamarca, and Boyacá, 1923–1945

	total 1923	return 1925	total 1925	return 1927	total 1927	return 1929
Antioquia	18	3	18	3	18	6
Cundinamarca	24	3	17	2	17	5
Boyacá	13	2	13	4	13	3

	total 1929	return 1931	total 1931	return 1933	total 1933	return 1935
Antioquia	18	4	18	6	18	2
Cundinamarca	17	4	17	2	17	2
Boyacá	13	2	13	1	13	0

	total 1935	return 1937	total 1937	return 1939	total 1939	return 1941
Antioquia	18	6	16	4	16	2
Cundinamarca	17	1	17	2	17	0
Boyacá	13	1	13	3	13	4

	total 1941	return 1943	total 1943	return 1945
Antioquia	17	7	17	6
Cundinamarca	18	5	18	4
Boyacá	13	2	13	3

Summary

	total representatives 1923–43	total returning in the following term
Antioquia	192 (100%)	49 (25.5%)
Cundinamarca	196 (100%)	30 (15.3%)
Boyacá	143 (100%)	25 (17.5%)

Source: Compiled from *Anales del Congreso.*

and the American Congress is the presence of a system of alternates and a generally high rate of absenteeism. In Colombia both senators and representatives are elected along with alternates who may be appointed to fill the seat if the incumbent does not wish to serve. As indicated in Table 11.6, about 20 per cent of the representatives elected to hold office give their seats to alternates. Furthermore, about five or ten representatives will simply disappear from the scene, their names (or names of possible alternates) not appearing in any roll call listing. In the votes themselves, even apparently important and close votes, one usually finds only about three quarters of the representatives or senators voting.

TABLE 11.6

Use of Alternates in the House of Representatives

Election date	Total members	Number of representatives who were replaced by alternates
March 1937	119 (100%)	20 (17%) July 1937
March 1939	119 (100%)	22 (18%) July 1940
March 1960	152 (100%)	31 (20%) July 1961

Source: Compiled from *Anales del Congreso; Anales de la Cámera.*

The phenomenon of alternates and absenteeism is a direct conse-quence of the status incentive of legislators. The position of alternate is, of course, a convenient way to share the prestige of office. But the practice has grown up because congressmen do not mind sharing their seats or simply forgetting about them. Once having obtained the title of representative or senator, Colombian leaders rapidly lose interest in Congress. They are not interested in actually doing the work of a legislator. When asked about their job, they classify being a congressman as *"aburrido"* (boring) or *"pesado"* (dull). It is a job from which they seem to get little, if any, satisfaction. In this way we can explain the curious paradox that Colombian leaders struggle fiercely at election time to become senators or representatives, but once elected they are casual or even reluctant about serving.

In the United States it is doubtful that legislators would ever es-tablish a system of alternates, let alone use it to any great extent. A congressman is elected to *be* the representative; he wants to do the job. The idea of turning his back on Congress after being elected would be distasteful or even incomprehensible to a man with a program incentive. It would be like going to a bridge tournament, registering, and then going home without playing. American congressmen, like bridge players, get their satisfactions from playing the game.

Briefly we may inspect some other areas of legislative life which are affected by the status incentive of congressmen.

Committees. Prior to 1945 there were no permanent committees in the Colombian Congress. At that time it was perhaps felt that committees were the answer to the age-old cry in Colombia of "congressional decadence." The reformers meant well but nothing substantial was achieved. Each house now has seven formal standing committees. The membership of these committees is large, ranging from about 14 to 38. Subcommittees are apparently never used. Some committees never meet; others meet a few times a session. After making daily inspections of congressional committees I concluded that the typical day (Tuesday, Wednesday, or Thursday; Monday and Friday are congressional holidays) would see the following committee activity:

> 3 committees—met for one or two hours
> 2 committees—met for less than 30 minutes
> 2 committees—had called meetings but no quorum was achieved and hence they did not meet
> 7 committees—did not meet

I estimate that the average congressman in Colombia spends about one hour a week in committee meetings. In the United States, congressmen appear to spend between 10 and 20 hours weekly in committee. On midweek days there will be from 30 to 50 committees and subcommittees meeting in the U.S. Congress. On Mondays or Fridays there will be between 10 and 20 committee meetings.

But even when they do meet, Colombian congressional committees do not resemble their American counterparts. Expert witnesses, with the infrequent exception of top administration officials, are not called. To my knowledge, no committee has ever had an executive (secret) session. The practice of exhaustive committee investigations into particular subjects is virtually unknown. Committee activity generally takes the form of (1) acrimonious debates scarcely connected with policy matters, as twenty or thirty congressmen make political attacks, or (2) boring rubber-stamp sessions in which a few stout-hearted congressmen sit through a reading of some document and drearily vote unanimous approval. In short, Colombian committees are not policy-making bodies. And how could they be policy-making bodies when their members do not wish to make policy?

Expertise and specialization. When congressmen are not interested in making policy they do not equip themselves to know about the problems of government. Colombian legislators are virtually without research or technical assistance. The Senate Library and congressional archives, with their tiny collections of lawbooks and scattered documents, employ about ten clerks. But even so they are grossly overstaffed, for congressmen seldom use these facilities. Congressmen have no offices and no secretaries. The committees have tiny staffs (usually one secretary and two typists) to handle paperwork, but nothing approaching a research staff.

Finally, few Colombian congressmen have acquired special knowledge on any area of legislation. American legislators have specialized in response to the complexity of governmental problems and the impossibility of knowing about all of them. If one wishes to have a decisive influence on policy, he must know about the policy area. But the acquisition of specialized knowledge requires effort. If legislators have no interest in policy, then they will not inconvenience themselves to become expert on specific policy areas.

Floor Debates. The House and Senate usually meet from about 6 to 8 or 9 P.M. on Tuesday, Wednesday, and Thursday. At least once a week the chambers will fail to meet, lacking a quorum, so each chamber has approximately five hours floor time a week. Floor time is largely spent either in dreary reading of documents and pro forma voting or in acrimonious debate, the purpose of which is to attract attention. By creating a scene the speaker gains publicity which enhances his status and advances his political career. As a consequence debates are characterized by personal charges, irresponsible attacks and condemnations and, frequently, *zambra* (physical violence). The observers in the galleries are free to cheer and shout down speakers.

Debates are customarily political and strategic, rather than upon substantive policy matters. Political scandals, accusations of corruption, favoritism, and administrative incompetence are favorite themes. Congressmen are as ready to accuse each other and Congress itself as they are likely to attack the administration.[4] Verbatim records of floor debates are not kept (nor of committee hearings); minutes give only a brief summary of what transpired.

These practices are again a product of the status incentive of legislators. Because American legislators have a program incentive, in the U.S. Congress many formal and informal norms are designed to prevent disruptive activity. Fist fights, cheers from the gallery, personal attacks, degradation of the institution, all get in the way of serious policy-making, and the rules of the legislature are intended to prevent such activity. Norms such as courtesy, deference, seniority, apprenticeship, and specialization (speak only on the subject on which you are expert) have developed because they facilitate policy-making.[5] Verbatim transcripts of floor debates and committee hearings are kept because what is said is intimately related to policy-making. Every day congressmen and administrators inspect the wording of testimony and debates to determine precise meanings, to get the facts absolutely correct.

Colombian legislators hold a status incentive and therefore they structure and employ their Congress accordingly. It is easy to imagine what some foreign mission would suggest if given $100,000 to propose reforms for the Colombian Congress: more staff, subcommittees, etc. But such reforms would treat only symptoms. If proposed they either would not be adopted, or if adopted, abused. Congressmen want short committee hearings because they are not

4. A sensational attack on Congress from within was made by Representative María Elena de Crovo of the MRL in the session of September 1, 1965. She captivated the House with scathing allegations of congressional corruption using, as props, a whip ("to punish the dishonesty of some parliamentarians") and a pistol ("to shoot the heels of those people who fail to respect me"). *El Tiempo,* September 2, 1965, p. 6, and September 17, 1965, p. 31; *El Espectador,* September 18, 1965, p. 13A; *Contrapunto,* August 26, 1965, p. 3. It was rumored that these colorful attacks were related to her interest in a Senate seat in 1966.

5. See Matthews, *U.S. Senators and their World,* pp. 92–117; Richard F. Fenno, Jr., "The House Appropriations Committee as a Political System," *American Political Science Review,* 56 (June 1962), 310–24; Nicholas A. Masters, "Committee Assignments in the House of Representatives," *American Political Science Review,* 55 (June 1961), 345–57; John F. Manley, "The House Committee on Ways and Means: Conflict Management in a Congressional Committee," *American Political Science Review,* 59 (1965), 927–39.

interested in working out policy; they want floor debates to be interrupted by clamor from the galleries because clamor is what they seek. Congressmen do not have greater technical assistance because they have no use for it. They are not interested in the exhaustive analysis of legislation and its effects. An illustration of the futility of rules which are in conflict with the incentives of congressmen is the law which states that no congressman should receive his daily salary if he is absent from Congress without an excuse on that day. This rule has been on the books since 1931, but apparently has never been applied.[6]

THE CONGRESS AND POLICY-MAKING

The most important fact about the Colombian Congress is, then, that in general *congressmen are indifferent to particular policy outcomes per se.* All of our inquiries about program differences between the parties (Chapter 4), factionalism (Chapter 9), party structure (Chapter 10) as well as the above examination of the nature of Congress lead to this conclusion. Because Colombian leaders have a strong status incentive, they have little interest in public policy for its own sake. I think this orientation is accurately reflected in an interview with an ex-representative from Cundinamarca:

Q. But aren't there people in Congress who are defenders of particular programs, who take a continuous interest in a policy . . . or defend. . . . Like agrarian reform, for example?

A. No, actually there are not. No one really has a particular interest. Take agrarian reform [1961]. The gringos [Americans] wanted an agrarian reform, so we did it—to please the gringos. We didn't care one way or the other. These issues come and go; it's all a matter of circumstances.[7]

6. In 1946 *Semana* (December 16, 1946, p. 8) noted that this pay deduction "has never been applied."

7. The reader should not conclude from this comment that Colombian congressmen are "reactionary" or conservative. That considerable attention to "agrarian reform" came from foreigners and not locally probably reveals more about the ignorance of these foreigners in perceiving real political priorities than any conservative tendency of Colombian leaders.

The observer who seeks to find a Left and a Right in the Colombian Congress is doomed to error if he makes a superficial study and is likely to go insane if he makes a careful examination. The search for a progressive or reactionary segment in the Colombian Congress is about as pointless as attempting to divide birds along the same lines.[8]

What, then, determines the behavior of legislators with a status incentive? How do Colombian congressmen, who have little interest in policy itself, respond to the issues that come before them? Votes are taken and frequently they affect policy. What makes congressmen vote as they do?

The answer is complicated and involves three elements which typically bear concomitantly upon the voting decision:

1. the strategic implications of the issue for the national factions
2. the popular-demagogic inclination to favor lower strata groups
3. the ignorance of and lack of interest in specific policies and details of policies

An important and frequently overriding determinant of a congressman's vote is the strategic implication of the issue for the faction to which he belongs. If it is clear that his faction stands to gain by voting "no," then the congressman will vote "no." In asking members of national directorates and congressmen about faction "discipline" it clearly emerged that they see two types of issues: "political" and "nonpolitical," or in our terms, strategic and program. Leaders defined a political issue as a matter which directly and obviously affected the political welfare of the faction. Illustrations include the election of a presidential designate, electoral laws, approval of high administrative appointments, and withdrawing support from an executive.

8. When I argue that Colombian congressmen are basically uninterested in policy, I strongly disagree with Albert Hirschman. Hirschman constructed an interesting model to deal with "reform" in the Colombian Congress based on the proposition that congressmen had strong policy preferences, that indeed they had strong preferences on all policy issues. On this point I believe Hirschman is mistaken and consequently much of his analysis is irrelevant for Colombia. Albert O. Hirschman, *Journeys Toward Progress* (New York, The Twentieth Century Fund, 1963), p. 292 and passim.

Nonpolitical or program issues were, in the view of the leaders, such matters as fiscal and monetary policy or social and economic measures. On strategic issues the leaders stated that faction discipline was expected; on program matters it was not. Leaders repeatedly pointed out that *on program matters directorates did not take positions and were not expected to take positions.* This is significant because it clearly reveals the lack of concern leaders exhibit toward program matters, compared with their concern over private, strategic matters.

In practice a division does exist between strategic and program matters, but Colombian leaders oversimplify the distinction. First, even on purely strategic issues it appears that "discipline" does not account for the cohesion which obtains in the voting patterns. When asked about the punishment of faction members who go against the faction on strategic matters, leaders were surprised and confused as if such a case were incomprehensible. When pressed to give illustrations of how discipline would be applied or to cite cases of punishment, leaders were curiously evasive.

In one interview with a member of a national directorate I finally got to the heart of matter of cohesion:

Q. What happens to the congressman who votes against his faction on a clear, what you call "political" issue?
A. Well . . . Well, it means that he is no longer in the faction; that he doesn't want to belong to the faction.

That is, the failure of a congressman to go along with a faction already indicates that he has shifted loyalties to another faction. He does not see the same risks and opportunities as other faction members and is, de facto, a member of a competing faction. Cohesion obtains within the faction on strategic issues because members share the same strategic perspective.

This cohesion does not represent the "discipline" of some other party systems. Threats and punishments are necessary where participants have prominent policy attitudes and have to be coerced into going along with the leadership on program matters. The carrot–stick technique employed in Great Britain and to a lesser extent in the United States to encourage party unity is necessary because legislators may have program preferences of their own which conflict with those of party leaders. Weapons of discipline are not necessary in Colombia because congressmen and leadership rarely care about program. On strategic matters all faction members have the same attitude; if they did not, they would not be in the same faction.

One matter, for example, which is always strategic is the election of presiding officers for each house of Congress. These three officers, a president and two vice-presidents, enjoy terms of only 60 days and customarily are not reelected. This practice is, of course, a response to pressure for the prestige of these positions; the rapid rotation in-sures that many legislators will attain the status of these posts. On May 4, 1965, the election for presiding officers of the House pro-duced an interesting but clearly strategic division. The supporters of Carlos Lleras for president in 1966, the Officialist Liberals and Ospinista Conservatives, backed one slate. The opponents of this candidacy, the Lauro-alzatista Conservatives, the Movimiento Revo-lucionario Liberal, and the Alianza Nacional Popular of Rojas Pinilla, united behind another slate.[9]

Many observers were astounded by this alliance. How could Laureanistas unite with Rojistas when Rojas had deposed Laureano Gómez in 1953 and after Gómez had been bitterly attacking Rojas for years? How could the MRL, which got votes by arousing anti-Conservative feelings of the Liberals, unite with the Lauro-alzatista Conservatives? How could allegedly "Rightist" ANAPO unite with the supposedly "revolutionary Leftist" MRL? Obviously neither histori-cal, nor personal, nor ideological considerations were important. The three groups had a common strategic goal: opposition to the candi-dacy of Carlos Lleras. Under the circumstances they could advance their common strategic goal by opposing the Llerista slate for House officers.

Strategic issues, however, are not clearly defined but shade into program matters so that virtually every item that comes before Congress has some strategic implications and therefore a tendency toward faction cohesion remains. That is, program issues such as taxes, budgets, labor reform, and public works often have—or are

9. *La República*, April 29, 1965, p. 7, and April 30, 1965, p. 8; *El País* (Cali), May 5, 1965, p. 21; *Semana al Día*, May 7, 1965, p. 9. Since neither side could obtain the necessary two-thirds majority, the House remained with the existing officers.

thought to have—strategic overtones. On these issues the directorates almost never take a position, either formally announcing that congressmen are free to vote as they like or simply ignoring the matter altogether. Nevertheless, faction members tend to vote together on such issues.

Typically, the most important strategic implication of program policies will be their impact upon the executive. Each faction adopts an orientation toward the president ranging from almost complete support to belligerent opposition. These strategies are determined primarily by the relative share of participation in the government (ministries, governorships) allotted to the faction, and the calculations made by faction leaders concerning the relative electoral benefits of support or opposition. In general those factions accepting posts in the government are government supporters, those without posts are opposition. However intermediate positions exist: quasi-support (accept ministries but reap electoral benefits from harassing the executive); or quasi-opposition (refuse ministries but tone down opposition to facilitate an alliance with a government-supporting faction or a larger offer from the president at some future date).

Consequently if a measure is supported by the executive and/or it appears that the executive will benefit from a measure, the tendency will be for opposition groups to oppose it and collaborators to support it. Opposition forces seek to disgrace and undermine the regime for electoral purposes. Their cry is that a drastic change, namely themselves, is necessary to rescue the country from chaos. Furthermore, groups outside the government oppose the executive because they must indicate that their support can be bought only at a price—a satisfactory number of government positions to their faction members. There will be an underlying tendency, then, for opposition factions to oppose anything the executive might want or need: monetary or fiscal measures, reforms of one kind or another. Conversely, those factions participating in the government have been "paid" and consequently will generally support what the government seeks.

SENSITIVITY TO THE POPULAR SECTORS

Compared to legislatures in other countries, is the Colombian Congress insensitive to popular demands? In view of the obvious lack of interest congressmen exhibit toward policy matters, it first appears that they do not care about the electorate and therefore may be expected to defy or ignore it. But this line of reasoning misses a fact of enormous importance. Congressmen care about themselves, and their own political advancement depends heavily upon electoral success. To fully understand this observation, it is useful to trace out some theories in detail.

The primary criticism directed at the Frente Nacional by both local and foreign observers is that it eliminates "democracy" from the policy-making process. If one accepts the classical model where the relative strength of parties serves to transmit shifts in the opinion of the electorate into policy, this criticism would be well taken. This model sees the parties (labels) expressing different policy tendencies, and as the electorate comes to prefer one tendency more, it votes more in favor of the party advancing that position. Consequently the party captures a greater proportion of governmental offices and thereby shapes governmental policy more in favor of the values party members hold. If an arrangement like the Frente Nacional, where the parties get the same number of congressional seats regardless of the vote, were adopted, the classical model would be undermined and the sensitivity to popular demands eliminated.

But this model assumes that the parties and party members have different policy programs. It assumes, in fact, that leaders have a program incentive and are seeking to put their different preferences into policy. Only if such differences arise between the parties will party competition serve as a transmission belt for popular demands. This classical model will not work if politicians are uncommitted to anything beyond their personal careers. It will not work because all politicians will adopt the immediately popular position.

I think enough has been said in previous chapters to demonstrate that Colombian leaders do correspond rather closely to the theoretical abstraction known as "selfish maximizers." Now it happens that Colombia uses and has used popular elections to select its leadership. Although these elections have frequently been less than perfectly free and unbiased, they have been basically competitive. Consequently, as predicted by the theory, Colombian leaders of all parties have adopted the same popular position.

The first implication of this observation is that criticisms of the Frente Nacional as "undemocratic" because of the parity arrange-

ment are misguided. There is not a conservative (small "c") party in
Colombia. The Colombian Conservatives have not operated as a
block to prevent reform; they have split into competing factions. And
none of these factions is opposed to anything popular—unless opposition is strategically convenient at the moment.

The other implication of the goal of electoral success sought by
Colombian politicians is that Congress takes on the coloration of a
popular-demogogic body. Colombian congressmen are inclined to
promise anything popular and avoid anything unpopular. And when
time comes to act, they are inclined to vote for anything popular.
One illustration of this attitude is the congressional tendency to resist
new taxes while readily approving more expenditures, thus often
leaving the budget drastically unbalanced (see Chapter 12). The
popular inclination of Congress is often obscured by the strategic
implications of issues. As we know from analyses of voter behavior,
citizens are seldom aware of or interested in specific policies and can
be deceived by their representatives now and again.

But the blessing of strategic opposition to particular measures is
that it is circumstantial and sporadic. Over a period of a few days or
years the context will change and the measure, particularly if it is
popular, will pass. One night Congress refuses to pass the judicial
reform; the next night it passes the same measure by a handy margin
(see page 260). Furthermore, there are limits to the wisdom of
strategic opposition to an apparently popular measure; it is important
not to give political enemies too much ammunition for their attempts
to identify you as a self-seeking demagogue or reactionary oligarch.

In Colombia we find the kind of politician upon which Anthony
Downs built his model of democracy: a man whose goal is to get
himself into office.[10] Leaving aside the complication of factions, the
Colombian politicians *really* correspond to his basic assumption that
politicians are maximizing officeholding opportunities. American
politicians, as is clear from a comparison with Colombians, fall far
short of meeting this ideal type. They have program commitments,
which have impeded the development of popular-demogogic policies.
In the United States Congress there are many men who believe that
the popular is not always right, that governments should hesitate to
intervene, that any policy should be carefully studied before it is

10. *An Economic Theory of Democracy* (New York, Harper, 1957).

approved. The opposition of these men is not strategic or momentary. Term after term they will vote against measures designed to relieve some immediate suffering or against some apparently popular reform. For this reason reforms in the United States are massive undertakings, battles waged on many fronts decade after decade.

In Colombia no such barrier to reform legislation exists. The basic goal of politicians, personal success, produces the *true* theoretical result: politicians highly sensitive to the whims of voters. There are few dedicated reformers in the Colombian Congress, men who work long and hard at devising programs and who are in politics to accomplish these reforms. But neither are there dedicated reactionaries, a fact that foreign observers invariably overlook. They think they see a strong reactionary element in Colombian leadership which calls for a dragon-slayer of the "moderate left" to combat it. This is pure romanticizing. Because they are sensitive to votes, Colombian politicians are sensitive to the popular clamor. Insofar as they care about policy, and providing that overriding strategic conditions do not interfere, Colombian congressmen are inclined to give the masses anything they appear to desire.

The idea that Colombian governmental policy is crudely reactionary is a preposterous misconception. Colombia has many modern, progressive, and socialist policies: social security, government housing, agrarian credit, expropriation of lands, protection of workers and trade unions, enormous price control, considerable national ownership of industry, free public education, and a progressive income tax. Virtually all these policies have been adopted in the interests of the lower strata. If in practice they do not work fully or do not produce the desired result, we cannot blame the Colombian Congress. The obstacles probably lie in inadequate resources, improper administration, and problems not amenable to easy, direct solution.

A popular-demagogic inclination of congressmen, then, is the second general determinant of voting behavior. Although strategic implications will frequently overlie this tendency, it emerges on many occasions: when strategic implications are unclear or feeble; when the issue has clear popular appeal; and over the long run as circumstantial strategic considerations cancel out.

CONGRESSIONAL APATHY AND EXTRAORDINARY POWERS

In assessing the importance of Congress in the Colombian system, one must make an important distinction. One aspect of congressional power is the ability to coerce the executive on important strategic matters; the other concerns the making of policy. If a majority of congressmen vigorously accuse the president of giving undue advantage to one faction, his life will be miserable indeed. When congressmen genuinely perceive that the executive is endangering their political prospects, they will unleash a holocaust of opposition and implacably block his wishes. When a clear executive-congressional struggle arises, Congress can drive a president from office or even, as I shall show in Chapter 13, constitutionally murder him.

But on policy matters, particularly details of policy, Congress does very little. This is so because legislators, with a status incentive, do not wish to have the bother of making policy. This point was well made in a thumbnail sketch of the Colombian Congress which appeared in *Semana*:

> A congressman works first of all on political tactics, and incidentally on laws. He is primarily a politician; additionally, a legislator. The nation, the taxpayers, the voters pay him . . . to make laws . . . but his occupation, which fills most of his working time and all of his leisure time, is politics [*política*, strategic maneuvering]. The Colombian congressman is not, therefore, a technician or a specialist.[11]

The article continued to describe the various types of congressmen. It noted the existence of a rare man

> who works quietly . . . to present into the hands of the Secretary at the precise moment the clause, the modification on which no one will argue and which everyone will approve; the legislator who makes a law single-handed, who substitutes himself, with the general approval of the rest, for the entire Congress.[12]

11. *Semana,* December 16, 1946, p. 7.
12. Ibid., p. 9.

We might suspect, incidentally, that Antioqueños would frequently be these rare types, owing to the difference in their incentives. I asked a representative from Cauca about this:

Q. Is there anything different about the members of Congress who come from Antioquia?
A. Yes . . . They're more tenacious.
Q. What do you mean?
A. Well, they seem to know more about administration. They are more experienced with governmental matters. They seem to be able to grasp things more clearly.

That there are occasional congressmen with an interest in policy-making in the Colombian Congress seems true; but there are not enough of them to carry out any extensive lawmaking. Furthermore, on any major piece of legislation the threads of strategic meaning would wrap committee discussion (what little there might be) into endless knots as members of different factions attacked and counter-attacked.

Congressmen, then, do not want to be lawmakers and they realize that a serious attempt to make laws would fail. Consequently, there exists the practice of delegating extraordinary powers to the executive branch to compose laws on difficult and involved subjects: taxation, tariffs, and comprehensive reforms (such as the judicial reform of 1965, noted below).[13] Usually the extraordinary powers are delegated by the passage of a short law stating in a few paragraphs the general outlines of the proposed reform. Typically such measures have strategic implications along the axis of opposition-support for the executive. When such delegations of authority are approved they constitute an abdication by Congress of the power to spell out details of policy. But this is a power Congress does not want. As we shall see in Chapter 13, Congress can be a tyrant over the executive, but a lazy tyrant.

The congressional lack of interest in policy becomes a third force —or indeed, a non-force—in voting patterns. That is, many decisions

13. The practice of delegating extraordinary powers seems to be as old as Colombia. It was practiced in the 1820s; see Bushnell, *The Santander Regime in Gran Colombia*, p. 13. Also see Salamanca, *La República Liberal, 1*, 178 ff., 213.

may be taken or not taken simply because congressmen are uninterested and unaware. One moment they may vote for something, another minute against the same thing. This erratic and inconsistent pattern may obtain on even the most important matters. To a certain extent such inconsistency is the product of shifting strategic winds. But often it can be attributed only to a superficial attitude toward policy itself.

It is this phenomenon of apathy and ignorance which led me to describe the congressional inclination as "demagogic." Legislators prefer popular things, but in a superficial sense. They do not examine the ramifications and long-run implications of policies. They glance at the broad lines of a policy. If it seems popular in an immediate sense, they are inclined to favor it even though it may have disastrous consequences later on.

I might summarize this discussion of the determinants of voting behavior by saying that congressmen are playing a game with three rules. The first rule is defend your faction. The second, do the popular thing. The third rule: remember that often the game isn't important anyway. It is possible to illustrate the combined impact of the three elements of legislative behavior by inspecting some typical cases of congressional action.

The judicial reform bill. In late 1962 the government sent to Congress a measure to give the executive extraordinary powers to elaborate and promulgate a judicial reform. *Proyecto* 223 consisted of a few short paragraphs setting forth the objects of the proposed reform and some general methods for accomplishing them. The object of the judicial reform was to provide a more just judicial system. The reform would include definition of some new crimes, alterations of certain punishments, an expansion of judicial facilities in rural areas, and speeding up the delays between arrest and trial. Fortunately, two of the votes on this measure were done on a roll-call basis in the House of Representatives so we may inspect the behavior of the factions on the issue.

The proposal for judicial reform powers had strategic implications of moderate proportions. Since it was proposed by the executive it tended to be an opposition-support measure. But it was not a dramatic measure nor highly publicized. It was not clear whether it was particularly popular; it was not clear that the executive stood to gain or lose popularity by its passage.

The first vote on Proyecto 223 in the House came on November 21, 1962, at the first reading, prior to referral to committee. As shown in Table 11.7, the vote followed faction lines. The Unionista Conservatives (Ospina-alzatistas), with four of the six ministries, were with the executive, Conservative President Guillermo León Valencia. The Officialist Liberals, with the six Liberal ministries, were also in favor, with a few defections. The Laureanista Conservatives defected somewhat, reflecting their position of quasi-support. They had two ministries but were dissatisfied with this share. The MRL and ANAPO were opposition groups, without any representation in the executive. The measure received the necessary two thirds required for approval under the Frente Nacional (notice the low voting turnout) and went to committee.

TABLE 11.7

Two House Votes on the Extraordinary Powers
For Judicial Reform, November 1962

Factions	Vote on first approval, Nov. 21		Vote on Article 3, Nov. 28	
	Yes	No	Yes	No
Unionista Conservatives	36	0	44	0
Officialist Liberals	38	3	38	8
Laureanista Conservatives	19	6	19	7
MRL	2	24	0	31
ANAPO	0	4	0	6
Totals	95	37	101	52
Total voting	132		153	
Total of House members	184		184	
Proportion turning out to vote	72%		83%	

Source: Compiled from *Anales del Congreso 1962*, pp. 2125–26 and 2238–39; *Organización y Estadísticas Electorales 1962*, pp. 90–99.

Only one week later, on November 28, 1962, the bill was back on the House floor, slated for article-by-article consideration and final passage. The session grew stormy. The first two articles were passed by voice vote over the increasingly vociferous objections of opposition members. The speaker acceded to the opposition request for a roll call vote on Article 3, producing the result shown in Table 11.7. The article just barely failed to obtain the required two thirds and therefore was defeated. The speaker then adjourned the session.

But failure was easily converted to success. The next night, November 29, Article 3 was simply brought up again and revoted (a standing vote, not roll-call) and passed 101 to 16.[14] What had happened, apparently, is that the shifting turnout had produced a sharp decline in the number of opposition members present on this night. But what was the "will of Congress"? Or, more specifically, what was the will of each congressman? In the United States a close vote would be reproduced almost exactly one day later. If a measure were to be revoted each side would take elaborate measures, sleeping in the congressional lounges if necessary, to see that every vote was available.

It seems clear that opponents of the extraordinary powers were not particularly committed to defeating the measure. Article 3 was defeated on November 28 because many of the opposition members happened to be present, because they were opposition, and because their emotions were aroused on that particular night. But the next day they were willing to ignore the measure and let it pass. The lesson for those who want to get things done in the Colombian Congress is not to excite strategic conflicts. Be quiet, noncommittal, undramatic. To force things through Congress, particularly with the two-thirds requirement, is difficult and frequently impossible. But far-reaching measures may be approved if they are slipped through unobtrusively. One parliamentary tactic practiced by the speaker (if he is a government supporter) is to terminate stormy sessions when an executive-support measure is under consideration to "*calmar los ánimos*" (calm the emotions). At the next session the matter may be quietly passed as the momentary strategic conflicts are forgotten.

The proposal for judicial reform was passed, therefore, in the House. Then, as reported to me by the House floor manager of the bill, the executive lost interest in the measure and the matter was dropped. In 1963, however, extraordinary powers for judicial reform were again proposed and passed by Congress.[15] Finally, on August

14. *Anales del Congreso 1962,* pp. 2319–20.
15. The House passed this measure by a vote of 93 to 27 on July 18, 1963; see *El Tiempo,* December 30, 1963, p. 21.

1, 1965, a comprehensive judicial reform, filling an entire book, was promulgated. The expectation, based on the earlier votes, was that the Ospinistas and Officialist Liberals would support the measure and the Lauro-alzatistas would be most likely to oppose it, since they had defected in greater numbers to oppose the reform in the two votes displayed in Table 11.7. But the result was quite different. The Lauro-alzatistas vigorously supported judicial reform, their paper, *El Siglo,* hailing it as "a national longing." [16] The Ospinista paper called it "a failure . . . a bureaucratic pork-barrel." [17] Officialist Liberal leader Carlos Lleras argued that it would have been better to spend the money on nursery schools.[18]

This shift in attitude toward judicial reform resulted from a changed strategic climate. When the judicial reform was promulgated, a Lauro-alzatista, Raimundo Emiliani Román, was Minister of Justice. This faction thought it would make electoral hay from the measure, presenting it as a popular and needed policy. Their opponents, the Ospinistas and Officialist Liberals, reacted against this move, reasoning that what was good for the enemy was bad for them. If the Lauro-alzatistas, through their Minister of Justice, were going to present the reform as their work, then the Officialists and Ospinistas would label it bad work.

The agrarian reform bill. Another interesting and often misunderstood case of congressional action was the agrarian reform bill, fought out in 1961 (law 135, December 13, 1961). This measure was contested along rather clear factional lines. The Laureanistas and the MRL opposed it, the Ospino-alzatistas and the Officialist Liberals supported it. While there were a few crossovers, the cohesion of the factions was quite high.[19]

A hasty observation might lead one to suppose that, at least as the battle was fought in the Senate, the Laureanistas were a "reactionary right" corresponding to the stereotype of selfish landowners opposed to reform. This supposition would appear to be supported by the

---

16. *El Siglo,* August 1, 1965, p. 11.
17. *La República,* August 1, 1965, p. 4.
18. *El Espectador,* August 8, 1965, p. 1.
19. *Semana,* January 16, 1961, p. 17; January 23, 1961, p. 10; April 13, 1961, p. 10; May 22, 1961, p. 13; June 5, 1961, p. 11; June 12, 1961, p. 11; July 10, 1961, p. 14; July 17, 1961, p. 12. Also see *El Tiempo,* October 5, 1961, p. 10; October 19, 1961, pp. 1, 19.

phrase sometimes used to identify the Laureanistas: *Conservador Doctrinario*. Who would be better candidates for the "reactionary right" than Doctrinaire Conservatives? Thus the agrarian reform issue could be presented outside Colombia as a conflict between a "selfish oligarchy" opposing the "moderate left" which was sincerely responding to the "reform or revolution" imperative.

Under close examination this interpretation crumbles into dust. First, one is hard-pressed to find landowners, selfish or otherwise, in Congress at all. For whatever reason landowners, farmers, ranchers, and cattle-raisers appear in small numbers in the leadership group (see Table 2.7 and Appendix Table 4). In many conversations with Laureanistas I detected no particular bias against peasants, against agrarian reforms, or in favor of landowners. A study of attitudes of the Lauro-alzatistas reveals no "reactionary" inclination (see Table 4.4). Furthermore, the MRL, generally alleged to be a "leftist" group, allied with the Laureanistas against the agrarian reform measure.

If we examine the strategic context, however, the behavior of the factions becomes intelligible. The Laureanistas were, from August 1958 to the March 1960 congressional elections, the closest friends of the Officialist Liberals and President Alberto Lleras. During the same time the Ospinistas and Alzatistas opposed Lleras and the Frente Nacional. But in the March 1960 elections the Laureanistas suffered a setback at the hands of the Ospino-alzatistas. The deterioration of their position produced several changes. First, in view of their lessened parliamentary contingent, the Laureanistas could not be given as many ministries. They lost, in particular, the Ministry of Agriculture.[20] As a result the Laureanistas shifted to a stance of quasi-opposition, harassing President Alberto Lleras to coerce him into offering them a greater share of the administrative positions. The Ospino-alzatistas were ready to enjoy the fruits of their opposition and at the same time became collaborators.

Furthermore, the Laureanistas were a declining faction in electoral terms. To recover their position they needed to adopt a visible, dramatic, appealing program before the electorate. For a smaller faction, a position of support is neither visible nor dramatic and is devoid of appeal. Hence, opposition was the obvious alternative. Finally, in 1962, a Conservative president would take office. Would the Laureanistas have a voice in deciding who he would be? Not unless they

20. *Semana*, February 13, 1961, p. 11; April 3, 1961, p. 11.

were sufficiently visible and belligerent to be considered an autonomous force. When the Ospino-alzatistas took up the agrarian reform measure, therefore, the Laureanistas would have practically renounced their independent existence by adopting the same position. The MRL also opposed the agrarian reform, a logical consequence of its position as a small group without any ministries.

The agrarian reform conflict, then, had little to do with the subject matter. It reflected the strategic relationships prevailing between the factions. *Semana* advanced this interpretation:

> Politics [this week] had as a "leitmotiv" the agrarian reform, not because this proposal might have meaning in terms of fundamental institutional change, but because centering upon this measure a skirmish over presidential succession is being fought.[21]

The agrarian reform measure eventually did pass because the Officialist Liberals and Ospino-alzatistas had a majority in both houses. In this case only a majority was needed for approval, for prior to the conflict Congress had already passed, as the constitution permitted, a measure which made a majority vote sufficient for passage of social legislation (Law 147 of December 11, 1959). That measure lapsed at the end of 1961 and has not been renewed.

The Chocó bill. The rejection of the bill to make Chocó a department in 1947 illustrates how fleeting strategic implications may be. Apparently neither Liberals nor Conservatives found any strategic objections to making Chocó a department when the issue came to a vote on the Senate floor in July. Everyone expected the matter to be approved readily. *Semana* reported what happened:

> But all of a sudden the demon of partisan politics arose, brought in by an incidental allusion to the last elections which [Liberal proponent of the measure Diego Luis] Córdoba made. The Conservatives closed ranks in a single block against making Chocó a department, with the cooperation of a few Liberals from Valle and Antioquia. The rest of the Liberals united in favor.[22]

21. Ibid., January 23, 1961, p. 10.
22. Ibid., August 2, 1947, p. 5. The department of Chocó was to be carved from portions of the departments of Valle and Antioquia. Chocó was made a department in the following year.

The bill lost by three votes—votes which could have easily been obtained if all the Liberals had been present.

The sales tax bill. An interesting illustration of congressional inconsistency is found in the history of the sales tax measure. Originally Congress passed the measure in the form of extraordinary powers during June-July 1963. The vote in the House was reportedly 114 to 32.[23] The sales tax was to have gone into effect at the beginning of 1964, but at the last moment President Valencia met with top leaders of government-supporting factions and a decision was made to postpone this unpopular tax until January 1, 1965.[24] Toward the end of 1964 congressmen began an attempt to rescind the sales tax measure.

The opposition to the sales tax was so clearly a popular stance that the popular-demagogic orientation of congressmen erased factional lines. The national directorate of the Officialist Liberals formally (and superfluously) announced that members of the Officialist congressional delegation were "left in freedom" to vote as they chose.[25] In the House the proposal to abolish the sales tax was overwhelmingly approved by 121 to 6 votes.[26] This action represented a dramatic reversal of congressional will. It can be accounted for by realizing that when the measure was originally passed in 1963 no one was paying much attention. The measure simply slipped through.

The reversal was even more immediate, however, for the House had just passed the budget which contained the sales tax as a revenue source. An Ospinista Conservative from Antioquia pointed this out to the House:

> Señor Representative Octavio Arismendi . . . said that the spectacle which we are witnessing demonstrates that the Parliament is structurally incapable of managing the fiscal policy of the nation. The fact that just a few days ago Congress approved a budget which included the income from the sales tax and today is discussing a bill which strikes down that tax demonstrates it quite clearly.[27]

23. *El Tiempo,* December 30, 1963, p. 21.
24. Ibid., December 28, 1963, p. 19.
25. Ibid., November 18, 1964, p. 1.
26. *Anales del Congreso 1964,* p. 1966 (session of November 24, 1964).
27. Ibid., p. 1901.

The most surprising development, however, occurred in the Senate. Judging from the sentiment in the House against the sales tax, one would have supposed that the Senate would also rescind it. But in the Third Senate Committee where the proposal lay awaiting approval, the agenda was altered at the last minute to prevent the sales tax matter from coming before the committee. Consequently the committee did not pass the proposal to rescind the sales tax, the Senate did not act, and the tax went into effect on January 1, 1965. The alteration of the agenda, moreover, was not a stormy matter. It was approved by government supporters as well as opponents, including one of the most belligerent opposition leaders, Alvaro Uribe Rueda, chief of the MRL Linea Dura.[28]

There is an explanation for this curious behavior. Since the sales tax matter was relatively out of sight in the Senate Committee, the popular-demogogic implications of the measure were greatly weakened. Moreover, committee members did not have to vote in favor of the tax, but merely for an alteration of the agenda. Government supporters were probably urged privately by the executive to let the matter die in committee, since the government desperately needed the sales tax revenues. The opposition members in the committee probably calculated that if the sales tax went into effect it would be unpopular and the matter could be exploited by the opposition.

This examination of the Colombian Congress supports some findings of Barber's study of freshmen Connecticut State Assemblymen, discussed earlier.[29] The group he identified as Lawmakers were individuals whose satisfactions came from working on policy, from translating their preferences into law. In our terms they had a program incentive. As we would expect, these participants exhibited a high willingness to return to the legislature and were active in legislative work.

Another group, the smallest in Barber's sample, were termed Advertisers. They entered the legislature for prestige and contacts. They had, it seems, a status incentive. The Advertisers had much in common with Colombian legislators. They were unwilling to return for a second term. Although they were active in a formal sense, their

28. *El Tiempo,* December 16, 1964, p. 15.
29. Barber, *The Lawmakers.*

activity was attention-getting (speeches, for example) rather than on substantive matters. They found the legislature a dull place and regarded legislation as if it were not their job to make it. What would a legislature populated largely by Advertisers look like? I think it might be described by the following hypothesis, drawn from an examination of the Colombian Congress:

> *H34. A legislature whose members have a status incentive will be characterized by:*
> 1. *chronic absenteeism in committees and votes*
> 2. *low committee workloads*
> 3. *few technical or research facilities for legislators*
> 4. *disruptive, conflict-provoking patterns of behavior*
> 5. *a popular-demagogic orientation toward program policies*

These findings about the Colombian legislature suggest that Americans may be misguided in their criticisms of the U.S. Congress. We are often impatient with such norms as seniority or apprenticeship. At least since Woodrow Wilson wrote *Congressional Government* in 1884 we have been mistrustful of the committees which guard their subject matter so jealously. We are annoyed when congressmen are reluctant to force a bill from committee. We find the club-like atmosphere of restraint stifling if not downright suspicious. We are unhappy to discover that congressmen frown upon colleagues who speak on subjects they have not studied. We are suspicious of the way congressmen use devices to hide their lawmaking activities from the public eye: closed committee hearings, secret markup and conference committee sessions, the teller vote. We vaguely suspect that in these private nooks and crannies corruption is flourishing.

An examination of the Colombian legislature suggests that these criticisms are somewhat misplaced. The above practices have evolved naturally and necessarily from the American legislators' desire to form policy and enact laws. Working on program is the reason why most of these men are in Congress and they have seen to it that nothing, perhaps even the electorate, greatly interferes with their goal. As a policy-making institution, as a body of men who examine exhaustively, deliberate calmly, and weigh thoughtfully, the United States Congress would seem a model legislature.

As a legislature sensitive to immediate popular demands, the United States Congress does not rate highly at all. Such sensitivity is inconsistent with the same incentive that makes congressmen such dogged policy-makers. They want to study matters in detail, examine consequences, allow things to "settle down." They want their policies to *work,* and workable policies require much study. American congressmen therefore tend to be cautious, and Congress takes on a conservative cast. And, I need hardly note, the program attitudes of many congressmen are expressed in opposing measures which happen to be popular in an immediate sense.

The Colombian Congress presents the opposite picture. As a policy-making body it is equivocal, clumsy, and superficial in the usual meanings of those terms. But it is extremely sensitive to immediate popular demands. There is little resistance to doing the popular thing immediately, no desire to study, investigate, or hesitate. Colombian congressmen get little satisfaction from devising policies. And they certainly are not inclined to advance policies that are unpopular. Their satisfaction comes from the prestige of office, and the conquest of higher office requires popularity. The Colombian Congress, therefore, becomes a popular-demagogic institution.

CHAPTER 12

THE BUDGETARY

PROCESS

Neither Congress nor the executive may propose an increase or new expenditure in the budget . . . if the increase alters the balance of budgeted expenditures and budgeted revenues.

Constitution of Colombia, Article 211.

The basic character of a political system is perhaps revealed most clearly in the nature of its budgetary process. Governments exist on money. Their most fundamental and enduring task is raising and expending funds. Where are budgetary decisions made? Who makes them? On what basis? The answers to these questions will reveal central characteristics of a political system.

Budget-making in Colombia is fundamentally influenced by the pronounced tendency of all participants to do the popular thing: spend money. In the administration, in the executive, in the Congress: nowhere can stingy, penny-pinching fiscal conservatives be found. It is popular to spend money, unpopular not to spend it. And it is unpopular to tax. Colombian politicians do not want unpopularity. Inexorably, then, this attitude fosters fiscal irresponsibility and deficit financing.

Since no person or institution will exercise downward pressure on the budget, Colombians have attempted to enact laws to do this job for them. Legally, the budget must be balanced (see epigraph above). The proposals for revenues and expenditures are submitted together and the totals must balance. But since no one can predict revenues with certainty, this item is adjustable and is usually inflated to produce the numerical equivalent of proposed expenditures. To block this dodge partially another law prohibits the government from claiming more than a 10 per cent increase in the revenue for an item over what that item actually produced in the preceding year. But it is difficult to apply this measure, given the constantly shifting revenue base. Furthermore, these laws are obviously not applied to supplemental expenditures.

The role of Congress in budgeting is actually quite limited. Early in July of each year the administration sends the proposed budget to Congress and it passes to the House Budget Committee. This committee is composed of two members from each department (36 members in 1965) to prevent excessive squabbling over inequitable distribution of funds to the different regions. The Budget Committee is a desirable one since through it representatives may provide certain benefits for constituents.

During September and October the House Budget Committee meets to consider the budget (both revenues and expenditures), in full committee, for about one hour on Tuesdays, Wednesdays, and Thursdays. Subcommittees are not used. Witnesses, with rare exceptions, are not called. Virtually no investigation of the budget items and agency uses of the funds is attempted. During September, I attended two meetings (sessions are public) of the House Committee. Both times I interviewed a member of the committee in the committee room while that member was participating in the session in progress. This was possible because the committee meeting consisted of a dreary reading by the committee secretary of proposed authorizations. At five- or ten-minute intervals there was a pause in the monologue and the few committee members still present in the room, including my respondent, slapped their desks in unanimous approval of whatever had been read. Later, in October and November, committee hearings became more lively as discussion and trading go on over certain regional expenditures.

The budget then goes to the House floor, Senate committee, and Senate floor quite rapidly. The budget must be passed by December 10. If it is not approved by that date, the previous year's budget is supposed to go into effect. Generally the Senate has only a few weeks in which to act, sometimes only a few days. In 1962, for example, the House did not pass the budget until December 5.

The net effect of congressional action on the budget is slight. Most items are left unexamined and unchanged. A small amount of rearrangement is effected as congressmen shift expenditures away from less obvious, less popular items to more visible, usually regional, matters. Occasionally the total amount of the budget is left unchanged; other times the total amount is increased somewhat over the executive proposal. In order to balance off these additional expenditures congressmen simply raise revenue estimates to the level necessary to produce arithmetic equilibrium.

As the year progresses, Congress proceeds to authorize supplemental expenditures for substantial amounts. These expenditures are necessitated by the undercalculation of costs or, to say the same thing another way, by administrators who overspend their allotments: e.g., the Ministry of Health hires too many officials, the Ministry of Public Works takes on too many projects. The end result is that authorized expenditures generally exceed income, often by vast amounts. In a real sense, Congress does not *budget* at all because it regards resources as if they were not scarce.

Actual budgeting, the allocation of scarce resources, falls to the Ministry of Finance, not by choice but through necessity. When claims are made upon the empty till for amounts appropriated, the Minister of Finance often attempts to refuse, or at least delay, certain payments. Strikes and protests of government employees are constantly produced by the government's failure to tender back pay. In September 1965 the schoolteachers struck for ten days, in part to coerce the national government to pay past financial obligations—back salaries, pension benefits, bonuses, and adjustments—totaling about 120,000,000 pesos.[1] Six months earlier, in March, a teachers' strike was threatened, again to get the government to pay salary debts.[2] Also during September 1965, there was a 17-day strike of employees of the Department of Justice, partly to compel the government to pay family bonuses granted in 1963 and a Christmas bonus decreed in 1964.[3] In December 1963 there was a partial strike of judicial employees protesting delayed salaries; the Minister of Justice insisted no money was available.[4]

Refusal to pay may work in some cases, but strikes and demonstrations are unpopular and embarrassing so the money must usually be found. One alternative is a new tax, but the executive is generally anxious to avoid the repercussions of such a measure. And Congress,

1. *El Tiempo,* September 2, 1965, p. 11; September 8, 1965, p. 14.
2. *El Espectador,* March 22, 1965, p. 2.
3. Ibid., September 5, 1965, p. 1; September 7, 1965, p. 1.
4. *El Siglo,* December 12, 1963, p. 15.

given its popular-demagogic inclination, will usually resist new taxes. Therefore, the executive often resorts to deficit financing, seeking approval from Congress for authority to borrow from the central bank. Congress apparently accedes to these requests in almost every case. They are made in response to some emergency demand—pay for schoolteachers or police—and superficially have no unpopular aspect, being "free" money. I asked a member of the House Budget Committee about his attitude toward supplemental expenditures and supplemental requests for deficit financing:

Q. When the Minister of Education overspends and comes to Congress for additional credits, don't you get angry? Won't you refuse?

A. No, because then you have a social problem on your hands. Imagine closing schools! . . . You have to give them the money.

The popular-demagogic inclination of congressmen usually serves to suppress the strategic implications of the budget as an executive support measure. Opposition factions in Congress allow the budget to pass because they do not want to be held responsible for the hardships of austerity. I asked a representative from the MRL about this:

Q. Generally speaking would you say the MRL opposes most proposals?

A. Yes, that's right. We're the opposition you see.

Q. What about the budget? Does the MRL oppose that?

A. (taking my arm and speaking in a lower voice) Well what happens there is that each member has projects for his region so it is rather uncomfortable to oppose it. We let it pass.

The December 10 budget deadline and the constitutional provision permitting, automatically, the use of the previous year's budget if Congress fails to pass the new one are a profound commentary on the congressional role in budgeting. In the United States it often happens that some budget bills are not passed by July 1, the new fiscal year. But invariably Congress passes measures enabling the departments to continue expenditures at the prevailing levels. No laws or constitutional guarantees are necessary to insure continuous appropriations. It is most improbable that the Congress would allow the administration to run completely out of legally appropriated funds.

It is highly probable in Colombia. The intensity of strategic battles could well lead Congress to coerce the executive by withholding funds. Faced with this threat of administrative collapse, the president would have to adopt illegal means to keep the administration alive. Either way a dangerous situation would arise: administrative disintegration or illegal presidential action. Colombian constitution-writers found it wise, therefore, not to leave the weapon of budgetary strangulation in the hands of Congress. It would be used.

Twice in recent years Congress failed to pass the budget by the December 10 deadline and according to law the previous year's budget should have been used. In 1947 the congressional failure to act was the result of a complex strategic fight between Liberals and Conservatives.[5] In 1962 a few senators on the Senate Budget Committee felt that the proposed budget was so tremendously unbalanced that it would be better to forget it.[6] In neither case, however, were expenditures held to the level of the preceding year. The use of supplemental appropriations enabled the government to increase budgeted expenditures substantially:

1947	364 million pesos		
1948	412	"	"
1962	3,386	"	"
1963	4,176	"	" [7]

Meaningful figures on the cash budget of the Colombian national government (actual revenues and actual expenditures) are not readily available. The deficit and surplus figures generally publicized in Colombia (and given to me by the Controloría General de la República) are wholly inadequate since they are apparently calculations based on legal constructs rather than the straight cash revenues and expenditures which actually obtain. They are so far distant from the cash budget figures I have obtained as to be practically meaningless. Nor can one construct more than loose approximations of deficits and surpluses from the revenue and expenditure figures given in the

5. *Semana,* December 20, 1947, p. 6.
6. *El Tiempo,* December 8, 1962, p. 25; December 11, 1962, p. 1.
7. *Anuario General de Estadística 1963,* p. 793. See also Tables 12.1 and 12.2.

TABLE 12.1

Cash Budget of the Colombian National Government
1961–1964 (in millions of pesos)

	1961	1962	1963	1964
Operating expenses*	1,515	1,914	2,509	2,878
Investment expenses	1,303	1,046	1,096	1,362
Total expenses	2,818	2,960	3,605	4,240
Revenues	2,199	2,114	3,069	3,847
Deficit	−619	−846	−536	−393

*Interest on the national debt is included but amortization of loans is not.
Not attributed at the request of the source.

Anuario General de Estadística. The expenditures given in this source, for example are budgeted expenditures and not actual expenditures.

Several international groups have worked on distilling cash budget figures from Colombian sources. One well-known international banking organization provided me with the figures shown in Table 12.1. These calculations show rather substantial deficits in the years 1961–

TABLE 12.2

Cash Budget of the Colombian National Government
1950–1962 (in millions of pesos)

	Revenues	Actual Expenditures*	Balance	Balance**
1950	494.2	524.9	−30.7	−10.7
1951	669.1	567.6	101.5	126.9
1952	703.7	733.0	−29.3	2.3
1953	839.6	854.8	−15.2	19.6
1954	1,042.9	1,065.6	−22.7	4.8
1955	1,442.5	2,139.3	−696.8	−664.9
1956	1,137.8	1,385.9	−248.1	−208.7
1957	1,227.1	1,296.6	−69.5	−14.6
1958	1,636.6	1,617.6	19.0	103.8
1959	1,916.1	1,861.6	54.5	291.8
1960	2,132.3	2,094.3	38.0	144.6
1961	2,130.7	3,113.1	−982.4	−862.3
1962	2,143.0	3,224.8	−1,081.8	−862.4

*Includes debt amortization.

**This balance is based on actual expenditures excluding debt amortization.

Source: "Joint Tax Program of the Organization of American States and the Inter-American Development Bank," *Fiscal Survey of Colombia* (Baltimore, Johns Hopkins Press, 1965), p. 16.

64. The Joint Tax Program study gives a more varied pattern of deficits and surpluses for the years 1950–62, reproduced in Table 12.2. Note that the 1961 and 1962 figures of Table 12.1 differ somewhat from those of Table 12.2. Obviously, compilation of cash budget figures is a complicated and uncertain task.

There is reason to suspect that the cash budget figures given in Tables 12.1 and 12.2 understate deficits because, among other things, they apparently do not include the losses incurred by the decentralized agencies. An indicator of deficits which might avoid this problem is the change in the total national debt. Presumably a deficit would cause the national debt to increase. Table 12.3 shows

TABLE 12.3

Increase in Colombian National Debt, 1950–1962
(in millions of pesos)

	Increase in Net Debt*
1950	−0.4
1951	3.0
1952	31.9
1953	16.5
1954	130.7
1955	−97.5**
1956	141.3
1957	374.7
1958	253.8
1959	−13.5
1960	104.6
1961	697.4
1962	2,282.2

*The change in the balance of internal and external debt, excluding accrued interest.

**This figure is clearly misleading. Examination of both the legal and cash budgets for 1955 shows that the government appropriated and spent funds vastly in excess of its revenues. Somehow the funding of this deficit was disguised or transferred to later years.

Source: Fiscal Survey of Colombia, p. 11.

that in all but two years (1950 and 1959) the national debt increased during the period 1950–62. In only two other years (1951 and 1953) was the debt increase modest (less than 4 per cent of government expenditures).

An inspection of the budgetary history of 1950–64, revealed in these tables, supports the following conclusions: (1) The general tendency in the Colombian system is toward deficit financing, frequently in quite substantial amounts. Whether one decides that expenditures should be cut back or that "Colombia is in urgent need of additional governmental revenues at all three levels of government" [8] is not a matter to decide here. (2) The tendency toward deficit spending is interrupted by years of nearly balanced budgets or moderate surpluses (1950, 1951, 1959). These surpluses, however, are not commensurate with the staggering deficits frequently encountered (1955, 1956, 1961, 1962, 1963). (3) No obvious relationship appears to exist between the kind of regime or the party in office and budgetary practices. In the two years of greatest "austerity," 1951 and 1959, there were different presidents of different parties. 1951 was a period of Conservative hegemony and violence. 1959 was during the Frente Nacional and relative peace with a Liberal president in office.

Apparently, the cycle of excessive deficit spending and moments of mild austerity is largely a response to shifting reactions to government deficits. As deficit financing creates serious inflation, begins to undermine the local credit system, and seriously damages the foreign credit rating of the country, increasing pressures come from local businessmen and international agencies for tighter fiscal management. These pressures are voiced in public opinion media, encouraging a general demand for austerity. Thus fiscal policy tends to follow a cycle of stemming one fiscal crisis and then plunging into the next.

A full discussion of the economic impact of Colombian deficits would be inappropriate here. It appears that inflation, which averaged about 10 per cent yearly during 1954–64,[9] is closely related to the amount and manner of deficit financing practiced by the national government. The uncertain fiscal climate makes it difficult for the government to avoid the most inflationary policy of debt management: borrowing from the central bank. Private individuals and corporations are naturally reluctant to purchase government bonds

8. *Fiscal Survey of Colombia,* p. 20.
9. Departamento Administrativo Nacional de Estadística, *Informe al Congreso Nacional 1964* (Bogotá, Multilith Estadinal, 1964), p. 21.

which might become valueless in a galloping inflation. Finally, one can easily imagine that the investment climate is impaired by the atmosphere of panic which often surrounds government finance.

The pattern of recurrent fiscal difficulties, I suggest, is the product of the popular-demagogic orientation of political leaders. Congressmen are not going to risk being accused of acting like stingy oligarchs, oblivious to the needs of the masses. Except in the occasional case when strategic considerations interfere, Colombian legislators will do the apparently popular thing. As a consequence, the fiscal crisis is a way of life.

The role of the U. S. Congress in budgeting offers a remarkable contrast. The members of the House Appropriations Committee have considerable seniority in Congress, usually come from safe districts, and have little fear of electoral reprisal. The committee can thus insulate itself from popular pleas for more spending. It is divided into twelve specialized subcommittees which meet in secret session and carry on lengthy cross-examinations of scores of administration witnesses. Hour after hour committee members conduct their investigations into each agency's requests and the past uses of funds. Members of the Appropriations Committee are characteristically hard-working, close-lipped, and, frankly, somewhat stingy.

The members of the House Committee are known as "guardians of the treasury." They see themselves as protecting the taxpayers' dollars against the assaults of administrators and clamoring citizens. In the usual case the House Committee can be counted upon to shave down the administration's budget. As a result the budget items finally passed by Congress are generally lower than the amounts proposed by the executive.[10] The House Appropriations Committee exhibits a pronounced hostility toward supplemental expenditures. Except for demonstrable emergencies, the overspending of an allotment infuriates committee members. Committee hearings bristle with rebukes to administrators who do not fully appreciate the congressional budget-cutting role. Compare the following excerpts, taken from House hearings on appropriations, with the attitude toward supplementals expressed by the Colombian appropriations committee member above:

10. These observations are drawn from: Fenno, "The House Appropriations Committee as a Political System"; Aaron Wildavsky, *The Politics of the Budgetary Process* (Boston, Little, Brown, 1964), pp. 41–56.

CHAIRMAN [Martin B. Madden]: Please tell the committee why you need this $9,500.

MR. ACKER: This additional money is needed because of the fact, in the first place, that we did not get what we estimated for.

CHAIRMAN: That is not a good reason. If that is the only reason you have, it is not worth a cent.[11]

REP. JOHN ROONEY: There was a reduction made in the amount requested of the Congress last year, was there not? [The item under discussion was the State Department appropriation for international conferences.]

MR. WILCOX [State Department]: Yes, sir.

MR. ROONEY: The budget estimate was $2.4 million and the Congress allowed $1.6 million; is that correct?

MR. WILCOX: That is correct.

MR. ROONEY: After the deduction by Congress what reductions were made by the Department in an effort to stay within the amount allowed?

. . .

MR. WILCOX: Mr. Chairman, I find it rather difficult to be precise in answer to your question. . . .

MR. ROONEY: Unless you start explaining what you did, I am going to assume, for one, that you just went merrily along the way, on the assumption you were going to present the supplemental request and that you did not attempt to condense your budget to meet the appropriated amount of $1.6 million.[12] [The Appropriations Committee subsequently disallowed a requested $800,000 contingency fund for international conferences, requiring the State Department to come back with a specific justification if such funds proved necessary.]

The different budgetary practices in the United States and Colombia flow from the differences in incentives. American legislators have a program incentive. They get satisfaction from managing a govern-

11. U.S. House of Representatives, Committee on Appropriations, *Hearing Before Subcommittee in Charge of Deficiency Appropriations,* 68th Cong., 1st Sess., 1924, p. 509.

12. U.S. House of Representatives, Committee on Appropriations, *Hearings Before the Subcommittee on Departments of State and Justice of the Committee on Appropriations,* 86th Cong., 1st Sess., 1959, pp. 958–59.

ment as an instrument of their preferences. Many have, of course, conservative preferences; they believe that government functions and government spending should be discouraged. They enjoy hammering out a "tight" budget. But even those who prefer an expanded governmental role in certain matters want to examine and supervise such expansion. The budget is their tool for accomplishing programs; naturally they examine it thoroughly and manage it soberly. For this reason American congressmen want to "keep politics out" of fiscal matters. They want to be insulated from the popular clamor, to do their managing calmly and exhaustively. "You don't just mess around with taxes," say the members of the U. S. House Ways and Means Committee.[13] But you *can* just mess around with taxes, as Colombian legislators have so dramatically shown. After witnessing the disorder created in Colombian finances by politicians who will not say "no" to popular clamor, one might view the "skinflints" of the U. S. House Appropriations Committee with a certain thankfulness.

13. Manley, "Conflict Management in a Congressional Committee," p. 930.

CHAPTER 13

THE

PRESIDENT

The political groups, the pressure groups and the conspiracies have not let me govern. I have had to maintain a permanently defensive position. One has to be a cowboy to remain astride this bronco which has tried to throw me so many times.

> *President Guillermo León Valencia in*
> *a statement reported in* El Espectador,
> *September 7, 1965, p. 1.*

There are forces of atomic potential in the Colombian political system. The strength of the status and employment incentives charges the system with enormous energy, as the tropical sun concentrates hurricane forces in the equatorial atmosphere. The political figure who most fears these forces is the president. He is situated in the storm track—or, in President Valencia's apt analogy, he sits astride the bucking bronco. Whatever analogy one choses, being president of Colombia is a nerve-wracking, taxing job.

Just how taxing is illustrated by the unhappy fate of Francisco Javier Zaldúa, elected president in 1882. As soon as Liberal Zaldúa came to office on April 1, 1882, a severe conflict broke out between him and the followers of Liberal Rafael Núñez. Historians differ in ascribing the responsibility for this clash. Some blame Núñez, as a ruthless ex-president (1880–82) seeking to maintain his hold on the administration to insure his election as president in 1884.[1] An admirer of Núñez argues that Zaldúa provoked the conflict by conspiring with the radical Liberal faction (opponents of Núñez) to destroy Núñez politically.[2] Leaving aside the matter of guilt, Zaldúa was implacably opposed by the Nuñistas who held a majority in Congress.

1. Rodríguez, *Hechos y Comentarios*, pp. 161–77; Puentes, *Historia del Partido Liberal*, pp. 345–47.
2. Indalecio Liévano Aguirre, *Rafael Núñez*, pp. 200–13.

At that time senatorial approval was required for presidential appointments of ministers. When Zaldúa attempted to compose a cabinet of men from different Liberal factions, the Nuñistas balked and their senate majority refused to approve any appointments unless the men were Nuñistas. Zaldúa attempted to give undersecretaries control of the ministries, but the Nuñista congressional majority responded by passing a law which obligated the president to gain senatorial approval for second- and third-level appointments and for military appointments down to the level of sergeant-major.[3] Zaldúa still refused to yield to the Nuñista demand for more (all?) administrative positions.

At that time the president could not leave Bogotá and remain president unless he obtained the permission of Congress.[4] Zaldúa was an old and infirm man who found the chilly and rarefied atmosphere of Bogotá unhealthy. Zaldúa and the opposition realized that a premature death could be expected if he were not given an opportunity to recuperate in lower, warmer regions. To further pressure the president, the Nuñistas refused him permission to leave Bogotá.[5] Zaldúa refused to yield and did indeed quickly die, on December 21, 1882, only nine months after taking office. Although the passage of time has probably embellished the legend of the "martyred president," Zaldúa's death does stand as a reminder of the ruthless and implacable forces that may be unleashed against a president.

The primary danger a Colombian president faces is the unyielding opposition of a substantial majority of the political factions. Though felt most directly in Congress, the opposition does not begin there. The congressmen respond to strategic conflicts as members of national factions. It is the national faction which becomes disturbed or infuriated. When the president finds that most of these factions vigorously oppose him, he faces problems not only in Congress but also at the departmental and even municipal levels. The volume of antipresidential opinion will also increase as faction newspapers and speechmakers take up a belligerent opposition stance.

Faced with a large, implacable opposition, the president finds it

3. Rodríguez, *Hechos y Comentarios,* pp. 173–74.
4. This rule was apparently based on articles 65, 67, and 77 of the Constitution of Rionegro (1863).
5. Rodríguez, *El Olimpo Radical,* pp. 166–67.

difficult to govern in any meaningful sense. Other institutions, particularly Congress, will block, undermine, and reverse his every move. If the president attempts to stretch or violate the constitution to bypass the roadblocks thrown up by the opposition, he will experience even greater fury from them. Mosquera (1867), Gómez (1953), and Rojas (1957) each discovered that arbitrary or dictatorial acts cannot quell opposition. All three were deposed in popularly supported coups. Another alternative for the harassed president is resignation. This option was taken by Marco Fidel Suárez in 1921 and Alfonso López in 1945. Many more Colombian presidents have been at least urged by different factions to resign.

It is easy to see why a president fears a sizable opposition and the immobilism it will produce. A president understandably wants to be a national hero, respected and remembered. Obviously he wants to avoid leaving office scourged and slandered, known as a man who wrecked the country. Consequently the president's goals coincide, except in rare cases, with political tranquility and a functioning government. To keep the opposition small and fluid is the primary task of the Colombian president.

THE INEVITABILITY OF OPPOSITION

Since Bolívar, Colombian presidents have faced an opposition which, at a minimum, may be described as healthy. Opposition of some leaders and factions will persist regardless of who the president is or what he does. An attempt at the forcible suppression of opposition results, as just noted, in even more opposition. The persistence of this opposition is reflected in the powers that Congress holds and often wields against the president.

This pattern is in contrast to the experience in some other Latin American countries where chief executives, for substantial periods of time, have succeeded in eliminating effective opposition. The legislature is servile, newspapers respectful, and speechmakers discreet. In Colombia dictatorships or quasi-dictatorships have never taken root. Somehow opposition always survived. One reason lies, I believe, in the high party identification, which affords opposition leaders an enduring base of support.

In the Latin American environment, dictatorships, such as the

Leguía regime in Peru (1919–30), can often be established with relatively little effort. One does not need to massacre thousands or imprison tens of thousands; one does not need to establish a vicious totalitarian police network or capture every fragment of organization and every opinion center in the country. Many Latin American dictatorships have been established without great difficulty, have functioned undramatically, and have been overthrown bloodlessly. Insofar as this pattern has obtained, it is inconsistent with the idea that there are many participants strongly devoted to the notion of freedom *or* to the particular dictatorships involved. The easy-come-easy-go dictatorship is consistent with the proposition that participants have private incentives such as status.

If it happens that through luck and clever management a chief executive successfully applies certain repressive measures, the distribution of opportunity for political leaders shifts dramatically in the president's favor. A few exiles, a few arrests, a little arm-twisting of newspapers, and most leaders are readily convinced that opposition is an unrewarding strategy. They are deprived of the means with which to gather their own support—the free use of their tongues and pens—and therefore side with the executive in the hope of rising up the ladder on good behavior. Of course, the executive will enjoy this support only as long as he appears secure. If it seems that a military coup may be provoked by an opposition strategy, then virtually everyone will desert to the opposition and a coup will indeed be provoked. Leguía headed a dictatorial regime in Peru for almost eleven years with little apparent opposition; he suddenly fell in 1930, reviled by everyone. In Guatemala the dictatorship of Jorge Ubico lasted thirteen years. In 1944, after a few protest demonstrations, the seemingly unshakable Ubico was toppled quickly and almost without bloodshed.

If party identification is high, however, party labels become an enduring resource for opposition leaders. The magnetic appeal of the executive is greatly diminished because any leader may dip into a vast reservoir of support, the masses of party-identified voters. In this way the inducements offered to leaders by the executive—such as the president's popularity and his control of administrative resources—are counteracted by the strength of party labels. Neither presidential demagoguery nor repression can greatly impair this base of support for opposition leaders, and consequently a dictatorship cannot be easily established.

An illustration of the tenacity of an opposition based on party-identified voters is the level of Conservative activity in the village of Garzón (about 10,000 inhabitants in 1936) in the department of Huila during the days of Liberal hegemony in 1935–36. At this time the Liberals were fully in control of the national government since the Conservatives had refused to run candidates in the 1935 legislative election. Nevertheless the Conservatives in this village regularly published a party newspaper, *Acción Conservadora*.[6] The paper reported a vigorous party life at this time, including a departmental convention with 64 delegates.[7] We note a list of 120 names of local people who sent their congratulations to the new national Conservative directorate and the names of 122 individuals who donated money to the Conservative fund "to buy freedom of speech from the Liberal regime of Alfonso López." [8]

In Colombia, therefore, high party identification seems to have facilitated the presence of an opposition and has provided leaders with a base of support whenever the executive attempted to gather up all the reins of power. Even if they were of the president's party, ambitious leaders could form opposition factions, rooted in the electoral, or even military, support of party identifiers.

High party identification always makes the opposition strategy a productive one for some leaders; paradoxically, it also insures that the president almost always has some support. As explained in Chapter 7, high party identification gives those leaders who collaborate with the executive an outside electoral resource so they may avoid the liability inherent in the name of an unpopular president. Leaders can, except in extreme cases, accept the benefits which come from collaboration without suffering disastrous consequences in the next election. They simply run as Liberals and Conservatives. Party identification, then, reduces both the risks of opposition and the risks of support and therefore makes it likely that any president will have some of each.

Where party identification is low, supporting an unpopular presi-

6. Copies available at the National Library in Bogotá.
7. *Acción Conservadora*, July 25, 1936, pp. 2–3.
8. Ibid., November 9, 1935, p. 2; June 6, 1936, p. 3; July 4, 1936, p. 3.

dent can be prohibitively risky, because leaders have nothing else on which to stand. For this reason the support of a popular and/or repressive president will quickly erode if he appears headed for a fall. The same leaders who cooperated hasten to condemn the "reactionary tyrant"; they lead demonstrations and parades against him. To have fought the dictatorship is an important credential for advancement under the next regime. Consequently in regimes where party identification is low we should expect an alternating pattern of periods of virtually unopposed presidential rule, owing to the executive's popularity and/or use of repression, and periods of extreme opposition to the president probably leading to a coup (hypothesis H18).

CITIZEN VIOLENCE AND THE LABOR MOVEMENT

I have pointed to the degree of party identification and its effect on executive support patterns as the explanation for the difference in coup probability in Colombia and in Peru. Regardless of how one explains it, the Colombian president is far less fearful of a military coup than the Peruvian executive. This fact has great significance for predicting the degree of executive sensitivity to violence and, subsequently, certain characteristics of the labor movement.

In Peru, where the executive is in greater danger of a coup, citizen violence poses an acute threat for the president. Demonstrations, parades, strikes, clashes with the police, opposition invective: these may provoke military intervention because they represent palpable evidence of society's profound antipathy toward the president. The Peruvian executive has, therefore, acquired the weapons necessary to intervene in the conflicts which provoke violence. In labor disputes and strikes, for example, the Peruvian executive plays a central role, frequently dictating solutions to strikes in private firms, solutions sufficiently generous to induce the workers involved to end the strike and concomitant agitation. This practice of settling labor disputes by executive decree has arisen because the president is fundamentally threatened by such conflicts. In this context the Peruvian labor movement has adopted a strategy of political bargaining: the coercion of the executive (not the employers) by actions which threaten to produce snowballing violence. And with this strategy, the Peruvian labor movement enjoys considerable success.[9]

In Colombia the executive is less sensitive to political violence. A wave of increasing unpopularity is unlikely to be touched off by violent incidents because the national factions supporting the president are anchored in party labels. They do not desert the president at the first signs of rough weather. Consequently, even when faced by violence, the president retains sufficient political support to forestall military intervention (hypothesis H18). The executive, therefore, need not intervene so readily or widely in labor conflicts. The Colombian labor minister does not decree solutions to strikes in private firms.

Since the Colombian executive cannot be readily coerced by worker demonstrations and clashes, the strategy of political bargaining is relatively unproductive for the Colombian labor movement. It has been thrust back upon the method of collective bargaining, consisting, essentially, of attempts to coerce the employer by a collective withdrawal of labor.

The basic difference between these two bargaining methods has a profound effect on the Colombian labor movement, producing many contrasts with the labor movement of Peru. One would expect, for example, that labor movement structure in Colombia would focus on the firm rather than the work center, since it is the employer (firm) that is being coerced. This pattern, with certain complications, does obtain. In Colombia if there are two plants of the same firm located some distance apart, there is only one union for both groups of workers. In Peru one would find two separate unions. Under political bargaining attention is concentrated not upon the firm but upon the nation's chief executive. Consequently the basic structural unit in the Peruvian labor movement is the simplest fighting unit, the work center or plant. In turn these plant-level unions form alliances for the purpose of effecting solidarity strikes with *any* other unit.

Another contrast with the Peruvian labor movement should occur relative to the length of strikes. It was reasoned in the Peruvian study that if coercion took place along economic lines against the employer, considerable time might elapse before the strike began to

9. See my *Labor and Politics in Peru* (New Haven, Yale University Press, 1965).

hurt. In most industries the employer has inventories and easily deferred orders so that the first weeks of a strike are hardly felt. Therefore strikes would be long under collective bargaining. With political bargaining, the executive is coerced by the buildup of violence and such a buildup reaches its peak quite quickly. Consequently strikes should be short. This analysis appears to apply to Colombia. A typical Colombian major strike (e.g. an important wage demand) lasts about two or three months and, in an unusual case, such as the Alotero or Gaseosas Colombianas conflicts of 1964–65, as long as eight months. In Peru a strike of similar significance would last three to four weeks, in an exceptional case about eight weeks.

It must not be thought, however, that in Colombia nothing resembling political bargaining takes place. The executive is often concerned about strikes which cause public inconvenience because they can affect his popularity, although not to the same extent as in Peru. Consequently, although executive involvement in labor disputes occurs much less often than in Peru, the Minister of Labor does on occasion attempt to mediate these conflicts. Even in the United States where collective bargaining is clearly the basic labor movement strategy, the president plays an important role in rail, steel, automobile, and dock strikes. But although elements of political coercion are found in both the United States and Colombia, the executive does not usually intervene to make binding decisions in labor disputes involving private firms. Political bargaining is not the primary labor movement strategy in either country.

BASIC CHARACTERISTICS OF PRESIDENTIAL BEHAVIOR

The Colombian president, then, is not greatly shaken by civilian violence itself. His activity is directed primarily to the task of attempting to satisfy, or at least not clearly antagonize, the political party factions. Since the demands of these factions concern strategic issues and not program policies, it follows that the president's role is largely that of balancing the various demands for positions in the government. President Valencia recognized this problem: "The parties are divided into groups and sub-groups, classes and sub-classes.

The governmental positions are not sufficient to give representation to all these groupings." [10]

Some groups will, of course, choose an opposition strategy because their strength does not justify participation in the government. They cannot expect an adequate number of positions; therefore they calculate that a vigorous opposition strategy will bring electoral success so that more positions may be demanded at a later date. But among the factions that are left, willing to participate at a price, there will still be more demands and expectations than available positions.

The national factions want positions (ministries, agencies, governorships) for several reasons. First, they constitute the rewards and honors sought by politicians. Secondly, they enable faction leaders to strengthen their faction by giving employment and favors to active followers. Finally, the faction and the individual leaders gain prominence and publicity which is useful for further advancement, particularly to the presidency. The Minister of Education is constantly dedicating new schools; a governor is opening new bridges.

The support strategy, however, entails a certain risk. Frequently the electoral strength of a collaborating faction will wane under the fierce attacks of the opposition. Government supporters may become tinged with the responsibility for the "crisis" and "inaction" alleged by the opposition. In Colombia the tendency for collaborators to lose electoral support is expressed by the phrase "power burns." Actually, of course, it is not power but the voracious opposition which burns. The liability of the support strategy must not be exaggerated, however. Party identification greatly cushions the danger of a vote loss and often collaboration results in no relative electoral decline at all. In general, a small faction will suffer most from a support strategy because it loses its visibility. Consequently, smaller groups (such as the MRL Linea Blanda and Linea Dura and ANAPO in 1965) are generally found in the opposition.

The varying degrees of support and opposition, however, are fluid and delicate matters, not determined by one variable. To a certain extent they depend upon how the president handles his position. In attempting to obtain the greatest support and maintain a fluid opposition, Colombian presidents generally try to: (1) be impartial,

10. Comment made to reporters, in *El Espectador*, March 14, 1965, p. 2.

(2) procrastinate on critical decisions, (3) reduce their visibility, and (4) be sensitive to immediate popular demands.

Impartiality. Since the essence of politics in Colombia is the quest for personal advantage, it follows that the most grievous injury one can inflict upon a faction is to impair its officeholding opportunities. Conversely, the way to please a faction is to afford it fair representation in the administration. Insofar as he is able, the president generally attempts to include all factions in his government on a fair basis and tries to be responsive to complaints of administrative partiality. He seeks to avoid favoring one faction against another. In this way he may hope to obtain the grudging support of most factions and avoid the implacable opposition of others.

In the selection of ministers, the president generally is guided by the congressional representation of each faction. Presidents have frequently composed mixed ministries, including men from both parties. And almost always the president will attempt to distribute ministries to different factions of the same party. Limits to presidential neutrality are usually established by groups already collaborating with the executive. In 1849, for example, in an attempt to give the Conservative congressional minority some administrative representation and thus mitigate hostility from that quarter, Liberal President José Hilario López named a Conservative, José Acevedo, as Minister of Foreign Relations. But the Liberals would not tolerate even one Conservative in the government. López was obliged to remove Acevedo to forestall implacable opposition from the Liberals.[11]

During his term (1962–66), President Valencia was faced by difficult distribution problems, particularly in dividing up the six Conservative ministries. Since there were three Conservative factions, the Ospinistas, the Laureanistas and the Alzatistas, roughly equal in congressional representation, Valencia decided to give two ministries to each one, a practice known as *"milimetría."* At first all three groups were tolerably satisfied, but after the Laureanistas and Alzatistas united in late 1964, the Ospinistas grew restless and, in August 1965, clamored for three ministries. Many local pundits criticized Valencia for sticking doggedly to the 2-2-2 distribution, failing to realize the potential advantage of such a mechanical distribution of offices.

11. Restrepo, *Historia de la Nueva Granada, 2,* 122; Roberto Echeverría Rodríguez, *Los Gólgotas* (1944), p. 146.

If ministries and governorships were allocated on the basis of an objective standard, the president could not be coerced, threatened, or blackmailed by competing factions seeking greater shares. By depriving himself of the ability to make decisions on this matter, Valencia could—and to a certain extent did—escape pressures for a change in the distribution. At the same time, however, Valencia lost his ability to discipline factions by trimming down their representation if they became hostile to him. Assured of their ministerial positions, Conservative factions, both the Lauro-alzatistas and the Ospinistas, practiced an intermittent "opposition from within." Although they held ministries, they occasionally harassed the government in Congress and in their press.

The influence of most presidents in determining their successors or biasing congressional elections has generally been minimal. Naturally, different factions make accusations of executive favoritism, but in fact the president usually makes an effort to insure that these accusations are groundless. The president may have his private preference about his successor, but he usually takes pains to show that his personal choice does not affect his official acts.

President Valencia, for example, frequently stated that he was a "first-rate Llerista," that is, a supporter of Officialist Liberal Carlos Lleras for President in 1966. But he emphasized in word and deed that this preference was not affecting his action as president:

> REPORTER: If the president is a first-rate Llerista, could not there also be first-rate anti-Llerista governors?
> VALENCIA: Just a minute. . . . There is a distinction. As an individual I can have whatever political sympathies I like, but as a ruler I have to be absolutely impartial. It is not true that Llerista or anti-Llerista machines are being established in the country.[12]

And Valencia, seeking not to antagonize Lleristas (Officialist Liberals and Ospinistas) or anti-Lleristas (Lauro-alzatistas and MRL), was impartial. Although both sides made accusations of presidential bias, neither really believed that Valencia was practicing favoritism.

In order to avoid provoking a large, infuriated opposition, then, the president generally attempts to walk a neutral path between the

12. *El Espectador,* March 14, 1965, p. 2.

warring factions. When favoritism is practiced it generally comes not from the president but from factions the president cannot curb.

Procrastination. Because the demands for positions frequently exceed the supply, the president often faces the unpleasant task of disappointing someone. An immediate resolution of such dilemmas is likely to drive the losing faction toward the opposition. But while the decision is suspended there is no losing faction and thus the president gains weeks of relative tranquility. Furthermore, the tactic of procrastination allows factions to edge away from ultimatums; e.g. "Unless we get three ministries we will not enter the government." Thus, the final outcome is less likely to produce a dangerous explosion. For these reasons presidents are likely to delay many weeks in making difficult decisions on the appointment or removal of ministers and governors.

In deciding certain policy measures the president is often well-advised to delay. If he acts quickly and decisively he may provoke charges of aribitrary behavior, leaving himself open to a barrage of opposition. It often serves a president to be criticized for inaction in a crisis; when he does act there is little ground for opposition. A tax increase, for example, may be quietly accepted if the president cleverly encourages the belief that he has delayed much too long in promulgating it.

Reduced visibility. You cannot coerce a man unless you can deny him something he wants. And you cannot shoot at a target you cannot see. In recognition of these maxims most Colombian presidents try to remain uncommitted and out of sight. In the United States we are accustomed to see presidents campaigning throughout the country in favor of certain programs, defending them in press conferences, congressional breakfasts, and speeches.

It would be unwise, however, for a Colombian president to adopt a similar stance. First, by indicating that there was something he wanted badly, the president would simply give the various factions in Congress something to withhold in bargaining for greater shares in the administration. In all probability, by giving congressmen material with which to coerce him, the president would make it less likely that his measure would pass. Secondly, by dramatically favoring something, the president would excite his strategic opposition. Noncollaborators, instead of absent-mindedly letting the measure pass, would be galvanized into firm opposition.

Consequently, the president avoids becoming dramatically committed to particular measures. He strikes a stance of disinterest, as if to say, "I think it's a good idea but I don't really care." Sometimes a president may shift attention away from himself by giving the job of advocacy to a special committee and to members of Congress. The agrarian reform law, mentioned in the last chapter, originated in a nongovernmental commission and its defense was largely the work of Senator Carlos Lleras. President Alberto Lleras appeared as little more than a sympathetic bystander. In 1965 President Valencia appointed a special committee of business and labor leaders to work out certain labor reforms and tax measures to be submitted to Congress. Many times the minister in charge of the particular measure will be a visible advocate, and the taciturnity of the president usually makes it seem that the minister is acting on his own.

Sensitivity to popular demands. Even if the president and his ministers were privately indifferent to popular demands, such an official stance would be politically unhealthy. A conservative or insensitive executive invites opposition by providing the factions with the opportunity to adopt a dynamic opposition stance. No matter what the president does some factions will insist he has squeezed blood from the masses. Even government collaborators will raise the cries of crisis and the need for reform. By taking clearly unpopular positions the executive would simply prompt supporters to desert him and reap the electoral benefits attendant upon opposition.

For this reason Colombian presidents are sensitive to immediate popular demands. They avoid unpopular actions and advance popular measures, even unsound ones. Budget deficits, price controls, and foreign exchange controls are some basic practices which grow out of this sensitivity. Matters that are easily controlled and highly visible such as bus fares or water rates are natural targets for opposition attacks and, hence, natural objects for stringent regulation. Of course, if rates are kept low to satisfy political pressures, utilities will have little reserve for improvements and expansion, with the result that service may be poor and incomplete.

Although the president generally tries to be popular, the best he can achieve is subdued unpopularity. The attacks of the opposition and the atmosphere of crisis generated by all office-seekers make it impossible to advance a credible claim to success. To be popular the Colombian president unbalances his budget to provide more schools, public works, housing, health care, and other governmental services. He then seeks new taxes to cover the deficit, so the opposition attacks him. He resorts to deficit financing but that causes inflation, so the opposition attacks him. He cuts back governmental services in an austerity program, so the opposition attacks him. The president cannot expect the horse to stop bucking; staying on is all he can hope for.

A brief case study serves to illustrate the importance of the above norms in making life possible for the executive. Toward the end of August 1965 the government sought congressional authorization to accept $400,000,000 in American aid loans. When the matter came before the House on August 19, 1965, a few members of the MRL vigorously opposed it; one even tore a microphone off the stand and threatened to throw it. The presiding officer wisely adjourned the session to allow emotions to cool. On August 24 the matter was again brought before the House, quickly brought to a vote, and passed in a standing vote of 105 to 27.[13] I happened to observe this particular session and noticed a number of MRL representatives standing in favor of the measure. This behavior perplexed me so I queried one of these MRL congressmen about his vote:

Q. How did the MRL vote on the American loan of $400,-000,000?
A. [laughing] We sacred cows of the MRL voted in favor.
Q. But why? Won't it help the president?
A. Maybe him or the next one. We just thought it was a good thing. Here's the money so why not take it?
Q. But . . . but López [leader of the MRL] says in his book *Colombia en la Hora Cero* that Colombia must be liberated economically, that the United States has enslaved . . . ?
A. [smiling] Listen: we didn't study the thing at all. I came on the floor and asked someone about it, he said it seemed okay so I voted for it. That's all.

So Valencia got what he wanted and opposition members helped get it for him. This victory was the result of astute manipulation of the presidency. First, Valencia had not antagonized the MRL by moves which impaired its political prospects. His position of impartiality had kept the MRL from focusing too much attention on him.

13. *El Tiempo,* August 25, 1965, p. 11.

Secondly, during August, while this matter was before Congress, Valencia had allowed the Ospinista-Lauro-alzatista conflict to simmer while he delayed naming a new ministry. At this time the Ospinistas were threatening to withdraw from the government if they were not given three ministries. But the Lauro-alzatistas would withdraw if the Ospinistas *were* given three ministries. By delaying the final decision until September 1, Valencia gained the acquiescence of both factions on the loan issue. If he had immediately named a ministry on August 7, when he first said he would, it is possible that the Ospinistas would have been jolted into opposing the measure.

Finally, Valencia kept the loan out of the news and avoided identifying himself with it. Except for the disturbance in the House on August 19, the matter was largely unnoticed. Few people knew that the issue was being considered; fewer still viewed it as "Valencia's measure." Thus by skillfully toning down strategic implications, Valencia took advantage of the congressional inclination to approve popular proposals.

Although the Colombian president has some strategies to keep politics manageable, he still is the prisoner of circumstances. If factions become implacably opposed to each other, the president will find it almost impossible to maintain his neutrality. No matter what he does, each group will accuse him of favoring the other and both will oppose him. Furthermore, opposition will increase as the presidential term advances. As elections draw closer and the fruits of office are nearly exhausted, the opposition strategy grows more attractive for most factions. Historian Eduardo Rodríguez noted this phenomenon in the term of Conservative President Miguel Antonio Caro (1892–98) in 1897:

> The government of Caro was weakening daily, because two thirds of the constitutional period [of six years then] had passed, which in itself is a cause of unpopularity for a government, no matter how good it might be.[14]

The president's problems, then, are often generated by circumstances beyond his control.

14. Rodríguez, *Diez Años de Política Liberal,* p. 39.

Although I cannot here extend this discussion of the Colombian presidency, perhaps this brief overview adequately demonstrates that his basic job is to keep the various national factions friendly, or at least not implacably hostile. The president's role in policy-making is secondary to his job as manager of the strategic relationships between the various party groupings. These relationships involve not only the positions of the factions at the national level but also the juggling of faction demands at the departmental level. The president is first a manager of the strategic conflicts in the Colombian system.

But again, as with the Colombian Congress, it is not accurate to equate a secondary interest in policy with a conservative or insensitive orientation. The executive, simply because the buck must stop somewhere, is sometimes forced to play an unpopular role, as in refusing payment of salaries when there is no money, or initiating a new tax to cover a growing deficit. But, as Colombia's inflated budgets indicate, the president is basically sensitive to popular, lower strata demands. Of course, one must not confuse this popular policy orientation with the ultimate effects of governmental programs, since between the two enter the problems of scarce resources and difficulties in administration.

CHAPTER 14

POLITICAL CONFLICT
IN PERSPECTIVE

¿Siempre tendremos que fregarse?
(Will we always have to foul up?)

> *Anonymous,* La Paz, o la Guerra *(Bo-gotá, Imprenta de N. Gómez, 1860),* p. 1.

Over one hundred years ago an anonymous writer, identifying himself as an artisan, pointed out the Colombian problem in plain and simple language. On the eve of the civil war of 1860–61 he asked if machinations and violence always had to be the pattern of Colombian politics. He saw civil war approaching and pleaded against the folly of it all: "I hear on one side the word *majority* and on the other, the word *majority*. Each party says it has it. How can that be?" And he was not far wrong in diagnosing the root of the problem. "Our ancestors fought and sacrificed for Independence; we fight because we are not on top." [1]

A century later the problem persists: is violence inevitable in the Colombian system? The problem, I insist, is basically political. It relates to the status and employment incentives of participants and the context in which the struggle for these rewards takes place. Any solution to the problem of violence must either alter the incentives of participants or the political framework which shapes their behavior.

This is not the view generally taken by students of comparative politics or American policy-makers. The popular position holds that deprived masses seeking to better their standard of living are the cause of political violence. It follows from this view, therefore, that acute political conflict can be reduced by socioeconomic progress, by popular reforms, by raising standards of living. Demonstrations for

1. *La Paz, o la Guerra,* p. 11.

more housing, for example, are ended by providing more housing.

Although superficially convincing, the privation explanation for political conflict may be highly misleading. It ignores participants, particularly leaders, their motives for participating (incentives), and the strength of these motives. And it fails to recognize the decisive role played by leaders in finding and focusing demands.[2] Movements of political violence seldom occur spontaneously. They grow out of a context defined by leaders, form over demands agitated by leaders, against targets identified by leaders and are often organized and directed by leaders. Given their critical role, it is of paramount importance to learn why leaders participate.

If leaders have what I have broadly identified as a program incentive, it seems plausible that their level of activity will be related to the demands they make. Leaders with a program incentive are drawn into political activity by the desire to accomplish policy objectives. Their satisfactions come from working for policies, from devising remedies for undesirable conditions. It would follow, then, that as programs are approved and put into effect, changes in participant activity should result. Some participants would withdraw from politics, having accomplished what they set out to do. Others would reduce their level of activity since the diminished severity of the problem no longer warranted strenuous efforts. Consequently, where a program incentive is found, leadership activity, and the resultant agitation, would bear a relationship to the solution of problems which disturbed leaders.

Some tentative illustrations of this phenomenon can be found in American history. Slavery, for example, was an issue which stimulated considerable participation: abolitionist societies, underground railroads, the John Browns. There were enough participants strongly aroused on this matter to found a new party, the Republican party, and ultimately to provoke a civil war. But when slavery was abolished, agitation rapidly subsided. Participants withdrew by the thousands, having accomplished their objective. Their object was apparently not to protect the citizen rights of Negroes or better their living

2. An illustration of the leadership role in finding demands and creating issues is Robert Dahl's account of the development of the urban renewal issue in New Haven under Mayor Lee; *Who Governs?*, pp. 117 ff.

standards, for no serious attention was given to these matters until almost a century later.

We might also suspect that the declining belligerence of European labor or socialist parties can be traced to a similar phenomenon. Fifty years ago the disadvantaged position of the workers stimulated participants whose program incentive was to better the lot of the workers. As workers gained more rights and benefits, the attractiveness of the worker defense incentive was reduced. Fewer participants were drawn into activity in response to it and those who remained active exhibited a lower level of concern. Consequently militant socialists and militant socialist parties have practically disappeared.

The impermanence of political reform groups in the United States is also attributable to a specific program incentive which weakened when the mission was accomplished. Reform movements often had the highly specific goal of beating the machine. Frequently participants with this incentive were successful in their own terms: they defeated the regulars and gained control of the city government. Their incentive then weakened since city government was "cleaned up," and they rapidly lost interest, enabling participants with more durable incentives to regain control. George Washington Plunkitt, an old-style New York politician, poked fun at the reformers, characterizing them as "only mornin' glories":

> Now take the reform movement of 1894. A lot of good politicians joined in that—the Republicans, the State Democrats, the Stecklerites and the O'Brienites, and they gave us a lickin', but the real reform part of the affair, the Committee of Seventy that started the thing goin', what's become of those reformers? What's become of Charles Stewart Smith? Where's Bangs? Do you ever hear of Cornell, the iron man, in politics now? Could a search party find R. W. G. Welling? Have you seen the name of Fulton McMahon or McMahon Fulton—I ain't sure which— in the papers lately? Or Preble Tucker? . . . They're gone for good, and Tammany's pretty well thank you.[3]

These remarks do not, of course, explain why a certain program incentive should emerge, nor why it appears when it does, nor why it

3. William L. Riordan, *Plunkitt of Tammany Hall* (New York, Alfred A. Knopf, 1948), pp. 23–34. James Q. Wilson has also noted the crisis reform organizations face when they win; see *The Amateur Democrat*, pp. 5, 365.

is as strong as it is. Presumably if a program incentive is strong, extreme levels of protest and violence are probable (hypothesis H4). But it does seem true that leadership participation, and consequently the level of political conflict, will bear a relationship to government policy if the incentive is of the program variety. If, for example, leaders with a program incentive are leading demonstrations for more housing, it is probable that when a housing program is established they will relax their efforts and fewer demonstrations will occur.

If, as in Colombia, leaders hold a status incentive, however, a radically different perspective is warranted. Status-motivated leaders participate not to effect any particular socioeconomic change, but to obtain status. Consequently the protests and violence they instigate are only incidentally related to socioeconomic conditions or governmental programs. Many conflicts may be over strictly strategic matters. The violence of 1946–53, for example, represented the working out of strong status and employment incentives through particular political structures in what I called a "defensive feud." Socioeconomic issues were peripheral. The many crises at the national, departmental, and local levels occasioned by withdrawals of support by different factions are products of the struggle for political opportunity and are little related to the presence or absence of particular governmental programs.[4]

Illustrative of the strictly strategic conflict is an episode which occurred in the town of Soacha, Cundinamarca (pop. 27,000). On September 6, 1963, some inhabitants of Soacha blockaded the main highway which runs southwest from Bogotá and passes through the town. Why? A sharp conflict between the former mayor and a majority on the city council had arisen over (1) which firm should be given a contract to build a new water main for the town and (2) the mayor's dismissal of, as he alleged, superfluous municipal employees. The two local treasurers sided with the council and refused to take orders from the mayor. The mayor responded by jailing them. Naturally this crisis provoked the intervention of the departmental secretary of Gobierno, who removed the mayor and appointed another.

4. This view is advanced by Guillén Martínez, *Raíz y Futuro de la Revolución;* also see Mauricio Guzmán, "El Faccionalismo: Supervivencia Medieval en América Latina," *Journal of Inter-American Studies, 5,* (1963), 465–70.

But the supporters of the first mayor protested this action by blockading the highway so that no traffic could pass. In response, the departmental secretary again intervened. He rushed to Soacha and, after conferring with leaders from the pro- and anti-city council factions, found a third mayor acceptable to both sides and the blockade was lifted.[5]

Beyond purely strategic political conflicts, it must be recognized that status-motivated leaders are going to find and agitate for popular socioeconomic demands. Since their advancement depends heavily on electoral success, they will energetically espouse any apparently popular position. And the more intensely these leaders seek advancement, the more fiercely they will press the demands, tending toward a generalized position of protest. Opposition leaders will insist that the existing regime has brought the country into a terrible condition, that basic reforms are necessary, and that if elected they will begin the march of progress.

In any country at any time there are an infinite number of potential demands or problems that could be made into political issues. Whether these demands are found, how many are discovered, and how much they are agitated depends heavily upon leaders. In a system where leaders have a program incentive of moderate strength, a few demands are agitated at one time, at a relatively low level of intensity. And as the government devises programs to meet these demands, agitation subsides.

But if leaders have a strong status incentive, they are never satisfied by any governmental program. Their level of activity is determined by their own status aspirations and not by the fortune of the programs they happen to advance. If the government builds 5,000 low-income housing units, politicians will argue that it is not enough. If it builds 50,000, they will charge that kickbacks were made to contractors, that the work was shoddy, and that people have to pay too much to rent or buy them. Regardless of what reforms are enacted and in spite of any progress that might be made, the level of political protest will not diminish and politicians will continue to insist that the nation is in its blackest hour.

An illustration of the connection between the struggle for political advancement and socioeconomic demands is the behavior of Lauro-

5. *El Espectador,* September 7, 1963, p. 2.

alzatista Conservatives in Bogotá toward Officialist Liberal Mayor Jorge Gaitán Cortez in 1965. For many months the Lauro-alzatistas had complained about discrimination practiced against them in the allocations of positions in the Bogotá municipal administration. Finally, on April 22, 1965, the Lauro-alzatistas withdrew support from Mayor Gaitán, convinced that Gaitán would not yield to their demands (see Chapter 10). On Saturday afternoon, April 17, 1965, Bogotá was hit by a severe rainstorm, a virtually unprecedented deluge which dumped several inches of rain on the city in a few hours. In one of the poorer sections of Bogotá, because the storm drains were inadequate and not properly maintained, the water rose to several feet in the street, entered the houses, and damaged the furniture in about five hundred homes. It was a newsworthy story and covered as such by the Officialist Liberal newspaper, *El Espectador*. But the Lauro-alzatista *El Siglo* lashed out in its page one headline, in great blue letters:

INDIGNATION IN THE SUBURBS AGAINST MAYOR
GAITAN CORTEZ FOR THE FLOODS

The subhead further inflamed the issue:

WHILE THE MAYOR MAKES A POLITICAL CAMPAIGN
THE SUBURBS ARE COMPLETELY ABANDONED, SAY
THOSE SUFFERING FROM THE FLOODS [6]

Upon reflection it appears that any government can be held responsible for floods, since they can always be prevented. In the United States floods occur quite frequently and do considerable damage. Why, for example, isn't Mayor Sam Yorty of Los Angeles scored for the mudslides and bridge washouts which occur yearly in that city? One might claim that it is too expensive to prevent all floods. But Mayor Gaitán made this claim and it did not satisfy the Lauro-alzatistas. He said that he had earlier proposed a 643 million peso master plan for a Bogotá water and drainage program, but that there were no funds to finance it.[7] The Mayor of Los Angeles is not held responsible because not enough political leaders are sufficiently desirous of advancing themselves at his expense. But a voracious Co-

6. *El Siglo,* April 18, 1965, p. 1.
7. *El Espectador,* April 20, 1965, p. 1.

lombian faction like the Lauro-alzatistas finds a flood an excellent pretext for unleashing a volley of abuse against the executive who stands between it and political positions.

The demands, protests, and conflicts agitated by leaders with a status incentive, then, bear little relation to objective circumstances or governmental policy. It is therefore inaccurate to say that protest and political violence can be prevented by economic progress, by (more) "reforms" or by foreign assistance. These measures do not affect the status incentive of leaders and hence will not alter their level of activity. Regardless of what actually happens in the socio-economic sphere, patterns of protest and violent activity will alter little.

I am not saying that is necessarily bad for Colombian leaders to find popular demands and harass the government (and the United States) with them. This we expect of leaders in any free system and the diligence with which Colombians perform the task makes the government highly sensitive to popular needs. It was partly the Lauro-alzatista outcry over the flood, for example, that prompted the Bogotá municipal government to give compensation to families that suffered damages from it. I am saying that the popular demands raised by Colombian leaders have little to do with their reason for participating, so that the resolution of specific demands will not diminish their participation.

There are many arguments for giving foreign assistance, ranging from the manifest American tendency toward altruism to the greasing of military alliances. But we are mistaken if we believe that in Colombia foreign aid will buy political calm and stability. Where leaders have a strong status incentive, it is possible to eliminate a disease, stabilize a currency, or expand agricultural production through foreign assistance without making a dent in the level of protest or the violence potential of the system. No matter how many problems are solved, status-motivated leaders will always find more.

REFORM OR REVOLUTION

The prevailing interpretation of politics in Colombia and most other Latin American countries does not adopt the view of political conflict advanced in this study. Instead, it is argued that the solution

to protest and violence is the passage of basic reforms. A selfish conservative element, the argument runs, is holding up these reforms
while the discontented masses increasingly demand them. Failure to
enact these obviously necessary measures will lead to violent mass
movements of revolutionary proportions. In a nutshell, the prognosis
for Latin American countries like Colombia is reform or revolution.

This conclusion is laden with serious errors. First, it contains a
heavy ingredient of utopianism. Almost without exception writers
defending this view fail to specify the reforms they have in mind.
They speak in the vaguest generalities about "agrarian reform" or
"basic restructurings" without spelling out specific proposals. It seems
evident that the construction of 1,000 housing units or a decreed
wage increase or a five per cent increase in primary school enrollment
do not qualify as "basic reforms" because such changes occur almost
constantly and go unnoticed. But what is a basic reform if it is not
such marginal changes added up over decades? The argument for
reform seems not to be buttressed by a scholarly examination of
specific problems, resources, possibilities and difficulties. Instead, it
is a vague wish that a magic law will be passed which will make
Colombia like the United States.

It is easy to see how the utopianism creeps in, for local politicians
are utopian. They must paint the present in the blackest blacks and
insist that some simple changes, which they will effect when elected,
will bring on the age of progress. A leader with a status incentive
has no interest in the careful examination of specific problems and
the exploration of real solutions. He seeks to advance and therefore
must offer the voters utopia. If he does not, others who do will
trample him.

I listened to hours of speeches by ex-Minister of War Alberto
Ruiz Novoa, a weak presidential candidate in 1965, to determine
the precise meaning of his electoral slogan *"cambio de estruturas"*
(change of structures). Aside from platitudes and vague generalities,
the only specific proposal I gleaned was that schools should be open
at night to increase educational opportunities—and he never made
clear just who would pay for this marginal reform.

Another overtone of the reform-or-revolution chorus is that little
or no reform has taken place. This conclusion is not arrived at
through a comprehensive examination of policies and programs in

effect, nor from a meaningful assessment of the possibilities for change, nor from a thoughtful comparison with other countries, including the United States. Instead one reasons logically from the utopian position that there are "basic reforms" which could be implemented tomorrow and consequently "reforms" must not be in effect today. When a writer insists that there are "reforms for which Colombia's lower classes have waited so impatiently," he can hardly be expected to believe that Colombia has practically all the reforms found in the United States, for it is the utopia of the United States in Colombia which these reforms are supposed to create.

But, as I have already suggested, it is not correct to view the policy orientation of the Colombian government as "feudal" or "conservative." In actuality it tends to be demagogic and popular. And without looking very hard the investigator begins to realize that Colombian legislation contains stacks of popular reforms, many more progressive than existing U.S. laws. And they seem to keep coming every year. On September 4, 1965, the government promulgated some new labor reforms (*Decreto Legislativo* 2351) which included, among other things, a measure requiring private employers to pay workers triple time (Article 12) for Sunday and holiday work and an expanded scale of discharge compensation. Under this new scale a worker discharged after working less than a year must be given 45 days salary; a worker discharged after five years service is given severance pay amounting to 125 days salary.[8]

At this point those arguing for reform shift their ground. The statute books, they agree, are loaded with reforms but these measures are not fully carried out. Again we must discriminate between the utopian and the realistic view of reform enactment. When the utopian speaks of enactment he is not interested in the marginal improvements which take place from year to year. He looks at general results and if ideals are not achieved—no poverty, 100 per cent literacy, everyone wearing shoes—then he concludes that achievement is inadequate. Again what he is looking for is a little United States and an idealized United States at that.

The realistic view of enactment takes into consideration the scarcity of resources and the enormous problems to be solved. If the government is already running fiscal deficits, then it is unreasonable

8. *El Espectador,* September 7, 1965, p. 7A; September 18, 1965, p. 1.

to expect more than incremental expansions of governmental services. Twenty years from now, regardless of the form of government, including a communist dictatorship, by American standards Colombia will still be a poor country. The best we can hope for is a series of marginal, undramatic improvements which journalists are unlikely to notice or which, if they are noticed, reporters are likely to exaggerate.

Adopting the realistic view of program implementation and progress, it appears that Colombia is doing reasonably well. From 1958 to 1963 the number of primary school students in public schools increased 41 per cent, from 1.27 million to 1.79 million, and the number of teachers increased 53 per cent, from 28,891 to 44,250, thus lowering the pupil-to-teacher ratio from 44 to 40.[9] In two years, from 1961 to 1963, the public electric companies increased gross production 27 per cent.[10] Certain other figures show substantial progress. From 1958 to 1963 domestic airline passenger-miles increased by almost 100 per cent.[11] The production of motor gasoline quintupled from 1953 to 1963.[12] The number of movie spectators increased from 45 million in 1952 to 72 million in 1963.[13] Real wages (i.e. wages corrected for inflation) of blue-collar workers in the manufacturing industry increased an unusual 20 per cent from 1961 to 1963. The real wages of white-collar workers in the manufacturing industry increased by four per cent in the same period.[14]

Put such figures in the hands of propagandists of a totalitarian state and they would be trumpeted around the world as demonstrating the dawn of utopia. But Colombians are never permitted to suspect that their country might be doing well. Too many local leaders find it in their interest to insist that the nation is in a crisis and nothing is being done about it. And many foreign observers, uncritically accepting local demagoguery, have adopted this perspective.

Finally, the analysis in this study contradicts the view that "mass discontent" is an autonomous phenomenon directly related to socio-

9. *Anuario General de Estadística 1963*, p. 208.

10. Departamento Administrativo Nacional de Estadística, *Informe al Congreso Nacional 1964*, p. 40.

11. *Anuario 1963*, p. 531.

12. Ibid., p. 604.

13. Ibid., p. 378; *Anuario General de Estadística 1951–1952*, p. 401.

14. Compiled from data in *Anuario 1963*, pp. 505, 507.

economic circumstances. What often looks like a "popular demand" is really the agitation of leaders motivated by a strong status incentive. Remove these leaders and "protest" will greatly diminish; Colombian politics would then resemble nineteenth-century American politics, when the needs of a backward country and suffering masses were moderately and intermittently pressed upon the government. Or transplant 50,000 Colombian leaders to the United States and Americans would quickly find that drastic reforms were needed immediately to stave off "disaster."

EVALUATING THE COLOMBIAN SYSTEM: A DIGRESSION

Mention of a few statistics suggesting socioeconomic progress in Colombia raises a larger question: How should we evaluate the Colombian political system? Without attempting any conclusive answer, it is helpful to review certain points that ought to be considered in reaching a conclusion. It would be hasty and unfair to condemn the opportunistic thrashing of Colombian politics on an a priori or emotional basis. Politicians with a private incentive such as status may be, in certain respects, desirable. The lore of political philosophy, of course, insists that political leaders be principled and idealistic. Although in the world of commerce we accept selfish motivation as natural and even necessary, a politician is considered immoral if he seeks private rewards.

But in terms of results, a politician seeking a selfish satisfaction may not be a total liability. If he is placed in a competitive, democratic environment which is fashioned to prevent violent excesses, he will be subject to the invisible hand of popular control and become highly responsive to immediate popular needs. Indeed, the American system is often thought to work in just this manner (although I argue that it does not). In a world where dictatorships stifle and ignore popular demands and where many democracies appear to delay unduly in passing apparently popular measures, this sensitivity ought to be highly valued.

But a government can be too sensitive to immediate popular demands. In the United States we often overlook this. Reform measures are typically tugged from politicians whose deep interest in programs leads them to impede policies with apparently deleterious indirect and long-range effects, regardless of their immediate popular appeal. In Colombia where politicians do not greatly concern themselves with long-range and indirect effects it is possible to see—although this is to an extent a value judgment—that not all apparently popular measures are ultimately to popular benefit. This conclusion would seem most apparent in the area of economic and fiscal policies: budgets, exchange rates, price controls, and wage legislation. Hence, while the sensitivity of status-motivated leaders is a positive feature, it also has undesirable consequences. Of course, it should be added, although many hastily devised governmental programs will be ineffective or contraproductive, the armies of status-motivated leaders, acting in a free environment, will provide the system with considerable feedback, causing the policies to be constantly adjusted to popular needs.[15]

One should be cautious, in connection with this matter of sensitivity, about employing the usual indicators of popular discontent, found in speeches, the press, and interviews, as valid measures of citizen deprivation. There is a great temptation to conclude that since Colombians are "protesting" more than Cubans or Canadians, they must be worse off. This conclusion would ignore the enormous importance of intervening variables—structures and incentives—in linking objective deprivation to political protest. The "popular discontent" that has characterized Colombian politics for over a century is a *normal manifestation* of a system intensely sensitive to popular demands. It should probably be regarded as a healthy sign; the greatest human deprivations typically occur without political protest.

Perhaps the most profound criticism one could make of the Colombian system is that there are so few genuine reformers in political positions. There are two basic requisites for achieving socioeconomic progress: a favorable governmental orientation and dedicated, persistent middlemen to shepherd programs year after year. Colombia

---

15. Not surprisingly, the congressional attitude toward new measures is not that every detail should be studied and all possible defects corrected before the law is passed. Instead, congressmen are inclined to pass the measure and let the difficulties which arise indicate the defects. In the 1936 debate on an agrarian reform proposal, for example, one senator argued that "since the matter of land tenure reform is a new thing in the country, the natural thing is to approve the proposed measure and if the law proves defective one can proceed to correct it." *El Tiempo*, November 5, 1936, p. 7.

has the appropriate governmental climate but not enough middlemen. Reforms do not make themselves. Men—many men—must
constantly implement them, a task that is, for the most part, undramatic and unnoticed. It is a task of investigating, tinkering, bargaining, and pushing around and through countless obstacles. This
task comes naturally to a politician with a program incentive; he
enjoys accomplishing specific goals. It is a task alien to a politician
with a status incentive.

The following description of one U.S. reformer, in the battle
against water pollution, illustrates the critical role of middlemen in
the process of reform:

Consider Mr. Spisiak.

He has a jewelry and real estate office on a street leading out
of Buffalo. He is of Polish descent and believes in those woods
and templed hills. For 28 years he has served without pay on
conservationist bodies. He got the National Water Conservationist $1,000 award in 1965, presented at the White House.
He turned the money into lesser awards—"I've never taken a
penny for my conservation work," he said, "and I never will."

In September, 1966, at the President's request he acted as
guide for Mr. Johnson in Buffalo on the United States Coast
Guard cutter Ojibway.

"LBJ stirs up a bucket of slop" says the caption under a
newspaper photo, "which contains a sample of Buffalo River
dredgings which are being deposited on Woodlawn Beach under
the supervision of the United States Corps of Engineers. The
dredgings contain toxic acids, oils, and tars."

The picture shows Gov. Nelson A. Rockefeller, Buffalo
Mayor Frank Sedita, and the President and Mrs. Johnson
grouped around Mr. Spisiak. The President wears a game look
over the pail.

Mr. Spisiak got the dredging stopped.

This July, he got a conviction of the Pennsylvania Railroad
on a charge of polluting the Buffalo River.

"It is the first time in the history of the Rivers and Harbors
Act of 1893 that we've got a conviction," he said exultantly.

That's the whole history of the new reform surge in conservation: the statute was there all the time but got lip service. Now things are moving.

Mr. Spisiak has a new move to annoy the Buffalo industrial establishment. He has supervised a color film . . .[16]

Such men as Mr. Spisiak are precious in any system. The United States has the good fortune to have such people plentifully distributed in political offices, from Congress to city councils. In Colombian politics they are rare. Consequently the process of reform lags considerably behind the legislative intent.

To say, therefore, that needed socioeconomic reforms in Colombia are being blocked by a conservative elite of top politicians (or shadowy "oligarchs") is to put the problem upside down and backward. It is upside down because top politicians are not conservatives but favor and promulgate popular measures in a steady stream. It is backward in suggesting that reforms can be made by the passage of national laws, whereas effective reforms require the quiet and persistent shepherding of political middlemen—in congressional investigations, in appropriations, in consultation with the administration, in action through the courts, in arranging bargains with interest groups and private individuals. Insofar as reforms have not proceeded far enough in Colombia, the main obstacle, other than a lack of resources, is probably the lack of these middlemen, not any conspiracy to keep the nation backward and downtrodden.

Program-motivated individuals are scarce in Colombian politics, but perhaps there are substantial numbers of such people located elsewhere: in the many community action groups (*Acción Comunal*) which carry out local cooperative projects of road-building, housing, school and water supply construction; in some quasi-governmental bodies such as electricity boards, regional development corporations, and the national job-training institute (SENA); in some corners of the administration such as agricultural extension and experimentation; in some interest groups engaged in cooperative projects for mutual benefit; and in certain industrial enterprises such as the extensive FORJAS metallurgical consortium. Many individuals active in these areas seem to have the deep interest in accomplishing specific projects indicative of a program incentive.

16. Richard L. Strout, "Polluted—'From Sea to Shining Sea'," *The Christian Science Monitor,* September 13, 1967, p. 1.

Interviews with these individuals suggest they do not enter politics for two reasons. First, they find politics too rough and too unscrupulous; they are thus outcompeted by individuals with the stronger status incentive and sufficient motivation to play the rough and unscrupulous game. Secondly, the institutions of Colombian politics, fashioned by politicians with a status incentive, serve to provide status and not program satisfactions. The hard-working reformer is likely to find himself frustrated and out of place in the circus-like atmosphere of the Colombian Congress, for example. The reverse occurs in the United States Congress, which is fashioned by and for "work horse," program-motivated politicians and where the status-oriented "show horse" finds rules and norms blocking the way to the satisfactions he seeks.

If the Colombian system can be criticized for not having enough reformers in political positions, it at least offers them other avenues. This, it would seem, is the great strength of a free, pluralistic political environment. Even if the national government were doing nothing—which is far from true—we should not suppose that some kind of dictatorship would necessarily be preferable. A dictatorship, particularly a totalitarian one, would choke off the hundreds of semigovernmental, cooperative, and private centers of innovation and reform which, in the long run, probably produce more decisive results than sweeping programs announced from above. Political freedom itself is a major instrument of reform.

IS COLOMBIA ON THE BRINK OF ANYTHING?

Inextricably bound to the reform-or-revolution belief is the view that most Latin American countries, including Colombia, are on the brink of disaster. "Time is running out in Latin America," we are told; these nations are at the "eleventh hour" or even the "zero hour." It is presumably because of these dire circumstances that "reforms" are so imperative. Because the crisis perspective so thoroughly permeates the literature on Latin America, it is worth examining in some detail. In what sense can it be said that Colombia is on the brink of disaster? What kind of evidence is there for such a view?

It should be clear by this point that we cannot accept allegations of crisis made by local politicians and citizens. As I have already suggested, in a system where a strong status incentive is found, aspiring leaders will invariably charge that a crisis is at hand. To advance their own careers they will insist that the present moment represents a critical, desperate situation, made so by the incompetence or malevolence of the incumbents. Thus a crisis will always be held to exist, almost regardless of the facts.

Even governmental supporters will adopt the crisis orientation. In the face of vigorous charges to the contrary, it is difficult and embarrassing to argue that the country is doing relatively well, that poverty and backwardness cannot be readily eliminated, that the idea of dramatic progress is a mirage. It is electorally suicidal not to meet opposition demagoguery with demagoguery. A young Officialist Liberal leader in the department of Tolima noted this problem:

> I support the Frente Nacional. I think it's a good thing. But when I go out into the neighborhoods to make contacts or to speak, it's awkward to support it. It's so much more comfortable to attack it—and it brings better results.

There is, then, a curious consensus that develops in a system where leaders have a strong status incentive. Opposition forces claim crisis to gain support and incumbents recognize the "crisis" to avoid appearing ridiculous or reactionary. Everyone agrees—there is a crisis. And naturally citizens will see a crisis as well, for it is all they hear about. I feel confident that any sort of opinion poll exploring citizens' attitudes toward their governments would show a substantially higher level of disapproval in Colombia than in the United States. This negative attitude, however, arises not from any specific socioeconomic condition but from the massive and continuous leadership "disaster" campaign.

Some writers have attempted to demonstrate a crisis in Colombia by pointing to electoral turnout. As is evident from Table 14.1, turnout in Colombia has generally been low, with between about 30 and 55 per cent of the electorate voting. One writer, for example, notes that in the 1960 elections "Voter abstention had been virtually 50 per cent. This climaxed a trend toward abstention that had been growing ever since the return of free elections." He continues, "The best interpretation of the abstention suggested less a public apathy than a broad demand for a more vigorous pursuit of reforms through the instrumentality of the bipartisan arrangement." [17]

But why should a writer seek to explain a "climax" of abstention when no such climax existed? The turnout for the 1957 plebiscite and the 1958 elections was abnormally high, indeed apparently the highest in history. And *the turnout in 1960 was still unusually high.* Where is the need for reform: in the statistics or in the mind of the writer?

In the 1964 elections, as seen in Table 14.1, turnout dropped rather sharply, but I am still not inclined to attach much significance to this change. First, turnout has been lower than the 37 per cent registered in 1964. Secondly, women, who vote less often than men, have been added to the electorate in increasing numbers since 1957 when female suffrage was adopted.[18] Third, the turnout in the 1966 elections was reportedly about 40 per cent, indicating no further decline since 1964.[19] Finally, it is difficult to argue that a specific relationship obtains between electoral turnout and some other condition since so many variables can effect the statistical degree of abstention. For example, probably the lowest electoral turnouts in the world (often less than 20 per cent) are recorded in Virginia, yet we hardly think of that state as balanced on the brink of disaster.

Another possible meaning of "crisis" might be the imminence of a communist takeover. Without minimizing the danger of this possibility in some other Latin American countries, Colombia is unlikely to "go communist" in the near future. One route to power would be the seizure of government by a tightly organized Communist party during a moment of anarchy. But this would require that the existing military establishment destroy itself by internal fighting. Such self-

17. Martz, *Colombia*, pp. 307, 308. Figures of the Registraduría Nacional del Estado Civil, which compiles electoral statistics, indicate that abstention was lower than given by Martz, about 42 or 43 per cent.

18. Calculations made from statistics of the Registraduría show that in the 1962 congressional elections four registered women voters turned out for every five registered men voters; in the 1964 elections three registered women voters turned out for every four men voters. From December 1961 to December 1963 the number of registered men voters increased from 3,256,711 to 3,530,834 or an increase of 274,123. In the same period the number of registered women increased from 2,605,692 to 3,090,104 or an increase of 484,412. Notice that the annual increase of even the male electorate exceeded population growth. Compiled from *Organización y Estadísticas Electorales 1962*, p. 257, and *1964*, pp. 133, 137.

19. *The New York Times*, May 2, 1966, p. 9; May 3, 1966, p. 12.

TABLE 14.1

Turnout in Colombian Elections, 1935–1964

Year	Offices	Proportion of registered voters voting (per cent) *
1935	House	33
	D. Assemblies	45
	City councils	54**
1937	House	34**
	D. Assemblies	33
	City councils	38
1938	Presidential	30
1939	House	52**
	City councils	40
1941	House	45**
1942	Presidential	56
1943	House	41**
1945	House	38
1946	Presidential	56
1947	Senate	56
1949	Presidential	40
	House	62
1951	Senate	32**
1957	Plebiscite	72
1958	Presidential	58
	Senate	68
1960	House	58
1962	Presidential	49
	Senate	58
1964	House	37

*The number of registered voters is the number of valid electoral identification cards outstanding. To conserve space, I have given data for only those elections which occurred at different times. In 1964, for example, elections for departmental assemblies and city councils were also held on the same day as the election for representatives, producing the same turnout.

**Turnout figures for these years are based on interpolations for the size of the registered electorate in that year.

Source: Registraduría Nacional del Estado Civil, *Organización y Estadísticas Electorales 1964,* pp. 134–36.

destruction, in turn, is likely to come about only if a coup and counter-coup are attempted, and at the moment a military coup is improbable in Colombia. Even if full-scale anarchy could be produced, it is doubtful that the tiny and divided communist movement could unobtrusively seize power and establish a dictatorship. Since Castro, too many Colombians have become sensitive to this possibility.

Guerrilla warfare seems an equally unpromising avenue. Judging from the Cuban experience, a guerrilla war can succeed in undermining the existing army only if there is a universal revulsion against the existing government. Such a revulsion is unlikely to be stimulated unless the government practices indiscriminate terror and repression. Only then would virtually all citizens and political leaders support the destruction of the regime *and its army*.[20] This ingredient of counter-terror has been missing under the tolerance and freedom of the Frente Nacional and consequently the army, acting in cooperation with local peasants and farmers, has steadily reduced the numbers of bandit-guerrillas.

In recent years the outlook for the communist cause in Colombia has been particularly bleak. In large part this unpromising situation has been the unintended result of the Cuban revolution. Instead of being the spark to light the tinder, Cuba has made communist victory more difficult in most Latin American countries. The example of Cuba stimulated many hotheads to attempt terrorism and guerrilla activity against free and tolerant regimes. Instead of provoking re-vulsion against the government, these "coffee-house revolutionaries," as one Colombian communist identified them in an interview, have stirred up revulsion against communism. In Colombia this reaction is particularly strong because the communists have supported those bandits of earlier years (1946–53) who later chose to call themselves Marxists or Castroites. More addicted to massacre than intelligent terrorism, these bandits appear to be the vanguard of communism in Colombia—clearly an unappealing vanguard.

On March 17, 1965, one of the last significant pro-communist guerrillas, Pedro Antonio Marín (alias Tirofijo), and his band of about 100 men assaulted the village of Inzá in the department of Cauca. They murdered sixteen villagers, including the local mayor, two policemen, several peasants, and two nuns. Naturally there was a public outcry. The press organ of the soft-line communists, *Voz Proletaria,* dutifully, if foolishly, approved of the assault but attempted to minimize the butchery of it. The death of the two nuns was "acci-

20. See Theodore Draper, *Castro's Revolution: Myths and Realities* (New York, Frederick A. Praeger, 1962), particularly pp. 13–14; Ernesto Guevara, *Guerrilla Warfare* (New York, Monthly Review Press, 1961); David Galula, *Counterinsurgency Warfare* (New York, Frederick A. Praeger, 1964).

dental" and no mention was made of the total number slain.[21] Guerrilla activity, rather than spearheading the advance of communism in Colombia, is becoming its kiss of death.

Castro has also made communist victory more difficult by stimulating a firm and conscious reaction against communism in Colombia. Before about 1960, communism was a distant reality and a vague epithet. Now the threat is felt more clearly. Local politicians find it more awkward to cooperate with communists, more profitable to attack them. Consequently it is now more difficult than ever for communists to form or penetrate large movements and organizations. Even if a state of anarchy should be produced, it is unlikely that communist groups could surreptitiously rise to power through it.

The last "crisis" I shall consider is the strictly political breakdown. As already stated, the fundamental problem of Colombia is the political conflict created by the competition for the private rewards of politics, status and employment. Depending on the institutional environment, this conflict may take relatively harmless forms: slander and invective, demonstrations and riots, periods of congressional immobilism, and perhaps the resignation of a president or, possibly, a military coup. More serious forms of conflict are the civil wars or protracted clandestine violence that I have suggested are actually periods of defensive feuding. The strength of incentives in Colombia creates forces that make it impossible to pronounce the system crisis-free. Whether the year be 1966 or 1826, Colombian politics has always held a potential for acute conflict. And quite frequently this potential has been realized. By American standards, then, Colombia has been on the brink of a political crisis, or in the midst of one, since independence in 1819.

But it is unproductive to match Colombia against the United States because incentives have apparently been so different. While certain socioeconomic changes may slightly affect the nature and strength of incentives in Colombia over the next few decades, it seems unreasonable to expect dramatic changes in this variable. The apparent durability of at least the leadership status incentive through

21. *Voz Proletaria,* March 25, 1965, p. 9. That the Colombian government permits the publication of such seditious material is remarkable refutation of the communist claim that "THERE IS NO FREEDOM OF THE PRESS IN COLOMBIA"; ibid., April 8, 1965, p. 4.

150 years of socioeconomic change argues against any significant alteration in the next few years.[22] An intense opposition and a certain amount of violence therefore are inevitable and simply normal in the Colombian system.

What would constitute a meaningful political crisis in Colombian terms is a sharp defensive feud which would cost thousands of lives and sow decades of social and economic blight. Is such a feud likely to occur in the period 1966–74? In Chapter 8 I discussed the defensive feud and tried to show how the Frente Nacional, by eliminating the reciprocal fears of each party about political exclusion, greatly reduces the likelihood of a defensive feud across party lines.

This argument is more than just theory. During eight years of operation, 1958–66, bipolar Liberal-Conservative conflict has been almost completely eliminated. The struggles now take place between shifting agglomerations of factions from both parties. Both theory and past experience indicate, then, that because of the Frente Nacional the political crisis of a defensive feud is now less likely than in almost any other period of Colombian history.

I would urge that the investigator discard the temporocentric perspective that the year in which he visits a particular Latin American country is the time of maximum crisis or danger. This unscientific and antihistorical view undermines serious research and can blind us to real dangers which may lie ahead. In Colombia, for example, the demagogic criticism of the Frente Nacional as the institution responsible for a supposed "crisis" has prevented Colombians from seeing these facts: that national affairs have gone along relatively well since 1958; that the Frente Nacional is largely responsible for the political calm; and that a genuine crisis probably lies ahead when the Frente Nacional expires in 1974.

22. Our hypothesis about the status incentive (H1) does offer certain avenues for speculation, however. For example, it might be possible greatly to reduce the status value of political office by packing illiterate, *ruana*-wearing peasants and peons into the highest positions: senator, minister, or even president. A more practical suggestion might be to abolish the presidency in favor of a plural executive. This change might reduce the pressure which now comes from the 50 or so top leaders who all believe that the presidency is within their grasp. Lowering this pinnacle of status by dividing it up among many individuals would weaken the motivation to seek it.

THE FUTURE

The parity and presidential alternation amendments known as the Frente Nacional were not enacted as permanent constitutional provisions; they will expire in 1974 unless extended by amendment. The Colombian constitution now requires that a valid amendment to the constitution be passed by a two-thirds vote in Congress in two successive ordinary sessions (Art. 218). A realistic appraisal of the nature of Colombian politics yields the conculsion that the Frente Nacional will not be extended. It simply will not be strategically convenient for two-thirds of the factions in two successive years to approve of an extension.

One strategic implication can be clearly seen even at this distance. The Frente Nacional is now held up as the major barrier to the utopia regularly promised by Colombian leaders. Six years from now many party leaders will argue as they do today. Once freed of the shackles of the Frente Nacional, they say, the country will move out of the crisis to an era of progress and happiness—with themselves at the helm, of course. Anyone who argues in favor of the Frente Nacional will be anti-utopian, satisfied with the existing "disastrous" state of affairs.

As it happens, the Frente Nacional can be blamed for very little. The major charge brought against it—that the parity arrangement negates the free competition of policies and prevents voter preferences from being translated into policy—is unfounded. *Policy competition is not salient in Colombia.* Even if it were, factionalism would provide a means for its expression. Those factions with the popular policy position would gain more seats—or the presidency—at the expense of the factions with the unpopular policy position.

The two-thirds majority requirement for passage of measures in all legislative bodies does create certain problems since it gives minority factions increased opportunity to wage a troublesome strategic opposition. But the two-thirds requirement is not a necessary part of the Frente Nacional. It was apparently adopted under the assumption that the two parties would form united blocs which would heatedly contest programs, or at least strategic issues. If such were the case, the two-thirds rule would prevent the defeat of one party by the other and necessitate compromise. But Colombian parties are not cohesive blocs; under the Frente Nacional they have divided into even more warring factions than before. They exhibit no tendency toward cohesion on socioeconomic issues or even strategic issues.

Apparently there has been only one straight Liberal-Conservative division in a congressional vote in the entire history of the Frente Nacional. At issue was a biazarre and ephemeral question: During the 1946–53 conflict, was a local Conservative leader in the department of Valle, who had recently died, an "honorable citizen" or a "ruthless murderer"? The vote, taken in the House on August 18, 1965, produced a unique partisan split: all the Conservatives (58) voted he was honorable; all the Liberals (52) voted he was a killer.[23] Thus the only partisan split under the Frente Nacional was produced by dredging up a strategic conflict more than a decade old.

The two-thirds rule, then, seems superfluous in view of the intra-party divisions and the absence of party cleavage on program or strategic issues. If the constitution could be amended to extend the Frente Nacional, this measure could be abandoned. In any case, as we have seen, the two-thirds rule does not present an overwhelming barrier to congressional action. If strategic implications are carefully subdued, measures may be slipped through a hostile Congress. Furthermore, if one subtracts the utopianism from the claim that "basic reforms are urgently needed," it becomes apparent that the executive already has a plethora of reforms, including just about everything a red-blooded American liberal could want.

The prognosis for the immediate future, then, is relatively encouraging. But about 1972 the critical moments will arrive. A Conservative president (1970–74) will be in office. Within both parties an intense fight will be taking place for the 1974 presidential nomination and the president will suffer the repercussions of these struggles. Underneath the intraparty struggles, the Liberals will begin to charge, with increasing conviction, that the Conservative president is permitting the persecution of the Liberals. The winner of the 1974 elections will attempt to form a bipartisan cabinet, as Ospina did in

23. *El Tiempo,* August 19, 1965, p. 3. The vote was actually over a Liberal proposal to call Conservative Minister of Communications Cornelio Reyes before the House for questioning for having attended the funeral of this leader. ANAPO, incidentally, voted Conservative.

1946. But his efforts are likely to fail as each side increasingly employs violence to protect itself against creeping fraud and political exclusion.

In 1965 Colombian leaders were strangely unconcerned about the expiration of the Frente Nacional. They felt that it had provided a "lesson" in tolerance and democracy that would be fully learned by 1974. But political systems do not learn lessons as schoolchildren learn to write. Leadership incentives are not altered by voicing platitudes. As far as can be seen, the necessary conditions for a defensive feud will still be present in 1974. There are no grounds for assuming a marked change in incentives. Nor is it probable that party identification has weakened sufficiently to permit the rise of large third and fourth parties or personalist organizations. I doubt that ANAPO will survive until 1974, at least as a party large enough to break a defensive feud between Liberals and Conservatives. Finally, the analysis of military intervention gives us no reason to hope that a defensive feud will be cut off more quickly than it was in 1946–53.

It does seem probable, then, that another defensive feud lies on the horizon. While it is not possible to predict the exact course of such a conflict, it is reasonable to expect that the period from 1972 onward will be characterized by a substantial increase in political violence. Then, Colombians will probably point to the Frente Nacional, which they now criticize so carelessly, as an era of progress and enlightenment.

APPENDIXES

APPENDIX I

THE UPPER
LEADERSHIP SURVEY

A survey of the Colombian upper leadership group was conducted by the writer during the period May-September 1965. The questionnaire consisted of a one-page sheet which was given to leaders to read and answer on the sheet (see translated copy). Virtually all of the returned questionnaires were distributed personally and collected personally. Experiments with mailing the questionnaire, a letter explaining its purpose and a stamped, self-addressed envelope proved unsatisfactory. Of about 20 questionnaires distributed in this way only about two were returned. In some cases (about 25) questionnaires were left with respondents who promised to return them by mail, but only about five were received in this way.

The sampling procedures were dictated largely by the requirements of feasibility. To achieve a reasonable geographic representation seven different departments were chosen for the survey, representative of the economic and cultural diversity of the nation. The number of respondents in each department was roughly proportioned on the basis of population, with the more populous departments having a greater number of respondents in the sample. An attempt was made to obtain approximately equal numbers of Officialist Liberal and Conservative leaders and to have Conservatives from both factions adequately represented in the sample. Appendix Table 1 gives the regional and party-faction distribution of the respondents. No attempt was made to obtain ANAPO or MRL respondents. It was decided at the outset that it would be excessively difficult to obtain a large enough sample of leaders from these smaller groups which seldom had established directorates in most cities and departments.

Instead of locating higher leaders as incumbents or aspirants for the positions identified in Table 2.1, the sample was obtained by finding members of departmental party directorates or municipal directorates of large (over 150,000 pop.) cities. It was reasonable to assume that individuals on these top party committees would be either holders of higher public offices or active aspirants for such positions. Tabulation of the public offices currently held by respondents in Appendix Table 2 shows that about 40 per cent of the respondents were holding higher public offices.

APPENDIX TABLE 1

Regional and Factional Distribution of Respondents
in the Upper Leadership Survey

Region	Ospinistas	Lauro-alzatistas	Independent Conservative	Officialist Liberal	Total
Antioquia	5	–	6	11	22
Cundinamarca	8	8	1	16	33
Valle	5	7	1	8	21
Atlántico	4	6	–	5	15
Tolima	4	2	1	8	15
Caldas	5	2	–	6	13
Cauca	3	2	–	6	11
Totals	34	27	9	60	130

It is unlikely that many people on these higher directorates not already holding higher public office would not be active aspirants for such offices. In several cases (Ibagué in Tolima, Pereira in Caldas, and the department of Atlántico) one or more party groups did not have an established directorate. In these cases I constructed my own list of higher leaders by asking various officials to name top leaders in the area. They were, for the most part, ex-members of directorates and would probably be on directorates when they were formed at election time.

The survey procedure consisted in visiting, first, the headquarters of the departmental and municipal directorates of the three factions to obtain lists of members and alternates of the different directorates from the secretaries of the directorates and bulletin boards. Usually these lists would contain about 30 to 60 names for all factions. Then, with the help of a telephone book, the secretaries, and other leaders, I found the addresses of as many as possible. Although many trips were made to suburbs, typically the easiest leaders to contact were the professional men with offices in the

APPENDIX TABLE 2

Public Office Held by Respondents in the Upper Leadership Survey, 1965

Senator	2
Member of the House of Representatives	14
Departmental Assemblyman	13
Municipal Councilman in city over 150,000	14
Other higher public office	10
Other governmental position (including public employment and small town mayor)	4
None	73
Total	130

center of the city. I attempted to counteract this bias by singling out women and those not in the telephone book and devoting extra energy to contacting them. Ten women (eight Liberals and two Conservatives) are included in the sample of 130, which seems to be a reasonable reflection of their frequency in the upper leadership group. The number of women in the higher legislative positions (Senate, House, departmental assemblies) and lower leadership legislative positions (city councils) for 1964 is given in Appendix Table 3.

APPENDIX TABLE 3

Composition of Legislative Bodies by Sex, 1964

	Men	Women	Total
Senate	97	1	98
House of Representatives	175	9	184
Departmental Assemblies	336	22	358
Municipal Councils	6,634	412	7,046

Source: Registraduría Nacional del Estado Civil, *Organización y Estadísticas Electorales, 1964,* p. 131.

The occupational distribution of respondents is tabulated in Appendix Table 4. While some overrepresentation of professional groups has probably occurred in the sample, I do not feel it is particularly serious. Judging from the frequency with which the professional title (Dr.) appears in front of the names of directorate members, it appears that about half of the in-

APPENDIX TABLE 4

Occupations of Respondents in the Upper Leadership Survey

	Liberals	Conservatives	Total
Big businessman, firm manager	3	3	6
Doctor	7	3	10
Engineer	3	2	5
Dentist	1	2	3
Lawyer	19	39	58
Cattle-raiser, farmer		4	4
University student	3	3	6
Comerciante, Negociante	7	4	11
Journalist	2	3	5
White-collar worker	5	4	9
Schoolteacher	2	1	3
Home–housewife	5	1	6
Miscellaneous	3	1	4
Totals	60	70	130

dividuals on these bodies (at the departmental and big-city level) are professionals.

It is difficult to calculate a meaningful rejection rate because the circumstances for non-responses were so diverse. Of all those presented with the questionnaire personally (about 160) only one refused to accept or answer it. But about thirty respondents who promised to answer, by mail or appointment, did not. Possible reasons for these failures range from the status value of making an American wait to a lack of interest in the matter. Possibly the rejections caused the more strongly status-motivated leaders to be underrepresented in the sample.

Although the poll has certain defects, it should be remembered that any such survey is a blood, sweat, and tears operation. An ordinary day of pounding the pavement and detective work to locate leaders would yield anywhere from two to a maximum of six or seven answered sheets. I estimate that I spent, not counting travel time between cities, about two hours of work for each returned questionnaire.

(Translation of the upper leadership survey questionnaire; the original appeared on a 9 x 13 sheet.)

Poll for Members and Ex-members and Alternates of Political Party Directorates

Directed by: James Payne
                Department of Political Science
                University of California, Berkeley, U.S.A.

1. What do you think is the most serious problem facing Colombia?_____
2. In the construction of housing do you believe the government should do (underline one)
   (a) much more   (b) more   (c) the same as now
   (d) less   (e) much less
3. Do you believe the government should control private industry
   (a) much more   (b) more   (c) the same as now
   (d) less   (e) much less
4. Do you believe the army should be
   (a) greatly increased   (b) increased   (c) the same
   (d) reduced   (e) greatly reduced
5. Do you believe that the influence of the Church in the government should be
   (a) much more   (b) more   (c) the same as now
   (d) less   (e) much less
6. In the legal protection of workers' trade unions do you believe the government should do
   (a) much more   (b) more   (c) the same as now
   (d) less   (e) much less
7. What foreign policy do you believe is best to advance the economic development of Colombia? (select one)
   (a) Depend more on the United States and the Alliance for Progress
   (b) Depend more on exports to Europe and the United States
   (c) Depend more on the United Nations and its agencies
   (d) Depend more on the other Latin American countries and the Latin American Free Trade Association
8. What is your opinion on the Latin American Free Trade Association?
   (a) That Colombia is receiving adequate benefits from the system
   (b) That the Association is too weak to be able to help Colombia
   (c) That the Association is too powerful for the good of Colombia
9. Your age_____   10. Your work or profession_____

11. Your age when you had your first public position (legislative or administrative)_____
12. The work or profession of your father_____
13. Your public office now, if you hold one_____
14. The party to which you belong (place an x)
    (a) Conservador Ospinista
    (b) Conservador Lauro-Alzatista
    (c) ANAPO
    (d) Liberal oficialista
    (e) MRL
    (f) Other_____

APPENDIX II

THE OCCUPATIONAL
PRESTIGE SCALE

The survey on occupational prestige was prepared jointly with Anthony Maingot of the University of Florida. In September 1965 a questionnaire was distributed to classes of students in the social sciences in three Bogotá universities: Los Andes, La Javeriana, and Externado de Colombia. The students were of both sexes, although predominantly male, between the ages of 18 and 25, and from the middle and upper strata. The translated questionnaire and directions explain the nature of the survey.

The 75 returned questionnaires were processed in the following manner. A score of from one to seven (as shown in the questionnaire) was assigned to each of the seven status-level columns. Then a mean score was computed for each occupation by adding all the scores given to that occupation and dividing by the number of questionnaires. It should be pointed out that the results of the survey estimate only *relative* social distance between occupations. They reveal little about absolute social distance (as compared with another country, for example) because respondents may be expected to employ the full range of the scale regardless of the social distance which exists between the highest and lowest occupations. Furthermore, the results cannot be usefully employed to show the existence or number of "classes." Seven positions were chosen because they seemed enough to provide useful discrimination but not too many to be confusing. The word "class" was employed because the students were familiar with it as a term of status level.

(Translation of the occupational prestige questionnaire.)

Survey on the Social Positions of Occupations in Colombia

Purpose: This is a survey to determine the actual social position of various employments or occupations in Colombia. On the second page there is a list of types of employment or occupational positions. We ask you to classify each occupation in one of the seven classes which appear in the columns to the right. You have to put an "X" in the column which corresponds to the class or social position which you think pertains to that type of work. The seven classes are:

1. upper-UPPER Class
2. middle-UPPER Class
3. upper-MIDDLE Class
4. middle-MIDDLE Class
5. lower-MIDDLE Class
6. middle-LOWER Class
7. lower-LOWER Class

In the classification we seek the prestige or social position which each occupation has *in reality* and *not* the prestige it ought to have.

	Class						
	1	2	3	4	6	5	7
OCCUPATION	upper UPPER	middle UPPER	upper MIDDLE	middle MIDDLE	middle LOWER	lower MIDDLE	lower LOWER
1. Comerciante							
2. Ministro (del Gabinete)							
3. Médico							
4. Empleado Público							
5. Ingeniero							
6. Hacendado							
7. Abogado							
8. Empleado Particular							
9. Odontólogo							
10. Rentista							
11. Funcionario Público							
12. Jefe de ventas de gran empresa (Coltejer o Bavaria)							
13. Contador							
14. Agricultor							
15. Industrial							
16. Periodista							
17. Estudiante Universitario							
18. Diputado al la Asamblea Departamental							
19. Profesor Universitario							
20. Maestro de Escuela							

21. Senador de la
    República
22. Carpintero
23. Representante
    a la
    Cámera
24. Arquitecto
25. Obrero
26. Sacerdote
27. Campesino
28. Consejal
29. Oficial del
    Ejército
30. Oficial de la
    Armada
31. Oficial de la
    Policía

APPENDIX III

LIST OF HYPOTHESES

ADVANCED IN THIS STUDY

H1. Status will be an increasingly strong incentive for leadership participation as (1) status-consciousness is higher in the society, (2) the status value of higher political offices is greater, and (3) recruitment to these offices is more open.

H2. In a society characterized by high status-consciousness and relatively weak barriers to upward social mobility, the supply of white-collar workers will be well in excess of that required by the economic system.

H3. In a society characterized by an oversupply of white-collar workers, not taken up by government, political participation will be a requisite for government employment (widespread use of the patronage system) and employment will be a strong incentive for political participation (active followers).

H4. When incentives for political participants are strong, intense political conflict is probable.

H4a. In a society characterized by (1) high status-consciousness, (2) high status value of higher political offices, (3) relatively open recruitment to these offices, and (4) weak barriers to upward social mobility, intense political conflict is probable.

H5. Where status is the incentive for leaders, there will be no differences between the leaders of different parties (or party factions) on program policies.

H6. Where program is the incentive for leaders, there will be differences between the leaders of different parties on program policies.

H7. In any system (status or program incentive) there will be differences between leaders of different parties on strategic policies.

H8. Where the incentive for leaders is status, leaders will enter politics at a relatively early age.

H8a.   Where the incentive for leaders is status, university students will be highly active in politics.

H9.   Where the incentive for leaders is program, leaders will enter politics at a relatively late age.

H10.   Where the incentive for leaders is status, leaders will retire from politics at a relatively early age.

H11.   Where the incentive for leaders is program, leaders will retire from politics at a relatively late age.

H12.   In those Latin American countries where the military was relatively small after independence, meaningful elections were frequent.

H13.   In those Latin American countries where the military was relatively large after independence, meaningful elections were infrequent.

H14.   In countries where meaningful elections are frequent, mass electoral organizations will be formed on a large scale.

H15.   In countries where meaningful elections are infrequent, mass electoral organizations will not be formed on a large scale.

H16.   The formation of electoral organizations on a large scale will produce a high degree of party identification so that major, permanent political parties will exist.

H17.   The absence of electoral organizations on a large scale will produce a (continued) condition of low party identification so that major, permanent political parties will not exist.

H18.   A military coup will take place when (a) vigorous civilian opposition to the chief executive is extremely (unusually) high and (b) when civilian support for the chief executive is extremely (unusually) low.

H19.   In Latin American countries where party identification of the electorate is high, military coups will be infrequent.

H20.   In Latin American countries where party identification is low, military coups will be frequent.

H21.   A defensive feud is likely in a system where (1) incentives for political participation are strong, (2) only two parties exist, (3) party identification with those parties is high, (4) the parties are decentralized, (5) partisan channels of communication (at least on strategic issues) exist, and (6) the military is prevented from intervening.

H22.   Factionalism will not occur where party identification is low.

H23.   Where party identification of the electorate is high and the incentive for leaders is program, factionalism will not be prevalent.

H24.   Where party identification of the electorate is high and the incentive for leaders is status, factionalism will be prevalent.

H25.   Where the incentive for leaders is status, leaders will be relatively sensitive to (changes in) the distribution of advantage for factionalists or new party leaders.

H25a.   In a system where status is the incentive for leaders, factionalism will increase as administrative resources are more dispersed among competing groups.

H26.   Where the incentive for leaders is program, leaders will be relatively insensitive to (changes in) the distribution of advantage for factionalists or new party leaders.

H27.   Where the incentive for leaders is program, the electoral system (SMSB, PR) does not affect the number of parties.

H28.   Where the incentive for leaders is status, a single-member, single-ballot electoral system will lead to the formation of two parties in each district (and probably to a two-party system).

H29.   Where the incentive for leaders is status a proportional representation electoral system will produce a multi-party system if party identification is low when PR is adopted.

H30.   Where the incentive for leaders is status a proportional representation system will not produce a multi-party system if party identification with only two labels is high when PR is adopted, unless a third party be based upon an ex-president.

H31.   In a country where the incentive for leaders is status, where party identification with two or three parties is high and where political freedoms are observed, there will be national party factions with these characteristics:

1. leadership positions will be allocated on the basis of each individual's electoral resources
2. higher leaders will have a relatively narrow margin of discretion in selecting lower leaders

3. the factions will be relatively cohesive in their behavior on the national political scene, except in elections

4. the behavior of the national factions will be primarily the product of a struggle over the distribution of political positions and the opportunities for political positions; their behavior will not be greatly influenced by the social composition of their membership, the nature of their electorates, or announced program policy positions.

H32.   In a system where status is the incentive for leaders, legislative turnover will be high.

H33.   In a system where program is the incentive for leaders, legislative turnover will be low.

H34.   A legislature whose members have a status incentive will be characterized by:

1. chronic absenteeism in committees and votes
2. low committee workloads
3. few technical or research facilities for legislators
4. disruptive, conflict-provoking patterns of behavior
5. a popular-demogogic orientation toward program policies

APPENDIX IV

THE USE OF INCENTIVE THEORY
IN THE FORMULATION
OF HYPOTHESES

A good theory should tell us more about the world than we already knew; it should predict relationships which are both true and previously unsuspected. Incentive theory may be manipulated in several ways to uncover such relationships. In this study I have treated incentives as a "real" variable, determined empirically through the use of in-depth interviews which probe for the respondent's interests and, hence, his satisfactions. In generalized form the discussion has followed this pattern:

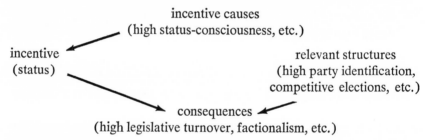

incentive causes
(high status-consciousness, etc.)

incentive
(status)

relevant structures
(high party identification,
competitive elections, etc.)

consequences
(high legislative turnover, factionalism, etc.)

Thus the arguments are empirical and testable at each point.

Incentives, however, need not be treated as observable. They may be purely theoretical assumptions which are not tested at all and, if one chooses, can be said to be untestable. One might say that in this study the phrase "status incentive" is not adequately measured and therefore all the hypotheses in the form "if status is the incentive for leaders, then . . ." are untested—and even untestable given the ambiguity of the operational definition for "status incentive."

This quite understandable objection may be disposed of by allowing incentives to become purely theoretical links. They will be assumptions which generate relationships, but which do not appear in the final hypothesis. One way to apply incentive theory is to connect the incentive causes with the consequences. Taking hypotheses H1 and H6, for example, we have

H1–6.   Where (1) status-consciousness is higher in the society, (2) the status value of higher political offices is greater, and (3) as recruitment to these offices is more open, there will be smaller differences between leaders of different parties (or party factions) on program policies.

In this fashion we can construct an entire series of testable hypotheses in which "status incentive" does not appear. Taken together, such a list of hypotheses becomes a prediction of what politics will be like in a system where the stated variables (including structures, where relevant) obtain.

The eight extended interviews with Antioqueño leaders, for example, are indeed skimpy evidence for any proposition about the incentives of this leadership group. But the predictions about deviant behavior of Antioqueños need not depend on the actual estimation of their incentives through interviews. Instead one may start with the observation that status-consciousness is lower in Antioquia. This condition may be assumed to produce a weaker status incentive and the *consequences* of this weaker status incentive will be predicted and observed. In effect we use hypotheses such as:

H1–8.   Where status-consciousness is higher, . . . leaders will enter politics at an earlier age.

Since we know that status-consciousness is not as high in Antioquia we can predict that the leaders will enter politics at a later age—as appears to be the case. In a similar fashion we can construct an hypothesis which predicts less legislative turnover of Antioqueños (H1–32), and again the prediction seems correct. It was unnecessary (albeit desirable) to test the intermediate assumption that the status incentive was less strong in Antioquia. But the chances of arriving at these predictions without making this assumption about incentives and without utilizing incentive theory seem remote.

Another way incentive theory may be used is to reason backward from one condition to the incentive which might have caused it and then predict other conditions which should be the result of this assumed incentive. Thus one could observe high factionalism (with party identification high and competitive elections) and reason that this phenomenon might be the result of a strong status incentive. Then, armed with the assumption of a strong status incentive, one could predict that some other conditions (low legislative committee workloads, for example) associated with the status incentive would obtain. In effect, one is constructing hypotheses in this manner:

> *H10–32. In a system where leaders are younger, legislative turnover will be higher.*

In this way all the hypotheses could be combined and restated to predict what conditions go with what. Incentive theory is necessary to derive these relationships but incentives are not mentioned in the final hypotheses.

One notes, for example, that the median age of Philippine legislators has increased from 35–39 in 1921 to 50–54 in 1962. Standing alone, this datum is a cold and isolated fact. But if we experiment with incentive theory, this observation may take on great significance. The increasing median age perhaps reflects a later retirement age. Perhaps such a change would be accounted for by a change in incentives, a decline in the importance of a status incentive? If this is so, what else should change? What about turnover? That should also decrease with a decline in the status incentive. We look back to the data and find our expectation confirmed: the proportion of House members with previous experience has increased significantly since 1921.[1] What we have done, in effect, is apply hypothesis H10–32 above.

It is possible, then, to use an incentive as a purely theoretical link which, while not observed itself, enables us to uncover unsuspected relationships between observed conditions.

It should not be forgotten, however, that the category of variables I have called structures are generally of great importance in shaping behavior. Dissimilar behavior may flow from the same incentives in a different context; similar behavior may result from different incentives being expressed in a different context. Legislators may be older, for example, because the legal age limit for office holding has been increased, not because the status incentive (if that was what it was) has altered. It is unwise, therefore, to apply incentive analysis too enthusiastically to systems one knows little about.

1. Robert B. Stauffer, "Philippine Legislators and Their Changing Universe," *Journal of Politics*, 28 (August 1966), 556–97.

BIBLIOGRAPHY

GENERAL WORKS

Barber, James David, *The Lawmakers,* New Haven, Yale University Press, 1965.

Busey, James L., *Notes on Costa Rican Democracy,* Boulder, University of Colorado Press, 1962.

Dahl, Robert A., *Who Governs?,* New Haven, Yale University Press, 1961.

Guzmán, Mauricio, "El Faccionalismo: Supervivencia Medieval en América Latina," *Journal of Inter-American Studies, 5* (1963), 465–70.

Fenton, John H., *People and Parties in Politics,* Glenview, Ill., Scott, Foresman, 1966.

McClosky, Herbert, Paul J. Hoffman, and Rosemary O'Hara, "Issue Conflict and Consensus among Party Leaders and Followers," *The American Political Science Review, 54* (1960), 406–27.

Snow, Peter G., *Argentine Radicalism,* Iowa City, University of Iowa Press, 1965.

Stokes, William S., *Honduras: An Area Study in Government,* Madison, University of Wisconsin Press, 1950.

Taylor, Philip B., Jr., *Government and Politics of Uruguay* (Tulane Studies in Political Science, 7), New Orleans, Tulane University Press, 1960.

Wilson, James Q., *The Amateur Democrat,* Chicago, University of Chicago Press, 1962.

SELECTED WORKS ON COLOMBIAN POLITICS AND POLITICAL HISTORY

Burnett, Ben G., "The Recent Colombian Party System: Its Organization and Procedure," unpublished Ph.D. dissertation, University of California, Los Angeles, 1955. An account of party history and an examination of certain political characteristics of the different departments: relative party vote, turnout, and literacy.

Bushnell, David, *The Santander Regime in Gran Colombia,* Newark, Del., University of Delaware Press, 1954. The only serious study of Colombian nineteenth-century history in English. A detailed and readable account of Colombian politics and society in 1821–26.

Dix, Robert H., *Colombia: The Political Dimensions of Change,* New Haven, Yale University Press, 1967. A useful account of aspects of Colombian political history and politics. Makes many of the usual neo-Marxist allegations (oligarchy, rigid, hierarchical class system, closed recruitment to political office) but offers neither the methodology nor the data necessary to prove such propositions.

Fluharty, Vernon L., *Dance of the Millions: Military Rule and the Social Revolution in Colombia, 1930–1956,* Pittsburgh, University of Pittsburgh Press, 1957. The usual allegations again, buttressed by the writer's own moral indignation and little else.

Gaitán P., Aquilino, *Por Qué Cayó el Partido Conservador,* Bogotá, Talleres "Mundo al Día," 1935. The rambling recollections of a member of the Conservative National Directorate, 1928–30. A rich and revealing account of Colombian politics from the inside: attitudes, activities, strategies, and the motives of participants.

Guillén Martínez, Fernando, *Raíz y Futuro de la Revolución* ("Colección 'Problemas de America'"), Bogotá, Ediciones Tercer Mundo, 1963. An excellent analysis of the roots, nature, and consequences of Latin American social structure. It incisively contradicts the prevailing views about class, caste, low mobility, and perpetual aristocracies and substitutes a picture of a fluid society characterized, from top to bottom, by a lust for honor.

Holt, Pat M., *Colombia Today—and Tomorrow,* New York, Frederick A. Praeger, 1964. A general survey of Colombia with a useful account of election procedures.

Hunter, John M., *Emerging Colombia,* Washington, D.C., Public Affairs Press, 1962. Observations and reflections of an American economist who taught in Colombia.

Martz, John D., *Colombia: A Contemporary Political Survey,* Chapel Hill, University of North Carolina Press, 1962. A readable account of recent Colombian political history, 1946–61.

Ospina Vásquez, Luis, *Industria y Protección en Colombia, 1810–1930,* Medellín, by the author, 1955. A serious study of the ins and outs of Colombian tariff policy, economic history, and its political aspects, 1810–1930.

Pérez Aguirre, Antonio, *25 Años de Historia Colombiana, 1853 a 1878: Del Centralismo a la Federación* ("Academia Colombiana de Historia: Biblioteca Eduardo Santos," *18*), Bogotá, Editorial Sucre, 1959. A well-organized account of episodes of political history, 1853–78.

Restrepo, José Manuel, *Historia de le Nueva Granada,* Vol. 1: 1832–1845, Bogotá, Editorial Cromos, 1952; Vol. 2: 1845–1854, Bogotá,

Editorial el Catolicismo, 1963. A compendium of historical data, political and economic, for the period 1832–54, organized chronologically.

Rodríguez Piñeres, Eduardo, *Diez Años de Política Liberal, 1892–1902,* Bogotá, Libería Colombiana, 1945.

——, *Hechos y Comentarios: Nova et Vetera* ("Academia Colombiana de Historia: Biblioteca Eduardo Santos," *11*), Bogotá, Editorial Sucre, 1956.

——, *El Olimpo Radical: Ensayos Conocidos e Inéditos sobre su Epoca, 1864–1884,* Bogotá, Talleres Editoriales de la Librería Voluntad, 1950. Useful, myth-debunking history. Briefly and readably explores the complexities of Colombian history that make it so difficult to find heros and villains.

Samper Bernal, Gustavo, *Breve Historia Constitucional y Política de Colombia,* Bogotá, Talleres Editoriales de la Litografía Colombia, 1957. A short but useful and clearly written account of some highlights of political and constitutional history, 1810–1945.

Sánchez Gómez, Gregorio, *Sociología Política Colombiana* (Ensayo Crítico), Cali, Sánchez Gómez Hnos., 1943. A provocative and perceptive discussion of Colombian politics and society: educational patterns, journalism, demagogy, and the political career.

Whiteford, Andrew H., *Two Cities of Latin America: A Comparative Description of Social Classes,* Anchor Books ed., Garden City, Doubleday & Co., 1964. A detailed account of social life in Popayán, Colombia (and Querétaro, Mexico). It is often unclear how the data lead to the general conclusions about social structure.

INDEX